The Journey Back

&

The Journey Onwards

the Journey Back

an autobiography by Eric Lewinsohn

The Journey Onwards

a biography by Peggy

First published in November 2021 by Immortalise

contact: info@immortalise.com.au

© 2021 Peggy

ISBN: print   978-0-6450377-5-3

        ebook 978-0-6450377-7-7

Cover design and typesetting by: Ben Morton

Cover image from Eric Lewinsohn

NATIONAL
LIBRARY
OF AUSTRALIA
A catalogue record for this book is available from the National Library of Australia

The Journey Back

&

The Journey Onwards

the Journey Back

an autobiography by Eric Lewinsohn

The Journey Onwards

a biography by Peggy

INTRODUCTION BY PEGGY

This book tells the story of the life of one man, a man who grew up in Europe, a man who left Europe to escape Nazi persecution, a man who spent most of his life in the English town of Hinckley.

He was an ordinary man who, particularly in his later life, had an impact on the lives of those he met.

He was an ordinary man to the world, but to me he was an extraordinary man, he was my father.

His name was Eric Lewinsohn

Since embarking on my mission to publish the story of my father's life I have received various reactions from people who are aware that I am doing this. They have all expressed the view that it is a good and worthwhile thing that I am doing and that it is a good thing that Dad's story is going to be available for people to read and, hopefully, to learn from.

It is a story of love, survival, determination, responsibility and, eventually self-gratification.

It is a story that I want future generations of our family to know.

It is a story that I believe is worth telling.

The two questions that I have been asked most often since embarking in this mission are:

"Why are you doing this?" and "Why now?"

"Why am I doing this?" As I have already said, it is a story worth telling, but my main reason for publishing my father's story is that I want to do it for him. When he wrote his autobiography my father desperately wanted it to be published but this did not come to fruition. He told me this in a letter he wrote to me in 1984. Well Dad, better late than never! Your story is going to be published as you wanted.

"Why now?" Well if I don't do it now it might be too late. I won't be around forever!

There was, however, an incident that occurred that was the catalyst in making me decide to take the plunge and make my father's dream come true. My youngest grandchild, Esther, chose the topic "To What Extent Did The Holocaust Impact The Following Generations Of Jewish Communities" for a school assignment. She came to me for resources to assist her in her research. Among these was Dad's manuscript. I re-read this myself and decided that I wanted to do what I had thought about doing in 2013, that is, to fulfil my father's wish to have his story published. In the book I have included more than my father's autobiography in the hopes of showing people the person that my father was and how others perceived him. My father was not perfect, none of us are, but he was the perfect father for me.

Contents

THE JOURNEY ONWARDS

THE JOURNEY BACK

An Autobiography by Eric Lewinsohn

PREFACE

- 1983 -

I suppose the thought of writing my life story had occurred to me sometimes during the last few years, but the opportunity to do so only presented itself when, by chance, I was forced into early retirement after a lifetime working as an engineer in a factory.

All of a sudden I felt the need to go back to school and to acquire an education in subjects that I have always wanted to do but never had the chance nor time to do before.

It is now a year since I first started at our local college to try to pass my examinations in English language and literature, a language which was not my own and in which I have never had a single lesson before.

At the age of sixty four I am the oldest pupil in our class and these last twelve months have been the happiest and most satisfying in my life as far as personal achievements are concerned, especially as I have just been informed that I have passed with an "A" Grade, which is the highest one can achieve. I am hoping to carry on, trying for higher levels in English and Sociology, a subject that I have always been interested in too.

It would be remiss of me at this stage not to thank the many friends who have helped and encouraged me to write this story.

My thanks go first of all to Theresa, who never tired of helping me by typing my hardly readable manuscripts. She must have spent countless hours sitting at her typewriter trying to decipher my writing. I shall be forever grateful to her. Then there is my teacher Ann, without whose help I could never have put it down on paper the way I did and who patiently showed me the way and corrected me where necessary. Then there are all those friends, in and out of college, who encouraged me at every step and last, but not least, there is Cosi, who first put the idea into my head to take up English studies and who, in her unwavering trust in my ability, did far more than I could ever have done myself for this story to to be written.

I have called this book "The Journey Back". I have thought long and hard about a title and perhaps this was the most difficult part of all.

By naming it "The Journey Back" I feel that, at this stage in my life, I am taking a look at myself and travelling back in time, right from the beginning to the present.

At my age I could probably be excused for feeling that perhaps it is the "Beginning of the End".

However, I would like to think that maybe it is only the "End of the Beginning", the start of a completely new life for me in the company of the many new friends that I have made.

DEDICATION

I dedicate this book to the memory of the two people who made it possible for me to be here at all, who, by their example, will always show to me what a perfect relationship and sacrifices between two people in love should be.

THIS BOOK IS IN MEMORY OF MY MOTHER AND FATHER.

– BLANKA AND FRITZ LEWINSOHN –

THE RETURN

- 1982 -

It was five o'clock in the evening when the plane touched down at Berlin's Tegel Airport. The journey from Gatwick had been uneventful and I had kept myself busy during the two hour flight by looking at some of the brochures and maps that had been sent to me. I had deliberately tried to shut out any thoughts of trepidation that I had about returning to Germany after forty five years. Whilst looking at the map of the West Berlin of today, I was pleased to see that many of the streets and squares that I had known so well still seemed to exist. What they would look like today I did not know, all I knew was they were still there – and I was back.

As I walked off the aircraft I could not help reflecting on the irony of the situation. When I left Berlin all those many years ago, I was hounded out with the threat of the Concentration Camp and death hanging over me by the Germany of Adolf Hitler – and here I was returning by invitation of the Lord Mayor of Berlin, to spend a week in his city, at his expense. In my breast pocket was the large invitation card which invited me to be his guest and telling me how honoured he was by my acceptance. Apparently, for several years now, the City of Berlin invited people who had lived there once, and had had to escape Hitler's wrath, to be their guests.

As I boarded the coach which was to take me to my hotel my fears and anxieties returned. What would I find? Had I done the right thing to return and to bring back nostalgic memories of my youth? Would it help me to turn back the clock? These past forty five years have been a lifetime and whilst I would not be able to bring back to life my loved ones who perished by Hitler's hand, it may help to soften the bitterness which is still in me and which seems to become worse as I grow older.

My hotel was on the "Kurfurstendamm", which, of course, is the most fashionable boulevard in Berlin. As the coach rounded the "Kaiser Wilhelm Memorial Church" it all came back to me. Although this church was now greatly reduced in height due to the direct hit it suffered during the war, it still looked the same to me as it did all those years ago, when I passed it practically every day, because we only lived about ten minutes away from it.

My hotel was about half a mile from the church on the "Ku-Dam", as the Berliner affectionately calls it, with it's brightly lit shops and cafes, where people sit outside and watch the rest of the world walk by. After I was shown to my room, which was very large and beautifully decorated, I unpacked, washed, changed and decided to have a stroll on the "Ku-Dam" before dinner.

I had a curiously detached feeling. Here I was, walking this familiar boulevard, where I had walked, courted, and even run and hid to escape from the Nazi brutes. No longer were there shops there that told you, in big letters, that the people who owned them were outcasts and inferior. No longer were the benches under the trees on the "Ku-Dam" reserved for the "Aryons" only and forbidden for anyone else to sit on. No longer did it say on the cinemas and theatres that people like myself were not wanted. No longer did I have to look over my shoulder to see if I was being followed by a brownshirt because I had to wear an armband with a "J" on it – and yet– it was the same old "Ku-Dam". I had come back and I was a free man.

I returned to the hotel and, after dinner, I sat in one of their comfortable lounges with a drink and at last I began to relax. Tomorrow I was going to look up some of the old places: first the Nollendorf Platz where we had lived, Hohenstaufenstrasse where my school was and Prinzregentenstrasse where I first started work. There was Victoria-Luise Platz, where I played as a child and the various cinemas and theatres if they were still there. According to the map the streets I mentioned still existed, so maybe some of the buildings did. That was tomorrow, but for this evening, I just sat and thought. On the radio someone was playing Brahms "Lullaby". The memories came flooding back. It was the first song my mother ever taught me and she used to sing it to me when tucking me in at night. But that was over sixty years ago – not in Berlin. It started in Vienna.

PART 1:
THE FIRST TWENTY YEARS

CHILDHOOD

I was born on July 21st 1919 at No. 2 Wurzingerstrasse, Vienna, Austria, the eldest child of Fritz and Blanka Lewinsohn.

Eric's first home in Vienna

My grandparents on my father's side, Alfred and Anna, had both come from East Prussia and, after marriage, had moved to Vienna, where my grandfather obtained a good job as a representative for a wine producing firm. They had three children, my Aunt Ella who was the eldest, then my father, and finally my Uncle Ernst, who was the black sheep of the family, but more about that later.

My mother's father Adolf, who was a barrister, died when my mother was thirteen years old and I never knew him. He was the victim of a flu epidemic, which also claimed the life of my mother's only younger sister Lilli, so my grandmother on my mother's side, who we all used to call Grossi, (short for grossmutter or grandmother)

1

had to bring up my mother on her own. Fortunately her husband had left her reasonably well off, so she was able to send my mother to High School, where she matriculated at the age of seventeen.

My mother met my father whilst she was on holiday with Grossi in Tyrol, and if there is such a thing, it must have been love at first sight. Whilst physically one could not imagine two people more different– my father was over six feet tall and well built and my mother was four feet eleven inches and slim– in every other aspect they were perfectly matched to each other.

When both families returned to Vienna they continued to see each other frequently. They went to concerts, the opera, football matches and for long walks. In March 1918, when my mother was eighteen and my father was twenty five they married.

Eric's parents Fritz and Blanka before marriage

Blanka and Fritz's wedding Day

I think it is appropriate to mention here, and it has bearings on later tragic events, how close my parents were to each other. From my early childhood, as soon as I was able to understand, it was obvious that their relationship was just perfect. They could not bear to be parted from each other. If they were invited out and they could not sit together they asked if their chairs could be next to each other, despite the fact that other people were making fun of their devotion. I can never remember them having a row nor hearing any harsh words between them.

Their love for each other had a tremendous impact on my brother and me and was certainly one of the reasons that we both searched all of our lives to equal it. I suppose we judged and compared our relationships in later years with theirs, trying to come up to their standard.

My parents were both of the Jewish faith, and although they were not orthodox, we observed the main Jewish holidays and customs in our house; however we also celebrated Christmas in the traditional way with a tree and many presents.

I remember very little about my first two or three years, except for what my parents told me. They were both very musical and I remember particularly well the evenings when my mother played the piano and sang me to sleep to the "Lullaby" by Brahms.

I suppose that my love of good music and opera was both inherent and encouraged by my parents. I was told that they took me to see my first opera when I was three years old. It was a performance of "Carmen" at the world famous "Staatsoper" in Vienna. I think it was a case of my parents not having a babysitter for that night, so they decided to take me with them. I was told that I behaved perfectly and that I did not take my eyes off the stage, which is really hard to believe, as "Carmen" lasts for about four hours and I cannot imagine a healthy boy of three sitting still for all that time.

It was shortly after this that my brother Hans was born. I was no longer alone to demand everyone's attention. There were two of us now and what a "bright pair" we were.

The house we lived in was in Poetzleinsdorf, a fashionable suburb of Vienna and not far from the famous Vienna Woods. The house stands on a corner and it has two upper storeys with the "Sonnenapotheke", the Sunchemist downstairs. I say "it has" because, when I went back to Vienna for a holiday after fifty years, some time ago, I looked up the house where I was born and it is still there, including the chemist's shop. We lived on the first floor in a large apartment, Grossi lived on the second floor in a smaller apartment and on the ground floor lived a family who acted as caretakers, and whose job it was to look after the house.

My father, who left school when he was fourteen and started work in a firm producing footwear, had risen from the shop floor through the office to become manager of the firm by the time that Hans was born.

An early incident, which could have ended tragically, occurred when I was five years old. My father decided to send my mother, Grossi and us two boys for a two weeks vacation at the famous spa of Poertchach, on the Woertherlake in Karinthia. This is a lovely mountain resort surrounded by lakes in Austria. He could not take the time off work himself, but came down at the first weekend. My mother and Grossi had made friends with another family in the hotel where we were staying. They were from Russia and could speak very little German. At the beginning of the second week it was decided to hire a boat to cross the Lake from Poertchach to Velden, which was on the other side of the lake.

It was agreed that Grossi would stay with Hans, who was only two years old, but that I would go with them. There were, altogether, six of us. My mother and I, the Russian, his wife and their two daughters, who were twenty and sixteen respectively, but from all accounts, the only two people who could swim were my mother and the sixteen year old daughter.

When we got into the boat my mother was at the back to steer, whilst the Russian and the twenty year old daughter sat on one side and his wife and sixteen year old daughter on the other side to do the rowing. I was put between my mother and the sixteen year old.

There is a large steamer, which travels every two hours between Poertchach and Velden, which are about eight miles apart. As one steamer leaves Poertchach the other one leaves Velden and they meet about halfway. I spent a week at Velden when I went back to Austria and they still ran. I used one and it brought back memories of a long, long time ago.

I do not know what went wrong, but we were only about one mile away from Velden, when suddenly we saw the big steamer heading straight for us, only a few yards away. When the operator spotted us it was too late to do anything and he sliced our boat into two halves longways.

I must have instinctively held on to the sixteen year old. Apparently I caught hold of her swimsuit and that saved my life. I was told that the Russian caught hold of my mother's leg, thereby hindering her from swimming properly. The main danger was, of course, that any one of us could have been caught up in the big worm of the ship's screw and crushed to death. The sailors jumped into the lake and brought the Russian, his wife and the twenty year old out safely. My mother swam to safety herself, but was frantic, because there was no sign of me or the sixteen year old girl. She was just about going to jump back into the lake to search for me when the sailors spotted the young girl, swimming around the steamer from the other side, with me holding on to her for dear life.

We were hauled up on to the deck of the steamer and put ashore at Poertchach. We made headlines in the newspapers that day, not only because we nearly drowned, but also because my mother had to walk through the fashionable resort of Poertchach wearing nothing but her bathrobe, which in those days, in 1924, was unheard of, and comparable to walking around in the nude today.

My father came down the same day, and it must have been an expensive holiday for him, because he had to pay for a new boat. I think all he cared about was that his loved ones were safe. I learned to swim shortly after that.

I have mentioned earlier what a "bright pair" Hans and I were. We were known as the "two little terrors" of Poetzleinsdorf.

We used to run along the streets and ring everyone's bells– and there were a lot of bells, because people lived in apartments and there was a bell for each apartment. On one occasion, whilst we were putting our two hands on every bell, the door opened before us and the caretaker of that particular house caught us and gave us a good hiding. We also went into the grocer's shop, ordering groceries to be delivered to our parents and neighbours, groceries that they obviously did not want. I understand that we got up to every trick in the book, with the result that most of the children in our area were forbidden to play with us, as we were a "bad influence".

When Hans was three and I was six I started to teach him to read and write by playing "school". I was the teacher and he was the pupil. I am afraid that I must have been a real tyrant to him, because I remember that, when he did not give the right answer, I gave him a good hiding, just as the teachers in school did in those days. However, it seemed to lay the foundation for a brilliant career for him. He was always "top of the class" at school. He later gained a university degree and has had a good job all of his life.

At about this same time I had my first encounter with the opposite sex. I had been given a "Lanterna Magica" for Christmas that year by my parents. It was the forerunner to the film projector, through which one filtered coloured slides of Grimms Fairy Tales etc. Our caretaker downstairs had a five year old daughter named Gretel. I invited her to come up and watch the film show with me. Once we were sitting in the dark, with papa working the projector, I realised that girls were different from boys and, in a quite innocent way, a kissing and cuddling session started. Our "romance" continued until the day I left Vienna, with me promising Gretel eternal love and telling her that she was the only girl that I would ever marry. I have often wondered what happened to her. I mention this here because there could be a possible link here to my relationships with women in later life.

Just a few months later something happened that should have been a warning to me to curb my impulsiveness and temper. My temper seems to mellow as I grow older, but my way of acting on impulse, rather than think about things first, has stayed with me all of my life, and has been responsible for many wrong decisions I have made.

We had a very large garden. It was full of shrubs and trees and Hans and I played in it whenever the weather would allow. That particular day we were having a game of hide-and-seek in the garden when a boy, who was about my age and in my class at school, stood in the road and peered through the railings of our garden. He probably only wanted to play with us, but for some unknown reason his presence annoyed me and I told him to go away. I warned him that, if he did not go I would throw something at him, but he just stood there and dared me to, so I picked up a large stone and threw it at him. I could have killed him. The stone hit him on the nose and broke it. When I realised what I had done I ran into home and hid under the bed in my room.

After a few minutes my father came in and told me to come out at once. There was a policeman in our lounge. My mother was crying, which started me off as well, and to complete the trio, Hans started to cry too. After the policeman had gone, having taken a statement and saying that the boy had been taken to hospital and if his parents wanted to they could prefer charges, in which case he would be back again, I got a well deserved thrashing from my father. The boy's parents did not press charges. I went to see him in hospital and afterwards he and I became the best of friends until I left Vienna.

It was shortly after this that I started having serious trouble with my ears. I had had diptheria when I was about four and most of the usual children's complaints like measles and whooping cough. I had suffered several bouts of earache but nothing serious. I now began to have violent earache. It was an infection of the middle ear, which resulted in me having my eardrums punctured to relieve the pressure. However, finally I became so ill that a mastoid operation was the only way to save my life. The inflammation in my left ear had spread and was threatening my brain. You must realise that I am talking about the 1920s, when a mastoid operation was a very serious step to take, as medicine was not as advanced as it is today.

My parents were told that I had a 50-50 chance of survival, but that an operation was the only way to save me. It was a Professor Alexander who operated on me and who saved my life. Unfortunately, about two years later, some crank, whose sister had died in hospital and who had a grudge against the doctor, shot him dead as he was leaving home one morning to go to the hospital. I made very slow progress after my operation and I was away from school altogether for nine months. For many weeks after being discharged from the hospital, I had to go back twice a week to have my bandages changed, as, in those days, the operation involved a big hole behind the ear, which I still have today.

I quite enjoyed these sessions at the hospital because the doctors used me as a sort of guinea pig to demonstrate my case to student doctors. They certainly made a good job of the operation because I never had trouble with my ears again, although it left me with a strong preference for my left side. I kick a ball with my left foot, hold a hammer in my left hand and I can write with my left hand as well as with my right.

So life returned to normal for me. My health improved and, at last, I was able to go back to school, although for a long time I was not allowed to take part in sports, especially swimming. As my eardrums were full of little holes I had to be careful, even when having a bath, that water did not enter my ears, as I would have lost my balance and drowned.

Life went on smoothly until the day in 1928 when my father's place of work had to go into liquidation. For the last three years he had been a part owner of the place. Economically, business had been very bad in Vienna for some time and a deep depression, which was probably the result of the Versailles Treaty and the fact that Austria had been Germany's ally in the 1914-1918 War, was becoming more apparent every day and many shops and factories went out of business.

My father's sister Ella, her husband and three boys were living in Berlin and my father decided to move us all to Germany, as there was more prospects of jobs in Berlin than in Vienna.

It was decided that, whilst my father was winding down his business and completing the process of moving home, I should go and live with my aunt and uncle in Berlin, until such time that my parents could join us.

I vividly remember saying goodbye to my parents. I was happy and excited, despite the fact that it was the first time that I was separated from them.

I arrived in Berlin with my Aunt Ella, who came to Vienna to fetch me, and I was immediately captivated by the place. In 1928 Berlin was the swinging Metropolis of Europe. It was the home of the great actors, scientists, doctors, singers, conductors and orchestras. You name it, Berlin had got it; it was the cultural centre of the world.

I was now living with my Aunt Ella, my Uncle Leo and their three sons. Heinz, the eldest, was eight years older than me, Max was two years younger than Heinz and Kurt was the same age as I was. Kurt and I became very close, he was the closest male friend I ever had. That is probably the reason that, when he died of tubercular meningitis at the tender age of thirteen, it took me a long time to get over his death. However, at the time I arrived in Berlin, that was still four years away. Four years in which Kurt and I shared everything, from going to concerts and to the opera, going to football matches and the first whispered secrets of puberty and sex. Our relationship was such, that we would tell each other everything, knowing that we could completely trust each other.

Another event that happened whilst I was at Aunt Ella's, and which had a lifelong effect on me, was that I was really introduced to classical music and opera by her son Max, who would later study music and become a Conductor in America. Max would take Kurt and myself to concerts and operas with the result that, by the time I was thirteen years old, I would stand in the queue for hours to get a seat or standing room to hear and see the greatest singers and conductors of all time.

Classical music and opera is a passion and love that has remained with me for all of my life, and has sustained and helped me to overcome many emotional issues that I have encountered.

Cousins Kurt, Heinz and Max

After living with my aunt and uncle for twelve months my parents and Hans finally came to Berlin, and we moved into an apartment of our own, in the same street that my aunt lived in, almost opposite.

I was now ten years old and had been accepted at the grammar school and so had Kurt. We sat next to each other at school and matched perfectly. Kurt was very good at sports, maths and physics, whilst I was better at languages, essays and music and we helped each other the best we could.

During those happy days an incident occurred which, at the time, left a deep impression on me and reminded me of a similar occasion some years earlier, only then I had been too young to understand.

I was sitting with my mother in a tramcar, chatting away happily, when a man who sat opposite us got up to get off, but before doing so he bent over my mother, spat straight into her face and called her a dirty Jewish pig. My mother went deathly pale and slowly wiped the spit off her face. The man gave a dirty laugh and shouted "Juden

Verrecke" – "Perish all Jews". The rest of the passengers in the tramcar said nothing and pretended to look somewhere else.

Something very similar had happened when I was about five years old and out shopping with my mother in Vienna. Some fat Viennese women pushed her at the counter of the store and called her a "filthy Jewess".

This second time I understood, and when we arrived home I asked my mother: "why"? She said she thought it was because she looked Jewish, but that was not what I wanted to know. I wanted to know why we were supposed to be different? I told her that my blood was the same colour as anybody else's and, to prove my point, I fetched out my pen knife and made a small incision into my finger, which nearly made my mother faint. I did not understand it then, I did not understand it later, I do not understand it now and I shall never understand it. I believe that was the day when I began to look with new eyes at someone black or yellow or different from us and realised that there is no difference at all, there is only one race on this planet and that is the "Human Race". We are all equal and we all have the same right to live and enjoy life, no matter what religion, colour or creed. I have practised this all of my life. Whatever other mistakes I have made, or hurt that I have caused people, I have always stuck truthfully to my belief of no prejudice whatsoever. I have tried to implant this on my family and friends, although I have not always been successful.

But back again to Berlin in 1931. The first rumblings of the Nazis were gaining momentum, yet let no-one believe that anti-semitism was not at least as great, if not greater, in Vienna, the City of Wine, Women and Song.

By now my father had gained a certificate as a qualified Chartered Accountant and was in partnership with two other accountants in a successful practice.

Kurt had been away from school for some time. He was getting bad headaches and running a high temperature, but the doctors did not seem able to find out what the problem was.

Once again I turned to Hans and the two of us would play school, which was an old favourite, only now we were both teachers and the pupils were the bare walls. Anyone coming into the room would think we were off our heads, talking to ourselves. We were also doing a fair amount of theatrical work, dressing up and singing and acting opera, where I would represent all the male singers and Hans the female ones. Once every few weeks we would give a "Gala Performance" with Mum, Dad and perhaps Aunt Ella, Uncle Leo and Kurt, if he was well enough, watching us. We would be in costume and I would be Ian Kiepura or Joseph Schmidt singing "A Song Goes Around The World" and Hans would be any of the other parts. We would have part of the lounge as a stage, with an old curtain drawn across, and lighting effect by a table lamp covered by different coloured paper. Oh, what fun we had. We were oblivious to the world outside. We wanted it to go on forever.

One morning I woke up and realised that I could not move. I had been ill with the flu for a couple of days, but I had seemed to be getting better. My mother called the doctor in. I remember it well because it was a Sunday and she did not want to disturb the doctor, but I was in terrible pain in my abdomen. When he arrived the doctor diagnosed acute appendicitis and I was rushed to the hospital and successfully operated on. I must admit that my appendix is an aspect of my life that I have never missed.

Kurt seemed to be getting worse. He would have a few weeks at school and then be in bed again for months. Still no-one seemed to know what was wrong with him. He had tests after tests.

Eventually a very famous specialist was called in. He diagnosed tubercular meningitis. I did not realise how ill Kurt was, although I spent most of my free time with him. First his speech went, then he lost the use of his arms and eventually he did not seem to be able to focus his eyes properly and he slept most of the time. Finally they took him to hospital. I remember the day in 1932, when my father came to our school to tell the headmaster that Kurt had died that morning. Something died in me that day too.

Four months later, Hitler came to power. Perhaps Kurt had been lucky after all. On January 30th 1933, when Hitler became Chancellor of the German Reich, I was thirteen years old. My childhood came to an abrupt end.

I did not know then, but I would learn the hard way, that never again would I be able to walk about in Berlin carefree. Never again would I be able to enjoy my opera or concerts without the threat that I might finish up in a concentration camp, because I was not supposed to be there to enjoy the music. That was reserved for the "Pure German Aryan Master Race" only, not for the sub human, depraved Jews.

Yes, my childhood was certainly at an end and a most bizarre adolescent life was about to begin.

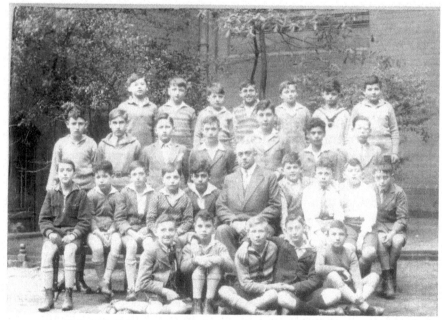

School photo—Eric is in the back row 3rd from left

Berlin school entrance

GROWING UP

How can one describe what it felt like to be growing up and Jewish under Hitler and his Nazi thugs? I can try to paint the picture as truthfully as possible, but surely the only people to understand completely are those who, like myself, were actually there and experienced it.

When Hitler came to power, economically, Germany was at its lowest ebb. There were six million people unemployed. Every morning there would be someone lying outside your door covered with newspapers. They had been "sleeping rough" because they had nowhere else to go. There had been several elections and successive governments during the previous two years. Violence was rife in the streets. The President of Germany was an old senile man of eighty five years, so the climate was just right for Hitler. A great many people were so fed up with the conditions that they were quite prepared to give him a chance, to see if he could do better than his predecessors; a great many people —except those who had read "Mein Kampf" and who knew what he meant to do.

It is only fair to say here that there were even some Jewish people who thought that Hitler might not be as bad as their friends and relatives tried to make out and, if he was – well, one could always get rid of him by having another election. How wrong they were!

Hitler left no-one in doubt that he meant what he said. Only two months after coming to power he gave orders for the "Boycott", which meant that all Jewish shops were daubed with paint. Stormtroopers stood outside these shops and any Germans defying them and going into these shops were jeered at and, in some cases, they were even marked with a stamp to show that they had been shopping in a Jewish shop. The same applied to hospitals, where Jewish doctors were not allowed to operate on German patients. One month later, all books by Jewish writers, paintings by Jewish painters and music by Jewish composers were seized and destroyed on bonfires, with the Nazis dancing around the fires.

16

Of course Hitler's access to complete power came with the death of President Hindenburg and the "engineered" Reichstagfire, which enabled Hitler to ban all other political parties in Germany and to become the head of and the dictator of the German Reich.

As far as I was concerned life seemed to go on as normal for a few months. My father went to his office as usual. My brother and I attended the High School or Gymnasium as it was called in Germany. We went to two different schools. Hans, being top of his class at the Primary or "Volksschule" got a free place or "Stipendium" at High School, whilst I, who was about average at school had to be paid for by my parents. I had attended the same school for about three and a half years when Hitler came to power. There were quite a lot of Jewish boys at my school,– I would say about 20%. We were all on friendly terms with one another, the Jewish boys and the other boys. We used to go to each others houses to birthday parties etc., and we all enjoyed one another's company. The same applied to the adults. My parents had many non-Jewish friends, with whom they played cards, went to the theatre with etc.

So outwardly nothing seemed to change for a while. Economically, conditions improved. Hitler took people off the Unemployment Register and put them to work building roads and "autobahns" at just a little more money than they had been getting when they were out of work. But for the record – they were no longer unemployed. After the Reichstagfire, Hitler's power became absolute by him dissolving all other political parties and by him having complete control of the media, the press and the radio. Hitler had a very efficient propoganda machine, under the direction of Joseph Goebbels, telling the people every day what they wanted them to believe, and people in Germany began to change.

I first noticed this by the attitude of some of my best non-Jewish friends at school. They gave a hint here and there, repeating some of the rubbish they either overheard by listening to adults or by reading it in the newspapers, and all sorts of excuses were made when I invited them to our home or suggested that we go for walks or to the cinema as we used to do. In our class there were about thirty five boys and about an eighth of them were Jewish. As a consequence of the non-Jewish boys behaviour towards us, we Jewish boys drew closer together until eventually there were two different groups.

When I was a child I had a good singing voice. I was a member of the school choir and even sometimes sang solo. Our music teacher, whose name was Herr Kalt (which is the German equivalent to Mr Cold), would insist that we carry on singing, even when our voices were breaking and we should have taken care of them. The consequence was that, after my voice changed, I lost my singing voice.

I remember one particular incident very well. It took place during our music lesson. It must have been about nine months after Hitler had come to power, and a new subject had been introduced into the schools in Germany. The subject was named "Science Of The Races", where the German boys were taught how superior they were to the rest of the world, because they were the Aryan Race. They were also told that the Jews were vermin and belonged to the lowest Races. We Jewish boys were made to attend these lectures and listen to what sort of scum we really were. On this particular day our music teacher, who had suddenly become very "Aryan minded", introduced a song that the Nazis used to sing and which included the words: "The Jews blood will drop from our knives". The whole of our Jewish contingent of eight boys refused to sing this song. We felt that it was bad enough that we had to attend the race discrimination lectures, but we were not going to sing a song with those words. To illustrate the mentality of the so-called "intellectual German professor", he innocently asked us why we would not join in. When we told him the reason he just could not, or would not, understand it and he said that if we felt like that we had better no longer attend choir practice and singing lessons.

We were glad to oblige him, but it did not save our voices. It was too late for that.

One of my favourite teachers at school was the one we had for Maths and Physics, not because I was particularly good at those subjects, but because of his personality. After Hitler came to power the

18

greeting "good morning" or "good day" was abolished and "Heil Hitler" was put in its place. Even small babies in their prams were taught to say that, before they could say "mummy" or "daddy" and they were also taught to raise their hands in the Nazi salute.

It was the same at school. No longer did we just stand up when the teacher entered the classroom and greet him with "good morning sir". Now he was expected to come in with his hand outstretched shouting "Heil Hitler", and the pupils were supposed to respond with the same. "We" the Jewish boys were exempted from doing this, because the Nazis felt that the Jews were "outsiders" and, consequently, not entitled to do that, – for which we were more than glad.

I know that this particular maths and physics teacher never stretched his hand out. He always made a fist, almost like the salute of the Soviets, and whatever he said was inaudible. It certainly was not "Heil Hitler". He just mumbled something under his breath.

For a long time I suspected that his sympathies lay in the opposite direction and I am afraid that I was right.

One day he was missing from school. When anyone asked the headmaster about him the headmaster would make some excuse. I saw the teacher once more before I left school, which was in the summer of 1934. I hardly recognised him. He used to be a tall, upright man. He was about thirty-five years old with a love for life and a smile for everyone. The man I saw was a broken old man, he walked like one and the most horrifying sight was his eyes. They used to be a clear penetrating blue. Now he had a patch over one eye and the other looked dull and lifeless. I later learned that he had been arrested by the Gestapo in the middle of the night suspected of Socialist leanings and sent to a concentration camp just outside Berlin. There they beat him up and gauged one of his eyes out. –Yes, that happened in 1934.

I think that here an introduction to the Gestapo and their methods, from the point of view of someone who saw them at work for six years, is appropriate.

The Gestapo, or Secret Police, came into being almost immediately with the rise of the Nazi Party to power. The concentration camps, although not a German invention, certainly achieved a notoriety. No-one in their wildest dreams would have thought it possible for human beings to invent such places.

The Gestapo's methods were quite simple. They mostly relied on people informing on someone, perhaps a person who had had a grudge against somebody for a long time, or even sons and daughters informing on their own parents. They always pounced first, without ever bothering to find out if there was any justification for the accusations and they always came in the middle of the night, when their victims were asleep.

I suppose one felt safer in a large city like Berlin, which at that time had four million inhabitants, than in a small town or village, where everybody knew everybody, and whilst one saw neighbours disappear and new ones moving in, one never thought that it would happen to them, as long as one did not dabble in politics and went quietly about their own business. How wrong we were again, and how little we understood the mentality of the Nazis. The worst of it was, the longer it went on for, with the truth being suppressed and people only being told what the Nazis wanted them to know, more and more respectable people in Germany began to believe what the Nazis told them. The people even began to practise some of the things that they were taught, so that after two or three years of Hitler's reign, practically the whole German nation became actively involved in supporting the Nazis, with the exception of a very small minority, who were unable to make an impression on the majority. Some people might say that this was not so and that there were many good and decent Germans who did not like what was happening. I can only speak from the opinion that I formed myself during my six years under Hitler, and I always argue that if that were true, why did they not do anything about it. No – the truth, as I saw it then and as I still see it today is, that as long as the people in Germany had a job and everything on the surface was running smoothly, what did it matter if one heard about these concentration camps and what went on inside them.

Perhaps, people said, it was exaggerated and it was much better to mind one's own business and to have nothing to do with these agitators.

Perhaps, they argued, the Furhrer was right about these Jews. They seemed to have all of the prominent positions in Medicine, Sciences, Arts and Commerce.

Perhaps the Jews were to blame for Germany's misfortunes after the War (WW1).

This is how they spoke, and it is surprising how intelligent people, if told the same story often enough, finally come to believe it.

So, this was the state of affairs in the summer of 1934 when I left school. For some time my parents had been discussing with me as to what I would like to do. I had always been very interested in the Performing Arts, the theatre and the cinema. I had also always liked to communicate with people by putting my thoughts to paper and, at one stage, would have loved to have been a reporter. That, of course, was out of the question because no Jew in Germany could be a reporter.

A client of my father, whose books my father used to audit once a year in his capacity as an accountant, had a small workshop, where he built and repaired film cameras. My father thought that, as I was not allowed to go to the Arts Academy, it might be a good idea for me to be apprenticed to this man. It would give me some initial technical knowledge of film cameras and, at the same time, I would gain some practical experience which would be useful later, if I wanted to continue in that area. My father was also taking into consideration that I was only fifteen years old and, at that age, one changes one's mind many times as to what one wants to be. There was, of course, the alternative, to carry on at school until my matriculation, but somehow I did not feel that I wanted to do that.

I had never been an outstanding scholar, perhaps I was more on the lazy side. Whilst subjects like History, Languages and Literature came easy to me and interested me very much, I always had to put a spur on in the last few months in order to pass my exams and move into the next form.

I also felt that the friendships that I had made at school prior to Hitler coming to power had been lost to me. I felt that I was being bogged down into a narrow circle of Jewish friends and I resented this to a certain extent because I have always liked to mix freely with people of all religions and creeds.

I have learned since, being born Jewish is something one cannot or want to shake off easily, but I have come to terms with it, and whilst feeling a certain affinity with being Jewish, that does not necessarily mean that one cannot be accepted for oneself and able to assimilate without being cast out by one side or another.

So, in the summer of 1934, I left school and started work in the little workshop. I think I made history in our family because I was the first manual worker. It certainly altered the whole future of my life, not only because I came from a middle-class background and went into a factory to become a manual worker, but it also certainly saved my life by allowing me to acquire a manual skill which enabled me to escape the clutches of the Nazis later on. It also determined my domestic life and the kind of people I was to meet.

If one believes in fate, which I strongly do, I think the day that I started work at 55, Prinzregentsstrasse, Berlin, as the only other member of the workforce to Herr Murauski, was the turning point in my life.

As I was to realise later on, gone were the dreams of, perhaps one day, becoming a reporter or a writer or even to become connected with the theatre or the cinema. In that small workshop, about five yards by five yards, with just two lathes, (one of them with a foot treadle and made by Herr Murauski himself), and a work bench, I learned everything there was to learn the hard way, which came in handy in later years. It provided me with the foundation to earn my own living at an early age. It also stopped any ambition I had to do what I really wanted to do.

Now that I have come to the end of my working life, sometimes, when I feel bitter because circumstances prevented me from following the ambitions that I had when I was young, I realise that my life has been a full circle and now at last, I am able to do what I want to, at my own leisure.

Although it was nearly fifty years ago, it seems to me, as if it was just yesterday, when I finished my first week's work at that little workshop and proudly walked home with the German equivalent of two shillings (less than 10p) in my pocket – my first week's wages.

Left: the workshop.
Eric's first job.
Eric in background.

Below: Eric's first employer,
Karl Murauski

23

THE LAST FOUR YEARS
IN GERMANY
(1934 – 1938)

I was now fifteen years old and, at that age, teenagers in natural surroundings, have the best years of their life. One starts going out to parties, meeting girls, going to dances, to the cinema, to the theatre or even to the opera.

I was no different from any normal young man. I liked to talk to girls and although I was not very interested in dancing, I loved to go to the opera, the cinema and to concerts. What was different was the fact that every time I went to see a play, a film, an opera or to a concert, I took a great risk. There were big notices at all of these places of entertainment which clearly stated that Jews were not wanted there. As a matter of fact the notices said: "Juden Verboten", which means "Jews forbidden" (Jews were forbidden to be there). Now I have always looked what one would term rather "Jewish". By that I mean that I had dark hair, hazel coloured eyes and a very prominent nose with a bend at the top, which I inherited from my parents who both had prominent noses. To anyone as race-conscious as the Germans were taught to be, it was not difficult to surmise that I belonged to that "Inferior Race".

The penalty, if one was found in a forbidden venue, was usually a stay in one of those concentration camps for a few weeks, with a warning that, the next time one could stay much longer. However, I must admit, that even at fifteen, I was so wrapped up in the theatre and music that nothing could deter me from going. As a result I heard some of the finest singers like Gigli and Kiepura in opera, Furtwaengler and Klemperer at concerts and I also saw some very fine plays with excellent actors. I assumed that the people who went to these feasts of culture were more interested in the music and the acting than in the politics of Herr Hitler, and perhaps I was right, because,

24

with the exception of one or two minor incidents, when I heard people discussing me and then saying that I could not be because there were big notices everywhere, I encountered no real trouble. Perhaps I was lucky. I have heard of people who were not so lucky.

By this time, every shop, restaurant or place of entertainment, if it were owned by Jews, had to display a big notice in its window indic-ating that it was Jewish. If a Jew wanted to buy something they had to go to one of these Jewish shops because the non-Jewish businesses had to display a notice that stated that Jews were not wanted there. It was more difficult if a haircut was needed because all non-Jewish hairdressers had to display a notice that they would not cut the hair of Jews. There were not many Jewish hairdressers about, so sometimes one had to travel quite some distance to get a haircut. I said deliber-ately the these shops HAD to display these notices, because many of them did not want to, not only for the reason of common decency, but also because many Jewish people were quite well-off and used to spend quite a lot of money in these shops. It is very difficult to explain all of this to anyone living in a free democracy like England and it must be very difficult to believe all of this unless one was actually there. It seems unbelievable that people would descend to such depths: all the more because if there were any big occasions, like The Olympic Games of 1936, that were held in Berlin, the Nazis used to remove all of these signs and notices before the guests from foreign lands arrived, so that, outwardly, everything seemed to be in order. However, the moment the visitors departed the notices were put back again. The same applied to the notorious "party" rag "Der Stuermer", which was produced by a man called Streicher, who was later hanged at Nuremburg. One cannot imagine the pornographic filth and pictures in that paper, which only dealt with the so-called crimes of all Jews. It showed photos of supposed rapes, incest etc. and, perhaps because the majority of the German people would not spend money on buying filth like this, the paper was displayed publicly at every few street corners in boxes, so that if people wanted to they could read it free of charge. In the whole of my life I have never seen anything so perverse and vulgar, but again, on big occasions these display boxes were empty until the visitors had gone home.

My brother Hans, who was now twelve years old, used to go to many concerts and other entertainments with me. Since Kurt's death we seemed to have drawn closer together. Perhaps it was the fact that, whilst he seemed to be the "little brother" to me when he was five and I was eight, the older I got the less it seemed to matter that he was more than three years younger than me and I found that I could discuss and share most things with him, as though we were both the same age. It was a closeness very unusual in brothers, and it has persisted to the present day, although for the past thirty years he has lived in Canada and we only see each other about every five years. Although today he looks every bit as "Jewish" as I do, in those far off days in Berlin he looked more like a "Nordic German" than anything else. He was blonde, and his nose did not curve till later on. People would have been hard put to denounce him as a Jew just by his looks. So, in a way, it was like having an alibi having him with me when I went out.

His German looks were very useful about three years later, when he had to rescue our grandmother from Vienna – but more about that later.

By now I had become quite hard-skinned to the German way of life under Hitler and at that time, at the end of 1934, it was quite possible, even for a young Jewish boy of fifteen, to enjoy life as long as he did not take part in any politics or political issues, kept his mouth shut and was careful with what he said to other people. I went to work, had one or two mild flirtations and queued up every Sunday morning outside The State Opera House to get a ticket for the performance that evening (in Germany theatres and opera houses were open on Sunday).

I was brought back with a big jolt to reality and what life was really like for a Jew under Hitler's rule in the summer of 1935.

Early in 1935 the so-called "Nuremburg Race Laws" had been passed by Hitler and his clique. This meant that, from now on, it was illegal for any mixed marriages between Jews and Germans. It was illegal for a Jewish boy to go out with a non-Jewish girl and vice

26

versa. Jews were not allowed to have a domestic help in their house if she was non-Jewish unless she was over fifty years of age. German prostitutes were not allowed to sell their bodies to non-Jewish clients. People who, until then, had thought they were non-Jewish, if they had a grandparent or great-grandparent of Jewish extraction, were declared to be Jews. Mixed marriages that existed with a Jewish member were investigated and the non-Jewish partner was advised to divorce their Jewish wife or husband. Hitler stated that he was determined that there should only be "pure Germans" in Germany. The segregation was almost complete.

The penalties for disobedience of these "laws" were very heavy. If one was lucky it was the concentration camp. If one was not so lucky, people were taken from their bed and were never seen again. Sometimes their ashes were sent to their families saying they had died from some "disease".

In this atmosphere of "racial purity" I ventured on my first holiday on my own. Until then we had always gone away together as a family, but now I was sixteen, and I felt that I could look after myself and fancied a holiday on my own. The place that I chose to visit was in Bavaria, in the mountains near Passau on the Danube. It was only about thirty miles from Hitler's birth place of Braunau.

I was very excited when I set off on the evening train from Berlin to Passau. I slept a little on the journey, but the trains in Germany in those pre-war days were not very comfortable, especially when one had to travel in a third class carriage which only had wooden seats.

However, nothing could deter my high spirits and when dawn broke, the scenery of the Mountains, with the sun just rising, was indescribably beautiful.

From Passau I made my way to the little village I had chosen, which was about forty five minutes away by bus.

When I arrived at the hotel where I was supposed to stay for the two weeks I was told that, although I would have all of my meals at the hotel, arrangements had been made for me to sleep at another house at the end of the village. I did not realise it at the time, but the reason for this was because I was Jewish. However, I was looking forward so much to this holiday on my own that nothing seemed to matter. I settled in nicely at the other house and, three times a day, I walked about a mile to the hotel to have my breakfast, lunch and dinner. The food at the hotel was excellent and so was the service, especially that of the hotel-owner's daughter, who was about my age, and who used to look after me. We started to talk to each other and found that we had a great deal in common. She also originally came from Vienna and she loved good music. After a day or two, in the evening after dinner, at about nine-thirty to ten o'clock, she started to walk with me to the house where I was sleeping. I was not really surprised when, on the third night, she kissed me goodnight.

The following day I did not see her at breakfast or lunch and I presumed that she was busy helping her mother in the kitchen. When I walked in for dinner in the evening she was at my table as usual. I could sense that she was a little upset and whilst she was friendly enough, she seemed to keep her distance. When she brought me my coffee, she said that her boyfriend would like to have a talk with me when I had finished my meal. Although that was the first time that she had mentioned having a boyfriend I still did not realise what was going on, until I entered the room she led me to. Inside were about twenty young stormtroopers in their SS uniforms and a radio was playing Nazi songs. At the top of the table was a blonde, blue-eyed boy of about eighteen or nineteen, who she introduced as Heini, her young man. As soon as I entered the room someone switched off the music and Heini asked me to stand in front of him. He then told me that Steffi, that was the girl's name, had told him about me. She had told him how she had walked me home the past two nights and, apparently, she had also told him that we had kissed goodnight. He then proceeded to tell me that he knew that I was Jewish and that, under the Nuremburg Laws, I had committed a serious offence. He told me that his uncle was a Commandant at the Dachau Concentration Camp, which was only about twenty miles away and that he had no choice but to get in touch with his uncle on the following day. Can you imagine how I felt? Here I was, a boy of sixteen, all on my own, with the prospect of being hurled into a Concentration Camp. I tried to explain that it was only an innocent holiday friendship, that nothing serious had happened, but I might as well have been talking to a brick wall. They were just sneering and laughing at me and enjoying every moment of it. He finally cut it short by saying that I would be hearing from him, and I stumbled out of the room and out of the hotel. I do not know how I got back to my lodgings. All the way I kept imagining footsteps behind me. When I arrived home I bolted my door and wrote a long letter to my parents explaining what had happened and asking them what I should do.

I slept very little that night and the next morning I took the first train to Passeu. I had something to eat in Passeu and posted my letter by express post. All that day I wandered about in Passeu and I spent about six hours in a cinema. I figured that that was the safest place to be. When it was dark I caught the last train back to the village. I slept very little again and the next morning I went up into the mountains with some food that I had bought in Passeu.

When it was dark I made my way back to my lodgings and there was a telegram from my father telling me to come home immediately. It was about eight thirty in the evening then and there was a train to Berlin at ten o'clock. I phoned for a taxi and managed to catch that train back to Berlin. The train was very full of stormtroopers and every time one of them walked past the compartment in which I was sitting my heart missed a beat. I thought that they had come for me.

I arrived in Berlin at six o'clock in the morning and my parents were there to greet me. Never had I been so glad to see them. Although I had only been away for about five days of the fourteen day holiday that I had looked forward to so much, it seemed as if I had been away for an eternity. I never went for another holiday in Nazi Germany on my own.

Back home and among the people I loved and, I suppose, being young, it did not take me long to get over this unsavoury experience. I never heard any more from Heini nor from Steffi. Perhaps they just enjoyed frightening me. Perhaps I was lucky.

Life for me went back to normal. Going to work every day, night school three evenings a week, and the opera or a concert at the weekend. Queuing up for a cheap seat in the gods, where one would not be noticed.

Towards the end of 1936 I joined a Jewish Youth Club. There were several of these in Berlin, some with strong zionist leanings and others where politics did not matter and where one read Shakespeare, Kipling, Bernard Shaw, Goethe etc. I joined one of those. My weakness for the fair sex continued and I took one or two girls from the club (it was a mixed club) out. It was all quite innocent, usually an evening at the pictures, followed by a cup of coffee or an ice-cream. I always remember one girl that I took out (her name was Irma), because she fell to sleep in the pictures and started snoring. The film was a Jeanette McDonald – Nelson Eddie one, very much the rage then.

I have often wondered why it is that so many trivial occurrences in our life seem to contribute to vital happenings. When Irma fell asleep I made up my mind that I would not take her out again, so when she suggested that next time she would bring a friend along, and perhaps I could bring someone too, I readily consented, hoping that I could palm her off on to someone else.

When we met the following week I brought along one of my former school friends with whom I had been keeping in touch and she brought F.

The reader will perhaps be surprised that I am starting to introduce people with just capital letters rather than by name. Whilst, until this stage, it has not mattered that I have used full real names, because the people have been either members of my family or they are not alive today. Other people are still alive today and they could be embarrassed by some parts of my story. I am sure that, if they ever read this account they will recognise themselves, but I think it is only fair that other people do not recognise them.

To return to my story, F was very good looking, perhaps a little on the plump side, but she was blonde, had grey eyes and a straight nose. You really could not call her Jewish looking.

My friend seemed to go for Irma, which suited me, and the four of us had a very enjoyable evening.

At the end of the evening I asked F if I could see her again and we made a date for the following week-end, when we went to Wannsee, which is one of the lakes surrounding Berlin, where one can swim or take a boat or a steamer ride, and in spring or summer one can have a marvelous time there. This started a courtship that was to last for the remainder of my years in Germany and beyond that. F belonged to the same youth club as me. She had not been for a while but now we went everywhere together. After about three months she invited me to her home where I met her parents. Her mother was a charming woman. Her father was a button manufacturer, a rather shy man who could not make conversation easily. He felt very German and he could not understand what was happening in Germany. He had fought for Germany in the First World War and I think he would have been the last man to want to leave Germany. He never did leave it until he was transported to his death.

I was the happiest boy on Earth. My father was still doing well in his partnership of accountants, and whilst my job was not what I had wanted to do, I was becoming quite skilled as an engineer. At night school I was becoming interested in subjects like Maths and Physics, which I had neglected when I was at school.

On top of that I had a steady girlfriend who liked good music. We went to the opera together and whilst she did not have a very sound knowledge and understanding of it she was quite content for me to explain it to her.

I think, at this stage, I should explain a little about F. She was easygoing but very inexperienced in many ways. For instance, at a later stage, I had to explain "the facts of life" to her, because her mother, who herself had a very strict upbringing, would never talk to her about anything like that. Looking back, after all these years, I

31

suppose, in a way, I quite enjoyed teaching her and explaining various things to her. Although she was not stupid she was not too quick off the mark and, therefore, I suppose I liked my role of being a little bit above her intellectually. I suppose there are some men who need a strong woman to lean on and there are others who like their women to look up to them and then again there are those who like them to be on the same level in every way. I dare say that, at that time in my life, I belonged to the second category. I am making this point because I feel that it will, to some extent, explain what happened later.

But I am digressing again. F and I became closer and closer and twelve months after we met we became engaged.

The world seemed to be a marvelous place to me despite Herr Hitler and his thugs. One heard of terrible things, but as I said before, as long as one kept quiet, behaved and was lucky, life seemed to go on quite normally for a seventeen year old.

The family. Eric, Blanka, Fritz and Hans (Jack) in Berlin circa 1938

And then the first bombshell fell! One day my boss asked me to tell my father that he would like to see him. When Dad arrived Herr Murauski told him that he was now going to be doing highly secretive work (armaments) and that he had been told that he would have to get rid of me as I was Jewish and, therefore, not considered to to be trust-worthy by the Germans. In all fairness, I think he was as sorry to see me go as I was to leave. He was one of those few Germans that I referred to earlier on, who did not agree with Hitler but were too afraid to do anything about it.

So, in the summer of 1937, I left work and entered a Jewish School of Engineering in Berlin as a full time student.

Shortly after that the second bombshell fell! For a very long time Hitler had had his eye on his native Austria. He wanted to annex it, and the majority of Austrians did not need much persuading, as they had always felt rather pro-German and anti-Jewish. We all know what happened, – Hitler succeeded, helped by Goebbels propaganda machinery and Von Papen's support of Schuschnigg and his government.

When the Germans marched into Austria our immediate thoughts were for Grossi (my mother's mother) who was still in Vienna. My other grandmother (my father's mother) had just recently moved to Berlin after her husband (my grandfather) had died at the age of eighty five.

One heard some gruesome tales after the Anschluss about the treatment of the Jews by the so-called"Gemutlichen" (kind hearted Viennese). They certainly did not need any lessons from their German masters. They rounded up the Jews in the centre of Vienna and made them wash the streets, throwing acid at their clothes and legs and jeering at them.

We knew that we had to get Grossi out of Vienna as soon as possible. But how? My father thought of an ingenious plan. I think I mentioned earlier that my cousin Heinz and my brother Hans looked very much like the typical "blonde, blue eyed Germans". I do not know where he got them from, but my father managed to get two Stormtrooper uniforms for Heinz and Hans to wear, and those two, disguised as two Nazis, went by train to Vienna and brought Grossi safely to Berlin. We must remember that Hans was only about

33

fourteen and a half years old at the time. It was quite a feat for someone of that age to dress up as and pretend to be a Hitler youth. So, once again, we were all together as a family.

Then came bombshell number three! For some time, since the beginning of 1938, the Nazis had been systematically "repatriating" Jews who originally came from Poland but had lived in Germany for a generation or even longer, had fought for Germany in World War 1 and had become German nationals. When I use the word "repatriating" it was of course, like everything else concerning Jews, done by force. They were taken from their beds during the night, allowed to take one suitcase each and loaded on to trucks, taken to the railway station and then sent East to Poland. Their monies and other belongings were confiscated by the "State". Of course the Poles in Poland did not want these people, and the majority of them were either put into ghettos or detained in camps. A third of Poland's population was Jewish and Poland is a country that became famous, or I should say infamous because of the Nazi progroms and their horrific persecution of the Jews there.

One family to whom this happened was named Grynszpan. They had a son, Herschel Grynszpan, who was studying at the Sorbonne in Paris. When Herschel received a letter from his parents telling him of their plight, his mind became so deranged that he bought a gun, went to the German Embassy in Paris and shot a minor German official named Ernst Vom Rath. Vom Rath was seriously injured. This shooting occurred on November 7th 1938. Was this just what Hitler had been waiting for? The impudence of it! How dare a "dirty Polish Jew" attack a "pure German"? Hitler gave orders for Goebbels propaganda machine to go into action.

Two days later, when Vom Rath died of his wounds, the fury of the Nazis knew no bounds. Hitler made a speech, telling the German people that if they chose to take the law into their own hands no-one would blame them. The date was November 9th 1938.

I went to school as usual. I had not been there for half an hour when I was called to the telephone. It was F. She told me that she had heard that that night there were going to be massacres in the streets, mass plundering and mass arrests of Jews. F had an aunt who was living on her own on the outskirts of Berlin. F and her family were going there and her parents suggested that my family go there too. I got in touch with my family and told them what I had heard. That evening we all went to Auntie P.'s house. There were about twenty of us altogether and we stayed there for two weeks.

The night of November 9th /10th 1938 has gone down in history as Kristallnacht or "the night of the broken glass". All Jewish shops were smashed in and the goods stolen, the synagogues were set on fire and about 100,000 Jews throughout Germany were arrested and sent to Concentration Camps. The "Dark Ages" had returned to Germany. The Nazis were dancing in the streets whilst the fires were burning Jewish properties everywhere.

The rest of the world looked on. After all, it was only three months since Hitler and Chamberlain had saved the world from another war by the "Betrayal of Czechoslovakia". Chamberlain had returned to England from "The Munich Conference" in Germany, saying that "there will be peace in our time". Chamberlain had said that one could trust Herr Hitler! The same Hitler who ordered the bonfire night and the burning of the synagogues on November 9th/10th. Still, if one can have "peace in our time", should one have "peace at any price"? What does it matter about a few synagogues? The rest of the world looked on.

During the fourteen days we spent at Frau P.'s pandemonium broke out in Berlin and also in the rest of Germany. There were some smaller towns where every Jewish male from the age of sixteen to seventy was rounded up and put into a concentration camp. Compared to that, Berlin and other big cities fared better, although it has been estimated that, out of the whole Jewish population of 500,000, at least 200,000 Jews were arrested on "Kristallnacht". Hitler got rid of the other 300,000 about four years later, except for those who were lucky enough to escape his clutches.

The Nazis certainly came for us on "Kristallnacht". Our maid was one of those German women over fifty years old who, as I said before, were allowed to work as maids for Jews. When we returned home she told us that they had come for us. F, by warning us and her family by inviting us to flee to Frau P's, had saved us. They had possibly saved us from death in a concentration camp. Those people who were arrested did not come out of the concentration camps alive unless they were able to prove that they could emigrate to another country.

Being involved with F affected my decisions and movements later and certainly accounts for me being alive today, although it did not save the rest of my family except Hans.

I have to explain here, that whilst the rest of the world was sympathetic to the plight of the Jews in Germany and Austria, strict quota restrictions allowed only a handful of Jews into every country each year. In addition to quota limitations one had to be rich enough to be able to support oneself and to start a business or factory to employ people of that particular country. This was very difficult because the Nazis only allowed each person to take ten reichsmarks with them if they left Germany. This was the equivalent of about fifty pence at that time. Unless one had already smuggled money out of Germany, or had funds in a foreign bank, it was impossible to meet the financial conditions required for immigration into other countries. The other option was if one could find someone in one of the immigration countries who would sign an "affidavit" for the migrant. This meant that the signer of the affidavit would guarantee to keep the Jew financially indefinitely. Young girls were accepted as au pairs this way.

As you can see it was very difficult to escape. There was a third way which was very dangerous. This is the option that we took, but details of that are in the next chapter.

Hitler was not satisfied with the physical damage that had been done to the Jewish population. There had to be something else and so he proclaimed new laws. These laws stated that, as from December 1st 1938 all Jews were forbidden to follow a trade or profession.

Every Jewish shop had to be sold at a ridiculous knock down price to Germans. No Jewish doctors, teachers, lawyers or accountants etc. were allowed to work after that date. In short, the livelihood was taken away from every Jewish person in Germany. Hitler imposed a "Juden-busse" for every Jewish person living in Germany. This was a penalty of five hundred reichsmarks for each person. As there were four persons in our family we had to pay two thousand reichsmarks.

For people who were lucky enough to emigrate during the following few weeks there was an additional financial levy, imposed on them for the magnificent gesture by the Germans of letting them leave Germany. This was in addition to any assets that one had in the bank, which were seized by the government. One was not allowed to sell one's home nor it's contents and one was not allowed to take the contents and other possessions with one. All that a person owned had to be left behind for the Nazis to plunder.

At last my father decided that it was time for us to leave Germany. Looking back I really cannot blame him for not daring to take the risk earlier. He had a well established business with his two partners. My mother had a dress shop that was thriving. It was certainly a big step for him at the age of forty five, with a wife and two sons, and with no particular knowledge of languages, to start afresh in a new country. I can fully understand why he did not take the risk earlier, but if we had left Germany earlier and my father had chosen the right country, he and my mother could have been alive after the War.

When we returned to our flat after the two weeks at Frau P.'s, hoping that events in Berlin had cooled down and that we would be comparatively safe, my father began to make preparations for our escape.

As I have already mentioned we had to choose escape method number three, as there was no time left for my father to contact his numerous acquaintances in other countries to ask if there was a chance of someone guaranteeing to keep us financially.

We did not have any assets in foreign banks so, therefore, there was only one option available to us. It was dangerous, and if we were caught we would be sent to a concentration camp where we would probably perish.

Anyone living in Germany at the time could see that Hitler was bent on War and on World Domination, even if some of the politicians of the Western World could not see it. Some saw it, like Winston Churchill.

Escaping was a risk that we had to take. We had nothing to lose. My father was not allowed to continue to work and conditions for the Jews could only get worse.

My father rallied all of the family around. Not just the four of us, but extended family such as cousins and uncles and F's parents as well. He explained his escape plan to them and invited them to join him. This was so typical of my father. Throughout his life he was always ready to help other people, regardless of the dangers to himself. It would be far more difficult to escape with a larger number of people than if there were just the four of us.

My Aunt Ella and Uncle Leo had been offered a job in Prague as married housekeepers to a wealthy family who had signed an "affidavit" for them and they accepted this. They had been able to get this job through their musical son Max, who had won a scholarship to the Academy of Music in Prague and had been studying there for the past two years. Later on, through the efforts of the daughter of Hearst the newspaper magnate, who heard him play there, Max managed to get to the U.S.A. where he still lives today.

Their eldest son Heinz had recently married a very pretty girl named Susi who was of Hungarian origin. They were very enthusiastic about my father's plan and immediately agreed to join him. Heinz had graduated as a doctor and would be very useful to us, not only for his medical knowledge, but also because of his German looks and the fact that he was always ready for an adventure.

Then there was my Uncle Ernst, my father's youngest brother. I referred to him in an earlier chapter as the "black sheep" of the family and so he was. For all of his working life he depended on other people to keep and shelter him. If this was not enough, when he departed a temporary home he usually took some of the host's valuables with him, knowing full well that, because he was a member of the family, the host would not prosecute him. One day Uncle Ernst had just left his wife Else, forcing her to fend for herself and their small daughter Erica. They had been divorced for a number of years. Despite the fact that my father had found Ernst a job in his office and Ernst had lived with us for some time and he had repaid this kindness by ransacking our silver tableware, my father was prepared to take him with us.

There was also Grossi, who we would not leave behind. My other grandmother, who had come to Berlin after her husband died, had recently died herself after a heart attack.

When Dad put his plan to F's parents F's father stubbornly insisted that he was going to stay in his beloved Germany. He thought my father's plan was far too dangerous and he was not going to risk the lives of his wife and daughter. As I said before, although a kind man, he was very weak. I think F's mother would have gone with us, but of course, she would not go without her husband.

As far as F was concerned, contact had been made with a family in London who were prepared to take F as a young au pair. This was organised through the daughter of Frau P. (where we stayed on and after Kristallnacht). This daughter of Frau P. had married an Englishman just after the First World War and she lived in London.

I was stunned. Whilst I had been completely for my father's plan until then, I could not imagine life without F. After all, we were engaged, even though I was only nineteen and she a mere seventeen. For the first and I think the only time, the man I loved and adored, - my father and I- we had a deep disagreement and row.

I said that if F was not coming with us then I was not going either. Some very harsh words were said by both of us, words that today I wish I had never said to him, but he made it quite clear that I had no choice in the matter: that I was not of age to please myself (in those days one had to be twenty one to do as one liked) and that I was going with the rest of the family even if he had to chain himself to me.

Looking back now, I know that it was his determination in this matter that saved my life. I only wish that I could have done the same for him and my mother and saved their lives when the time came for them to die.

The final preparations were made. There were eight of us who were going to try to escape from Hitler. My father, my mother, Hans and I, Heinz and his wife Susi, Uncle Ernst and Grossi.

On December 22nd 1938 our party of eight left in separate groups for Cologne on the first step of a daring escape. Officially we took only ten reichsmarks (about fifty pence) each with us. We only had the clothes we wore and some socks, stockings and underwear to change into, the shoes we had on our feet and a clean shirt. Unofficially we took a lot more, enough to last my parents for the next two or three years.

It was a cold, grey winter morning when we said our goodbyes to the rest of the family on Berlin's Anhalter Station. I had eyes for one person only. F had come to say goodbye to me and we were both crying like children – which of course we were.

Little did we know then that, within less than two months, she and I would be reunited in the land of all free men.

ESCAPE TO FREEDOM

Between the two world wars there was a strip of land called "No Man's Land" between Germany and Belgium. It had changed hands so many times between these two countries that, in the end, neither of them wanted it. It was only a few miles long and it was, more or less, a neutral zone. The few inhabitants who lived there freely communicated between both Germany and Belgium. They were mostly farmers. They were all rather poor and generally lived on the sale of the products from their land. The nearest town in Germany was Aachen, which was only a few miles away. Aachen was quite a sizeable town with plenty of shops.

Suddenly their fortunes changed! When Hitler had been in power for about three years and the Jewish refugees began to try to escape from Nazi Germany, the people of "No Man's Land" realised that they were sitting on a goldmine.

As I have previously mentioned, only those lucky enough to have had funds invested abroad prior to Hitler's advent and could provide work for the unemployed in the country of their immigration, or people who knew someone who would stand as guarantor for them, could emigrate from Germany legally.

The rest of the unfortunate ones had to take a risky chance and try to get smuggled out. This is where the people from "No Man's Land" came in. They realised that most Jewish people had some assets in Germany, either in money or jewellery. Jewellery was as good as, or even better, than money, and most Jewish people had been converting their money into jewellery, as one never knew, from one day to the next, whether the Nazis would confiscate any monies held in the bank.

So, from about 1936 onwards the people of "No Man's Land" offered to help the Jews to get out of Germany "at a price".

It started in a small way at first, but as things became worse from month to month for the Jews under the Nazi regime, the smuggling of

41

refugees developed until, by 1938, it had become a thriving business for the poor farmers of "No Man's Land". The more desperate the Jewish people were to get out of Germany the higher the price these people charged for human lives and property.

At the end of 1938 the charge was one thousand Reichsmarks for each human being plus twenty per cent of the value of the jewellery that was being smuggled out. To ensure that the correct price was paid for the jewellery the Jew had to get it valued and show proof of what it was worth before terms were agreed upon.

In 1936 my father and his partners were appointed as liquidators of a big jewellery firm, and from 1936 until "Kristallnacht" one of their jobs was to value jewellery that belonged to Jewish people. There were many Jews who were desperate to get out of Germany and my father, in his usual way of helping anybody, offered his services free of charge. He helped them try to get their assets in banks converted and advised them on what sorts of jewellery to buy for the best resale value once they got out. Because of this he knew all about the people of "No Man's Land". He had kept this information in the back of his mind, in case he was forced to flee the country in this way.

I will now explain what actually happened. The Jews met the people from "No Man's Land" on German soil. That is when the Jews paid the fee for getting out and they also handed over all of their valuables.

These people, who were free to cross the border between Germany and "No Man's Land" at least twice a day, smuggled the goods out of Germany to their farms. This was done mostly by women with babies in prams that had false bottoms. These women used to go into Aachen every day to do their shopping. Very rarely were these prams searched. There were a few isolated instances when a search occurred and then the Jews lost all of their belongings and were doomed, but it was all done in a very secretive way, and I still today believe that probably the customs officers got their cut out of it and closed their eyes to it.

To understand this one must understand that to get out of Germany into "No Man's Land" was not very difficult. The Germans wanted to get rid of the "dirty Yids" and the difficult part only started when they tried to get into Belgium. If the escapees were caught they would be sent back to Germany and put into a concentration camp. Your guess is as good as mine as to who kept all of the gold etc. One thing is certain, those unfortunate ones who were caught never saw it again, nor for that matter, were they themselves ever seen again.

Looking back now, after all these years, and putting it on paper, it sounds absolutely crazy, taking such a risk, but to a Jew it was the only chance, and even if it failed, at least they had tried. They knew with certainty that it would not be long before there was that knock on the door in the middle of the night. So what did one have to lose?

We left Berlin on December 22nd 1938, on our way to the border with Belgium.

We arrived in Cologne the same evening. My father had booked us into a good class hotel near the Dome. Good old dad! He was doing everything in style, right up to the last moment.

The next morning mother and father went by train to Aachen, which is only about thirty miles from Cologne. They met up with and settled all of the details with the people to whom we were to entrust our lives.

Hans and I were left to our own devices. After looking around Cologne we decided to have a ride on the steamer on the Rhine.

It was a cold, clear day with plenty of sunshine and we went to Godesberg. It is a lovely little town and it was one of the places where Hitler met Chamberlain during the Munich Crisis. We went into one of the quaint little cafes and ordered coffee and cakes. The coffee arrived, and whilst we were waiting for the cakes, I noticed two men looking at us and then they spoke to the waiter. I heard the waiter say that he did not think we could be, as there were big notices outside. We never finished that coffee, which by the way was delicious, nor did we see any of the cakes. We just got up and left. Once outside we walked as fast as we could. One could see that those two men were "Gestapo" and we made our way to the nearest park. It was a lovely park, but it was spoiled by the writing on the benches. On one side there was a row of benches marked "for Jews only" whilst on the others it said " forbidden for Jews". Of course, the segregation in public parks had been going on for some time, and all of the large parks in Berlin had their special benches for Jews, but as I hardly ever went to a park, I had not taken much notice. I know that from that moment, any regrets that I had about leaving Berlin, even leaving F disappeared. All I could think about was getting out alive from this hell. For the first time in my life I felt a real hatred, not just for the Nazis, but also for the rest of the Germans who had allowed themselves to be misguided by these devils. I am afraid to say that it is a feeling that has stayed with me throughout all of my life.

When Hans and I got back to Cologne our parents were back and a deep feeling of gratitude to my father and mother rose up within me. I went up to them, put my arms around them and kissed them both. My father looked at me and then he hugged me – he understood.

D-Day for us was the next day, December 24th, Christmas Eve. It had been decided to go on that evening because, in true sentimental German fashion, the border guards would be celebrating by drinking and singing, and my parents assumed that they would probably be less likely to be awkward or severe.

We left Cologne just after lunch and made our way to Aachen. When I say we, I have to explain that my father had briefed us all that morning on how we were to behave. First of all we split up into three groups. There was my father, my mother Hans and I. There was Heinz and his wife Susi and then Grossi and Uncle Ernst. We were all to sit in different compartments in the train to Aachen. When we arrived in Aachen the three groups were each to go their separate ways. We were all to meet at a certain cafe at five o'clock, but to act like complete strangers, as if we had never seen one another before.

That part of the plan went like clockwork and I thought it was rather funny, walking past my grandmother, uncle or cousin without any sign of recognition.

The next stage of the plan was that at five thirty a person would walk into the cafe and ask for "Herr Vogel" (Mr. Bird), upon which first the four of us would get up, pay our bill and slowly leave the cafe. The other two groups were to do the same within five minutes and leave separately. We were to be picked up by three different cars and taken to the border which was outside of town.

Well, no-one came at five thirty, no-one came at six o'clock. By six fifteen I could see that my father was getting restless, because we could not sit in this cafe indefinitely without attracting attention. My father kept re-ordering coffee and cakes and so did the other groups. I love a good cup of coffee, but I think I must have drank about six cups that evening. I was commuting between our table and the toilet.

Finally, at six thirty, the door opened and a big gruesome looking man came in and shouted at the top of his voice for Herr Vogel. My father told him that he was Herr Vogel, and the man told my father that the car that he had ordered was waiting. We slowly finished our coffee, paid and went outside.

There was a big black car in the street and I remember entering it with trepidation, thinking, what if it is a trap and the Germans were inside. However, that part of the plan went off alright. The driver of our car apologised for being late, but explained that they had done so deliberately, to give the guards more time to get merry.

To this day I cannot understand why there was all of this secrecy in the cafe, unless it was because one never knew if the man sitting next to you was a member of the Gestapo, or some-one who would denounce you just because he did not like the look of you.

We arrived at the border just after seven o'clock, with the other two cars and the rest of our party arriving shortly after us.

At the border we were all huddled into one big room. They knew that we were Jews of course, from our names and from our German passports with the big "J" in red letters, and the name "Isaac" added to every Jewish male and "Sarah" added to every Jewish female. In fact, everyone in that room must have known that we all belonged together.

I do not think they cared. Although there were a few bottles on the tables, they seemed quite sober to me and, with their typical "German efficiency", they proceeded to interrogate us.

First of all they looked at the sheets of paper in front of them to check whether we were wanted by the Gestapo. Once they had satisfied themselves that we were only an ordinary family who just happened to be Jewish, that we had never been involved in any political plot to do Herr Hitler any harm, and that we had never belonged to any political party, they told us to get undressed.

The women looked at the men and we knew the reason why. There were no female officials present, so that meant that the women were going to be body searched by men. At least the women were saved the humiliation of undressing in front of us, they were taken to another room. A couple of years later, the Nazis were not so particular. They made women and men undress together – before they shot them or gassed them.

After the women left we men undressed. I do not want to go into detail about how they searched us. Let it be sufficient to say that, with typical German efficiency and thoroughness, they probed every part of our anatomy. I understand that they did the same to the women, for whom it must have been a terrible ordeal to be externally and internally examined by these men, who, in their sadistic way, probably enjoyed it.

Needless to say, they found nothing, no hidden pearls or jewels stacked away in some cavity of our bodies. We knew what the penalty would have been! All of our possessions were already in the hands of the men who, we were hoping, would lead us to freedom.

This examination took the best part of an hour, but eventually we were all told to get dressed again. We were then again all assembled in one room and addressed by the man in charge. He told us that we were now leaving Germany legally and entering Belgium illegally. He said that, from this moment onwards we were no longer Citizens of the German Reich but we were "Stateless Jews" for whom there would be no "protection" if we were caught by the Belgians and sent back. If this happened the German Government would have no alternative but to take us into "protective custody" (concentration camp) as undesirable "Jews". When he finished his speech he told us we could leave, and we did.

When we got outside we walked through a wooden barrier and we were in "No Man's Land". It was dark and cold with plenty of snow on the ground. We stumbled along for about two hundred yards and then we heard a whistle followed by another whistle. There was a streak of light from a lamp and then we saw three men who told us to follow them. We must have walked for about a mile when we arrived at a large farm. We entered and there was a large room with a huge coal fire. There was a big table in the centre of the room and a large lady greeted us. She invited us to sit down and then I had one of the best meals of my life. First there was soup, piping hot and delicious, then we had meat, potatoes and vegetables (made from their own produce), followed by home-made cake.

After dinner the lady showed us to our rooms. Hans, Ernst and I slept in one room, Grossi, Susi and my mother in another room and Heinz and my father in a third room.

I do not think that I have slept more soundly in all of my life. Perhaps it was the thought that there would be no knock on the door in the middle of the night. Perhaps it was the realisation that the first stage of our escape had been successful. Although the more difficult part still lay ahead of us, I slept like a little child until about nine o'clock the next morning.

It was Christmas Day 1938. It was a beautiful crisp cold day with plenty of sunshine. I got dressed and went downstairs, where most of the others were already sitting at the table eating breakfast.

After breakfast the man of the house called us all together. He told us that we would not go across the Belgian border that day as had been planned, but we would be going on the following day, December 26th. The reasons for this, he explained, was that on December 26th, although most Germans would still be celebrating Christmas, it would not look as suspicious as it would if we were to cross on Christmas

47

Day. In Germany they do not have an equivalent of Boxing Day and many essential services return to normal on this day. A great deal more is made of New Year's Day than Christmas Day in Germany. He told us to consider ourselves as his guests and to come and go as we liked whilst we were at his house.

I went outside and started exploring the farm. It was a big place. I strayed into the cowshed where one of the farmer's sons was milking the cows. I watched –fascinated. To me, a boy from the city, this was a completely new experience. The boy asked me if I would like to have a go –so I did. I do not know if I mishandled the cow, but by the noises she made she did not seem very pleased with the way I did it.

In the afternoon Hans and I went for a walk and we talked and talked, wondering how we were going to cross the border. My father, if he knew, had told us nothing about it. Perhaps he did not want to worry us,–or perhaps he did not know the details himself. Needless to say, we spent a very pleasant day on the farm.

I remember that we had roast goose for dinner and it was absolutely delicious. In the evening we sat around the fire listening to music and talking. We all went to bed early. Each one of us knew that the next day would be one of the most important days in our lives.

We were woken up at about eight o'clock by the farmer's wife telling us that breakfast would be ready soon. We had a very large breakfast, with eggs and sausages.

After breakfast we were called into another room and there was the man who had come for us at the cafe and another man who my father seemed to know. I learned later that this was the man who was in charge of the whole operation. He was the man that my father had met and made all of the arrangements with on the day he had left us in Cologne.

It was explained to us that, at eleven o'clock, two lorries would arrive. We were to split up into two groups of four and we were to be hidden in these lorries. The lorries would travel for about ten miles to the Belgian Border. There they would be examined by the Belgian

Customs Officials and that it would be absolutely essential for us to remain perfectly still and quiet during that time. If we were found we would be returned to Germany by the Belgian Authorities. If everything went all right we would travel for a further ten miles in Belgium. We would then be transferred to two cars which would be waiting for us. These cars would take us to Antwerp but, for all that time, we had to remain split up and try not to communicate in any way with the other group, in order not to arouse any suspicion.

The lorries arrived on time. We all embraced each another and the people on the farm wished us the best of luck.

I now want you to imagine that you are looking into the back of a large lorry. There is a big open space, full of cases of merchandise. If you look further on, at the end of that space, there is a partition and the driver's cab is on the other side of that partition. Well, our lorries were built like that, the only difference being that the partition was held in place by four large screws. When these screws were removed the partition came away and behind it there was another partition and this one was the back of the driver's cab. The space between the two partitions was about twelve inches, just enough room for a person to stand with his back against the other wall. The width of the cab was large enough for four people to stand like that, side by side. We piled into that small space, and once we were in, the first partition was screwed back into place and then the cases of merchandise were stacked against this partition. In the ceiling of the cavity there was a small hole to let air in.

Hans, Ernst, Heinz and I were in one lorry. My mother, my father, Grossi and Susi were in the other. And then – we began to move. How can I describe what I felt during that journey? I remember thinking that that is how it must feel if one is buried alive. It was very uncomfortable and every time the lorry hit an uneven patch in the road our heads hit the ceiling. I remember wondering what it must be like for my father who was over six feet tall and large. I remember worrying about how he would feel, caged in like that, with the heart condition that he was suffering from. He had angina. It seemed like hours although it could have only taken us about twenty minutes.

And then – we stopped!. I could hear the voices of the Belgian Officials and I remember thinking and praying, "Oh God, don't let any one of us cough or sneeze". The voices of the customs officials were quite close as they examined the cases of merchandise.

And then – it was all over and we moved again. We looked at each other and when we had travelled a few hundred yards and we were sure that no-one could hear us, we turned to each other as much as we could and shook each others hands and we started to laugh – and cry – and sing. I can't remember what we sang, it does not matter. We had done it! We were free! We could hear the other lorry behind us. We were free! We had escaped Hitler's Hell.

The rest of the escape was relatively easy. We stopped after about twenty minutes and the partition was unscrewed. We were in the middle of a country lane with woodland on either side, and there were two cars waiting for us.

The journey to Antwerp took us another five hours. We stopped several times for toilets and for a cup of coffee and something to eat. We did exactly as we had been told. We sat at different tables and we did not speak to the others. We did not have to speak. We just looked across at one another and the look in our eyes said more than any words could have. I noticed that my father was carrying a heavy looking briefcase that he did not have before. It must have contained all of his valuables and jewellery. That was all he had in the world and it was expected to keep him and his family for the next few years. The people of "No Man's Land" had smuggled it out of Germany for him.

We arrived in Antwerp just after five o'clock in the evening. It was dark and we booked in at the "Hotel de Gare" (Station Hotel). Our room had a balcony and I went out on to it to look around me. Everywhere was brightly lit with Christmas decorations. Our room looked out on to Antwerp's Main Street. I looked and looked again and then I realised what was different. There were no swastikas, no flags, no people walking about in brown uniforms with Nazi armbands, no marching nor goosestepping, the air was clear. Even the stars seemed different, and the people. The people seemed happy and unconcerned.

They did not look into one anothers' faces with suspicion. There were no lorries driving up suddenly, with uniformed men jumping out of them and, often, dragging people into them.

I was seeing something that I had not seen for nearly six years. I was seeing people in a free country. Everyone was minding their own business. I was one of them. I had arrived. I was free at last.

That night I prayed for the first time in many years, thanking God that he had delivered all of us safely from Hitler's inferno.

EXILE

I have called this chapter "Exile" because I feel that the short period that I lived in Belgium was a sort of transit stage between my childhood and youth under the Nazis and my life of freedom when I arrived in England.

I liked Antwerp very much. It was lively and gay, a kind of little Paris. As soon as the Christmas holidays were over my father took us to the local police station to register. I have to explain what actually happened in the case of refugees who entered Belgium illegally.

Provided you did not get caught at the border and were sent back to Germany, once you arrived at a city where you intended to stay, you registered with the police. Although you were there illegally, and were liable to be transported back to Germany at any time, people were never sent back. I know it sounds crazy if you consider that, if you were caught at the border you were sent back, yet once well inside the country they did not extradite you. One condition of this was that you had to have been in the country for seven days. As your exit date from Germany was stamped in your passport you did not go to the police to register until seven days after leaving Germany. After three months the Belgian authorities would send you a letter, telling you that your permit in Belgium had expired and directing that you please move on. As there was nowhere for you to go, except back to Germany and to a concentration camp, you appealed against this directive and you were granted a permit to stay for another three months. After this second three months you got another letter telling you to leave and you appealed again and so on. This went on indefinitely. In effect it meant that, once people were able to reach Belgium proper, away from the border, the authorities would not send them back to Germany.

We had moved out of the hotel and had taken a small flat in Rue de Bex, quite a respectable area of Antwerp. There were five of us living in that flat, my father, my mother, Grossi, Hans and myself. Heinz, Susi and Uncle Ernst lived in a separate flat in the same house.

52

Once we had settled father proceeded to try to convert his jewellery into cash. He got quite a nasty shock! Antwerp is one of the major diamond centres of the world and, because of this, the prices offered to him were not as high as he had expected, but he still got enough for us to live on, moderately, for about two years. My father knew that he would never get a work permit in Belgium so he started to put feelers out and make enquiries about other countries including England, investigating the possibility of investing his money in someone's business to provide work for the unemployed. As I have said before, if one could actually prove that one could provide employment, there was a possibility of that country accepting you to live there.

As for myself, after the initial two weeks or so of enjoying my newly found freedom, including being able to sit in cafes and generally move about without fear, I was beginning to get bored.

I enrolled in an evening course at the local Technical School. The course involved doing practical work on the lathe, thus giving me more manual experience. It was a good job that I could read drawings, because I could not understand a word they were saying. Although both French and Flemish are spoken in Antwerp, and I did have a little knowledge of French from my schooldays, I did not know Flemish at all, and that was the language that was used predominantly.

In the second week of January, F left Berlin for London, where she had been accepted by an English family. They had stood guarantor for her and she was to live with them as a companion/au pair.

I now saved all of my pocket money every week, and instead of spending money going to the cinema etc., I phoned her in London, from Antwerp, every weekend, speaking to her for about five minutes. Now that I was living in a free country, without the threat of Nazism, my longing to be with her had returned, and I felt completely miserable except for the few minutes each week when I spoke to her on the telephone.

One evening I had a long talk with my parents. I discussed with them the fact that I was thinking of applying to go to England and, if that application was successful, would they mind me leaving them. They were very sensible about it. They realised that I would not be allowed to work in Belgium. They also realised that if by any chance I did manage to be able to go to England, I could probably be useful to my father, by establishing contacts there which could be helpful in enabling him to eventually start a business there.

I knew that, at that time, there was a scheme in England where refugees who had manual experience, such as carpenters, engineers, electricians etc., were allowed into the country to work as Trainees for thirty shillings a week (about one pound and fifty pence). One condition was that, at the end of the training period, they would leave the united Kingdom, not to go to Germany of course, but perhaps they would be accepted into the U.S.A. or another overseas country.

As there were very few Jewish people who had actually learned a manual trade, application numbers were not very high. Most Jewish people had their sons and daughters trained in academic professions or business, and for these people, there was very little chance of being allowed to enter England.

The next day I sat down and wrote a letter to the British Home Secretary. I outlined my experience in practical and theoretical work in Engineering, endorsing my application with the relevant references that I had from Berlin.

Within a week I received a reply from London, thanking me for my letter and stating that they would try to get me to England within four weeks.

I must admit that I was elated. I could not think of anything else except that I might be reunited with F very soon. The time seemed to drag. When, on February 9th 1939, the letter arrived endorsing my travel permit and permission to enter the U.K. my joy knew no bounds.

I made preparations to leave, and the date set for my departure, and for the first real parting from my parents in my life, was February 16th.

I was sailing from Antwerp to Harwich on the night boat and F was to meet me in London at Liverpool Street Station the next morning.

When the day for me to leave arrived I felt very happy and very sad too. Here I was, nineteen years old, protected as I had been for the whole of my life by the love and care of my family, and now I was plunging, on my own, into a new life, in a new country whose language I did not understand and could not speak and yet – that was where I wanted to be because the girl I loved was there.

Looking back after all of these years, there is no doubt that the only reason that I came to England was my love for F. Had I not done so, my fate would, most probably, have been the same as my parents, and I would not be alive today to tell my story. It is so strange, the role that fate plays in one's life. There was another time, a few months later, when I was married and I saw my parents for the last time. My mother implored us to stay with them in Belgium. Had we done so we would not have survived.

But back to February 16th. When it was time to leave we all went to the quay and after saying goodbye to everyone I went aboard. It was ten o'clock in the evening when the ship sailed out of Antwerp harbour. The lights of Antwerp twinkled in the starlit sky. I stood on the deck, waving goodbye to my loved ones, and to Antwerp, the city that had been my refuge from Hitler's Hell for seven weeks, the city which I will always have a nostalgic liking for because of this. In the distance the lights of the lighthouse showed us the way out from the Schelde to the sea. I stood on the deck for a long time, reflecting on my childhood and my youth, and looking ahead, even with some trepidation, to my adult life that the ship was taking me to.

There was a tap on my shoulder and the steward advised me that my sleeping quarters were ready. After my first whiskey, I thought it only appropriate to try one if England was to be my new home, I went to bed. I did not wake up until six thirty in the morning, when the steward shook me and told me that we were in England.

PART 2:
THE NEXT
FORTY FIVE YEARS

THIS "ENGLAND"

Most people, who are born and bred in England, take everything here for granted. They have their little moan and grumble about the authorities if things are not going their way. That is what is so magnificent about England. One can stand up and speak one's own mind, even on a box in Hyde Park in London. It is all so natural to the lucky boy or girl who grew up here and has never known any different. Can you imagine what it felt like to some-one like me, who had just escaped from a country where the best years of my youth were spent looking over my shoulder, checking to see if anyone was watching me and getting ready to denounce me.

From that moment, February 17th 1939, at seven o'clock in the morning, when I first set foot on English soil, I felt like I had been born again. I fell in love with this country there and then. It is a love that has grown during the years that I have been living here. Today I feel as though I have always lived here. I do not think that I could feel any more patriotic if I had been born here. Very often, when I talk with other Jewish people who escaped Hitler and made their home here, I find that their patriotism to England is not as great as my own. I get the impression that they still consider themselves Jews, who have adopted England as their country because it gave them refuge and, since then, probably a good living. I am surprised that many of them still seem to believe the old Latin proverb; "ubi bene, ibi patria", meaning "where life is good, that is your country". I seem to be different from many of them and indeed, very often I find it difficult to convince British born people that I feel as much for this country as they do, in some cases perhaps even more. Many people cannot understand how a person who was not born here can feel so deeply patriotic. I think I said earlier that I have always believed being Jewish is just a religion and, whatever country one lives in, one must try to assimilate and mix as much as possible with the people of that country. I think one should adopt their habits and manners and try to get them to accept you as one of them. Unfortunately, many Jewish people who were lucky enough to be accepted into this country still tend to stick closely together among themselves, therefore forming a group of their own and isolating themselves from the rest of the British community.

Someone once said to me that he always felt as if he were on the outside looking in on the rest of the world because he was Jewish. It need not be like that. If one tries, to the best of one's ability, to behave and act as the British do, and the people believe that you are genuine and really love their country as much as they do, they will accept you.

Let me make something quite clear. Being Jewish gives one a certain affinity and, of course, a sympathetic approach to anything concerning Jews throughout the world. That feeling is never lost and I think that it is right to feel this way. Many Jewish people who converted to the Christian faith realised that they had tried to take the easy way out, and they found that they were not accepted by either the Christians nor by the Jews. Having said that, I do not mean that because one is born Jewish, a fact that one has to accept because one cannot choose where or as what one is born, that one has to feel exclusively that way for all of one's life, shutting out allegiance to the country where one lives. Both can exist side by side. I have spent some time here expounding my patriotism because I feel that, having lived here for forty four years and been an Englishman for the past thirty six years, it has some bearing on the way my adult life in England developed.

Let us get back to that February morning forty four years ago. I went through the English customs and I did not understand one word that the customs officer said. I then boarded the train to London. In those days the railways in Britain were still privately owned and I was taken to a lovely Pullman coach to have my first English breakfast. Apparently, in those days of Private Enterprise, breakfast was included in the price of a boat/train ticket.

Being used to a continental breakfast, which usually consists of rolls, butter and marmalade with the occasional boiled egg on Sunday, I could not believe my eyes when I saw what was put in front of me. First there was porridge, followed by eggs, bacon, sausages, tomatoes and mushrooms and also toast and marmalade and my first English tea, which was new to me as well, as in Europe tea is served with lemon, not milk. I have, since then, got used to English tea but have always preferred coffee.

By the time I had finished my breakfast the train was approaching the outskirts of London. I must admit that, at first glance, I was not very impressed. All I could see were rows and rows of chimneys and dirty old houses. I was soon to change my opinion of London, later that day. The train rolled into Liverpool Street Station.

I looked out of the window and there was F. I can still see her today. A small, forlorn figure in a blue winter coat and a beret perched on her head. I waved to her frantically and then she saw me. A minute later we were in each others arms. I remember marveling at how good her English sounded to me. As far as I was concerned I might as well have been in China, I could not understand a word.

The first thing we did was go to the offices of the Jewish Refugee Committee in Bloomsbury as I needed to register with them. There were hundreds of people there and we spent all morning in their office. They made an appointment for me to meet the boss of the firm where I was going to work. The appointment was for the following day. As my knowledge and understanding of English was nil, one of their officers was to be with me at this appointment. They asked me where I wanted to stay in London. As F's employers lived in Willesden I asked for lodgings in that district. They made a phone call and I was fixed up with a furnished room in Willesden. Finally they gave me one pound to cover my fare to Willesden. I was reminded not to forget that I had to register with the police at Willesden Police Station as soon as possible as an alien.

When we left their offices we went for lunch and then F asked me if I would like to have a look at London. We went to Piccadilly Circus first and from there to Trafalgar Square. We looked at Buckingham Palace, Whitehall and the Houses of Parliament. We crossed Westminster bridge and looked up and down the Thames and I knew then, that to me, London was and still is the most beautiful city in the world. I was overawed by the splendour and majesty of it all. It was a good job that I had left my suitcase at the station. It was a very tired, but happy couple who made their way back there.

After collecting my luggage we travelled by tube to Willesden. We went to the address that I had been given and rang the doorbell. A not very pleasant, elderly Jewish woman opened the door. As soon as she saw F she stated that no girlfriends were allowed in the house, so I pretended that F was my sister. She gave us a funny suspicious look and then took us upstairs to my room. It was simply awful. There was newspaper on the floor instead of carpet or lino. It was winter and freezing cold and the gas fire was broken and didn't work. There was a bed, a chair and a wardrobe. I made up my mind, there and then, that I would not stay there any longer than I had to.

At last F and I were alone and we talked. F told me about her job. Although she was very grateful to the family for helping her to escape from Germany, once she got there things were not what she expected. They were a young English couple and they were very orthodox Jews. They had two small children and although F was supposed to be treated as one of the family, they treated her as a servant. They liked to go out every night and left the children with F. When she told them that her fiancee was coming to England, and she asked for the day off to meet me, they made a great fuss and did not like it at all. They told her that they did not know that she was engaged and, if they had known that, they would not have consented for her to live with them. Of course she was homesick too. She had been very close to her parents and she started to cry. I tried to cheer her up as much as I could and, eventually, it was time for her to leave. We arranged to meet at the weekend.

It was only about six o'clock and I felt quite hungry. I looked out of the window and saw that the shops were still open. I put on my coat and ventured out. The first shop that I came to was a fishmonger. I have always liked fish, especially the smoked kind that is popular in Europe. I bought some fish that looked like smoked herrings, which are ready to eat and don't have to be cooked. They were "kippers". I also bought some bread rolls, butter, coffee, sugar and milk.

I went back to my room. I buttered the rolls, skinned the kippers and put them on my rolls "raw". I did not sleep very well that night. I needed to go to the toilet every half hour. Since then I have always cooked kippers before eating them.

The next morning, none the worse for my first experience of English food, I made my way to Bloomsbury House to meet my new employer. He was a Hungarian Jew. He had a Press-tool factory in Highgate, which was quite a way from where I lived. This made me even more determined to find new accommodation as soon as possible. We arranged for me to start work on Monday morning. It was Friday, so I went back to Willesden and registered at the local police station. There I was issued with a little Aliens Registration Book which I needed to use until I became a British citizen, which was in 1947.

I decided to go to the cinema that evening. When I got back to the house at about eleven o'clock and let myself in with my latchkey I could not believe my eyes. There was an army of mice running up and down the stairs. I have always had a dread of mice. I don't know what it is, they just give me the creeps. I ran upstairs as quickly as I could and barricaded myself in my room.

The next morning I met my neighbours, a very nice elderly couple from Germany. We started to talk, and when I mentioned that I was starting work in Highgate on Monday, they said they knew of an address in Hampstead where I might be able to get a room. They told me that Hampstead was not very far from Highgate. F came over at lunchtime. She told me that her employers would like me to come for tea that afternoon.

When we arrived at F's employer's house I was greeted by a very brash young woman. Over tea and cakes she told us what she intended to do. She said that she had discussed it with her husband and if F promised to do all of the hard work in the house, such as the washing, ironing and cleaning, they were prepared to allow her to spend every Saturday with me. I looked at F and she nodded.

I thanked her for the tea and we went out. We decided to go over to Hampstead to look up the address that had been given to me and then to go to the cinema.

The house was on the corner of West End Lane and Finchley Road in a very refined area of London. When we rang the bell, a tall dark haired woman answered the door. I introduced myself and we were invited inside. As it happened there was a room to let. Mrs. S came from Austria originally. She had married an Australian and had lived in London for the past twenty years.

She made both myself and F welcome immediately. When I told her that we were engaged she said that she was very broad-minded and that F could visit me whenever she wanted to. Looking back, perhaps it would have been better if she had been more strict on visiting rules.

She then showed us the room. It was beautiful, large with carpet on the floor, a gas fire that worked, a large bed, a wardrobe, dressing table and two easy chairs. It seemed like a palace to me, particularly after the other place. It was twelve shillings and sixpence (about sixty five pence) a week, the same as I was paying in Willesden. I immediately took the room and I paid the first week's rent there and then. I told her that I would move in the next day, Sunday, if that was all right.

We took our leave from Mrs. S. and went to the cinema. When I got home everyone was in bed and the mice were having the time of their lives.

The next morning I told my landlady that I was leaving. She flew into a rage, making wild accusations about F and myself. She finished up by saying that she wanted a week's notice or a week's rent in lieu. I gave her another week's rent, packed my suitcase and thanked the neighbours for giving me the address in Hampstead. I never could understand why such lovely people stayed in that area. Perhaps it was handy for his place of work.

I arrived at West End Lane at lunchtime and I was invited to have lunch with my new landlady and her family. I was introduced to her husband and their lovely daughter S, a young girl of about fifteen, with dark hair and eyes. I thought that my troubles were over but perhaps they had only just begun.

WORKING FOR A LIVING

I had been working at my first job in England for about a month now. It was, of course, my first proper job and I was determined to make a go of it. The first few days were very trying, because I did not understand a word that was being said. Whilst I was able to read the technical drawings and work my machine, I found it extremely difficult to convert the English (imperial) system of inches and fractions of inches, as I was used to metrical measurements. This is rather ironical because, over the last ten years, when metric has become the norm in England, I have experienced the same difficulties again only in reverse because, over the years working here I have become so used to the imperial system that anyone would have thought that I had never heard of the metric system, and yet, I was brought up with it. There were numerous other "happenings" in those first few weeks.

One evening I asked my landlady what a certain four letter word meant. It was a word that was often used by the men at work. After the first few blushes, she explained to me that it was a rough English expression for having intercourse. I replied that I could not understand why the people at work used it when they referred to the job or to the machine. I have since learned that it is a universal word in the English language. I have used it myself many times during my working days in the factory. Today, of course, people use this four letter word on television, in the theatre and on the radio etc., but then, in 1939, it was not used outside the workplace.

The place where I worked was rather small. About thirty people were employed there. It was a press-tool factory and the work had to be very precise. The people there were quite nice to me. They had a good laugh at some of my English but it was all in a good-hearted manner. Later on, when I had mastered a few words of the language, they started asking me about Germany, but I could tell, by the expressions on their faces, that they did not believe me and that they thought that Hitler was not to be taken too seriously. Time, and places like Auschwitz have, of course, proved them wrong, but, in those far off days, my stories of persecution and concentration camps seemed unbelievable to the average, decent British workman.

My pay was fixed by the government. As a trainee (this was the term under which I had been allowed to enter England and work here) I was paid thirty shillings a week (about one pound fifty pence). If the reader wonders how I managed on this the answer is that I did.

My rent was twelve shillings and sixpence a week (sixty two and a half pence in today's currency). One must realise that, in those days, eggs were sixpence a dozen and fish and chips was fourpence. I did manage, and on Saturdays, when F was allowed to spend the day with me she would cook a dinner for me when I came home from work at lunchtime. In those days the working week was forty eight hours and included Saturday morning. As I said, when I got home on Saturday, F would be there cooking a meal on the gas ring in my room.

After lunch we enjoyed each others company. We were young, very much in love, lonely and inexperienced. Today all of these things are taken for granted in our permissive society, however, in those days, it was frowned upon unless one was married,– but after all we were engaged, hoping to marry one day and we only had each other in a new world and a new country. In the evenings we went to a concert or to a film.

I was determined to learn English as quickly as possible and, for that purpose, I collected every newspaper that I could get hold of and sat up late at night to read them. If there were any words that I did not understand (and there were plenty) I asked Mrs. S (my landlady) to explain them. I had always been rather good at languages at school and, after a relatively short time, I began to dream in English. I knew then that I had mastered it! Until then, every sentence I wanted to say I first mentally translated from German into English before I spoke. Once I started to dream in English I lost that habit and began to think in English.

As I said at the beginning of this chapter, I had been in my job for four weeks. It was Saturday lunchtime and I was in a very happy mood as I boarded the bus which was to take me home and to F. As I mounted the steps to my room I realised that I could not smell food cooking. I thought that something must have happened and that F had been unable to come over.

She was there but I knew immediately, just by looking at her, that something had happened. She asked me if I minded if we went out for lunch as she had not felt in the mood to make a meal and she had a lot to tell me.

When we settled down in a small cafe around the corner she began to tell me the bad news.

The previous day she had been called to Woburn House (the Refugee Committee) and had been subjected to a harrowing interrogation. Apparently Mrs. C (her employer) had decided that she did not want to keep F any longer. She used the excuse that she did not realise that F was engaged when she agreed to take her. She said that she felt that F would be better placed somewhere else, preferably away from London and away from me.

The woman gave F a really harrowing time. Eventually she informed F that arrangements had been made for her to be an au pair to a doctor's family near Shrewsbury and that she was to leave for that destination in two days time.

We were both stunned. It meant that we would only see each other very seldom because of the distance and the travel costs, which were impossible for either of us to afford. That apparently was the idea behind it all. Both Mrs C and the Refugee Committee were determined to break up our relationship. Neither they nor we knew it at the time, but it was already too late for that.

I have often wondered since, which direction my life would have taken if it had not been too late. All we knew on that day was that it might be a long time before we could be together again.

As a matter of fact it was only four weeks later when I received a letter from F that was to change everything. In the letter she explained to me that she thought that she might be pregnant. She asked me to come to Shrewsbury as soon as possible so that we could discuss things. You may think that I was shattered by the news. To tell the truth I was not. I was rather pleased. All I could think of was that, if it were true we would marry and be together all of the time. I did not stop to think about how I would support a wife and a child (there was no Family Allowance in those days), nor did I think of how I would break the news to our families. All I knew at that moment was that no longer would I be alone and that we would manage somehow.

That weekend I went to Shrewsbury and we made an appointment to see a doctor. Although F's employer was a doctor himself, obviously we did not want to consult him. We went to a doctor in Shrewsbury, giving my name and pretending that we were married. He confirmed that F was almost three months pregnant.

Over a meal we discussed what to do. Both F and I needed permission to marry from our respective parents as we were both under twenty one, and in those days, that was the age when one could marry without parental consent. We decided to write to our parents immediately explaining the situation and to ask for their permission to marry. As soon as permission was received I would set the wheels in motion in London by going to the Refugee Centre to explain matters and also by making arrangements for the marriage at a Register Office. We could always have a Jewish wedding at a later date if we wanted to. In the meantime F was to say nothing to her employer. I remember looking at F and I knew what was in her mind. Her upbringing had been very strict and she was terrified about what her parents would say. I had no fears on that score because I knew that my parents would always help me if they could.

We parted with a heavy heart. I remember feeling very loving, tenderly looking at that little girl of seventeen who, hopefully, was soon to be my wife. I felt really grown up, yet I was only nineteen myself. Looking back on what happened later on, it was doomed not to last from the beginning, but that evening as we said goodbye at the station, we both felt very loving towards each other. In later years I have tried to analyse why it went wrong and I have come to the conclusion that because of our circumstances, both victims of Hitler's persecution, both cast outs, away from our families, both alone, we only knew that we wanted to be together, regardless of our young age, inexperience and lack of security. It is, perhaps, because we felt so lonely and insecure that we went into marriage completely unprepared, knowing only that we wanted to be with each other.

My parents were marvelous, just as I had expected. F's parents were very difficult. They wrote a very strong letter to me and to my parents. My father told them to be glad that we were so fond of each other. I think he also told them a few home truths. They grudgingly gave their consent to our marriage. Later on, after the children were born, they really melted and became very affectionate. Neither they nor my parents were alive when our marriage went wrong. I could just imagine F's mother saying "I told you so".

With the permissions of both sets of parents in my hands I went ahead with the preparations. I dreaded the interview with the Refugee Committee but, unexpectedly, they were quite amiable and even gave me an allowance of one pound per week once I was married. My father also offered to send me one pound each week, so I would be two pounds better off. I felt rich!

It was arranged that the wedding would be at Hampstead Register Office on June 5th and we intended to stay at my lodgings for at least another few months. However, about three weeks before the wedding, something happened that made me decide to move as soon as we were married.

I mentioned earlier that Mrs. S (my landlady) had a daughter who was about fourteen or fifteen years old. She and I seemed to get on very well together despite the fact that she was highly strung and lived her life out of books. Because I felt lonely without F, I encouraged the daughter to come to my room in the evenings. We would sit on the floor and talk and read. What happened was perhaps my fault, but one evening when she came into my room she threw herself into my arms.

She told me that she loved me, asked me not to marry F and threatened to kill herself. All of a sudden she started to undress herself and asked me to sleep with her. It took all of my persuasion to get her out of my room. I had a sleepless night, wondering if she would be foolish enough to harm herself. Needless to say she didn't and she hardly spoke to me for the remainder of my time at that address.

It was shortly before this incident that Hans came to England. My father had managed to secure a place for him at Maidenhead College so he could continue with his studies. I was very happy to have my little/big brother near me again. By now he was a lot taller than I was. I am also glad to say that when I introduced him to Mrs. S's daughter she immediately turned her affections to him and, I believe, they have been good friends ever since.

F came to London on June 4th, the day before the wedding. She slept at Mrs. S's house that night and on June 5th 1939 we got married. F's Aunt Erna and Uncle Karl were present to represent F's family and Hans and my Uncle Max were there for my family. Uncle Max had been born in England. He had always had a British passport and had managed to get out of Germany quite easily. He kept a boarding house in Swiss Cottage

After the wedding F and I went shopping and began to look for new lodgings. I never told Mrs. S about my encounter with her daughter. They both attended the wedding, but I was determined to move. I also felt that I needed to be nearer to my place of work in order to save on bus fare. After a few days we were successful and found lodgings with a very nice young couple in Highgate, about twenty minutes walk from my factory.

The storm-clouds were gathering over Europe, but we were oblivious to it. We had each other and my parents had asked us to visit them in Belgium in August. They had rented a cottage at Kalmtout, on the Dutch border and wanted us to join them before the baby came.

We were both looking forward to that. Little did we know how difficult it would be for us to get there. We also did not know that it would be the last time that I would see my parents.

69

LAND OF
HOPE AND GLORY

It was a glorious summer, that summer of 1939, the last summer of peace. We had moved into our new lodgings and we were very happy. I went to work every day and when I got home in the evening there was F and a dinner waiting for me. We were looking forward to our holiday in Belgium with my parents. We were going to Belgium on August 6th which is the beginning of the traditional holiday week in London. I intended to stay for two weeks although, in those days, one week was all that one was allowed off work, but I intended to send a letter from Belgium, making some excuse, perhaps that I was not well, in order to clear myself.

We were still holders of German passports, so F had to go to the German Embassy in London to apply for our visas. She came out with the visas plus a great big "J" stamped in our passports, showing that we were Jewish. Even here in England, the Germans still exercised their mad ideology and there was nothing that we could do about it, because once one entered the German Embassy one was on German territory. One took a risk going there. People had been known to disappear and shipped back to Germany, so perhaps we were lucky just to have the "J" inserted in our passports.

Next we went to the British authorities to obtain their permission to go to Belgium and to make sure that we would be allowed to return to Britain. If all of this sounds very complicated please do not forget that we were aliens and refugees too, and at that time regulations were very strict.

The final part of the formalities was to obtain an entry visa from the Belgian authorities and that was where we came unstuck. They put every conceivable difficulty in our way, making the excuse that we were German refugees and, for all they knew, we may not want to leave Belgium to return to England. I could have laughed in their faces. I left Belgium and came to England because I could not work in Belgium, and for me, Belgium was too near to Germany anyway. However, it was red tape all the way. They said that they would have to make further enquiries before we would be issued with visas. It dragged on until the day we were to leave, and still no entry visas. That morning I hit upon an idea. I told F that I would go to the embassies of countries that had a border with Belgium and see if I could get visas for our entry into any one of them. If I was lucky we would go to that country and, once inside that country we would apply for a tourist visa to go to Belgium for a few days. I made a list of the countries concerned. These were France, Holland and Luxemburg. I first visited the French Consulate and I was in luck. Without any problem I was issued with visas for us to visit France. I phoned F and told her to meet me at Victoria Station, from where we would catch the boat train to Paris. Everything went off like clockwork. We arrived in Paris at five o'clock the following morning. After checking in at a cheap hotel for a few hours sleep we were ready to go to the Belgium Consulate when it opened at ten o'clock. We had no trouble whatsoever in obtaining tourist visas for Belgium from them.

I had sent my parents a telegram from London before we left, informing them that we were going to Paris to try to get a Belgium visa there. I now sent them another telegram from Paris, stating that we would arrive in Brussels at midnight. We then decided to have a good look at Paris before our train left for Brussels in the evening.

Everything went off without a hitch and when our train drew into Brussels Station my parents were there to greet us. From there we made our way to Antwerp, where Hans joined us a few days later. As a student he did not encounter any problems visiting his parents. We had an absolutely marvelous two weeks with my parents, the second week being spent in the little border resort of Kalmtout where my parents had rented a house. But, like everything else, the holiday had to come to an end.

The day before we were due to leave my mother implored us not to go back to England but to stay with them. As gently as I could, I explained to her what England already meant to me and that I could never live anywhere else. With tears in her eyes she promised to try to join us there as soon as possible. My father had already made contact with some acquaintances he had in London and, as the only way for him to be accepted into England would be to start up his own business and employ people, the first steps in that direction had been taken. Of course the war put a stop to those plans. As a matter of fact, if the war had broken out six months later, my parents would have been safely in England and they would not have suffered the horrible fate that they did. My decision to return to England saved my life.

Finally it was time for us to leave and, as long as I live, I will always remember those few last moments at Brussels Station. My mother took hold of Hans and me and made us promise to look after each other, a promise we have kept up to this day. When the train began to move I stood at the window waving goodbye to those two dear people. My father had his arms around my mother who was crying unashamedly and I thought that I could detect a tear in his eyes too. I stood there until I could no longer see them. My heart was heavy with grim foreboding, as if I knew that it was the last time that I would see them.

We arrived back in London in the early evening. The date was August 22nd 1939 and the headlines in evening papers carried the news of Hitler's non-aggression pact with Stalin. War was inevitable, and barely a week away.

When we arrived home there was a letter there for us from the Belgium Consulate, expressing their regret, but stating that they were "unable" to see their way to issue us with a visa to visit Belgium. We both thought that was very funny and I realised then that there is always a way of doing things if one is determined enough and accepts the challenge. It is a philosophy that has stayed with me for all of my life and I have always been intrigued by and excited to accept the challenge.

That weekend, the last weekend of peace for six years, we went to Alexandra Palace, which was quite near to us and we sat in the deckchairs listening to the band. I remember this particular Saturday afternoon. The band played some music that I had not heard before and, all of a sudden, everyone stood up and joined in singing. The music was Elgar's "Pomp and Circumstance" and the song was, of course, "Land of Hope and Glory". I was deeply moved and it has remained one of my favourite songs throughout the years, just as Elgar has become one of my best loved composers.

That evening we went to the West End and saw, of all things "Hell's Angels" with Jean Harlow, a film about the First World War. When we came out of the cinema the sky was lit up with lightening and thunder and after those warm days the rain came tumbling down. It was a suitable prelude to the next day which was September 3rd 1939.

After listening to Chamberlain's speech on September 3rd confirming that we were at war and, after the panic of the first air raid warning a few minutes later, we settled down, wondering how it was going to affect us, as aliens and German citizens in British eyes, although we were stateless as far as the Germans were concerned.

The next morning at work the men were laughing and joking, saying that it would all be over by Christmas. How wrong they were! My boss at work gave me a rise of five shillings a week, which was more than welcome, as I would not be able to get any money from my father now.

We had to register with the police as "Refugees from Nazi Oppression", but otherwise nothing changed. I had been considering looking for another job because once the baby arrived it would be difficult to manage on the money I received. I made tentative enquiries and was told that now there was a war on I would not be held to my terms as a trainee, and if a firm was prepared to apply for a work permit for me to work for them that was quite in order. I had no intention, however, of changing my job until after the birth of the baby, as all of the arrangements regarding the midwife had been made.

My eldest son, Ralph, was born on December 31st 1939, a few hours before the New Year chimed in. I now began to scan the papers seriously looking for jobs and I went for interviews. Eventually I was lucky and I secured a position in Croydon. The pay was five pounds a week, which was about three times as much as I was getting in Highgate. We proceeded to look for accommodation and we found a self-contained furnished flat in Upper Norwood, about twenty minutes bus ride from my place of work. For the first time we had a place of our own.

We settled in nicely and received regular letters from my parents. I even acquired a taste for beer and I went regularly, every Friday evening, for an hour, to a pub just opposite our home. The pub had atrocious blackout.

The war seemed very far away. Poland had been conquered by the Nazis within three weeks and we were now in the stage of the "phoney war" with Chamberlain assuring us that Hitler "had missed the bus". Shortly after Hitler invaded the Scandinavian countries and then, on May 10th 1940 Belgium and Holland were invaded. Chamberlain was forced to resign (thank goodness) and Winston Churchill became Prime Minister.

Then the Blitzkrieg went into France and there was Dunkirk and no Maginot Line. These were anxious days with the invasion of Britain seemingly only days away. I was working a twelve hour shift every day and worrying myself to death, wondering what had happened to my parents. Eventually I received a letter from them. They were both safe in what was called "unoccupied France". My father was interned in the "Camp de Gurs" near Perpignan, but my mother was free and living in Marseilles, giving English lessons.

My parents were able to see each other quite frequently as my father could go out on parole. They asked us to send them clothes parcels which we gladly did. Slowly, bit by bit, I was able to find out what had happened to them. On May 10th they had been in a tramcar in Brussels, where they had been living for some time, when they were arrested by the Belgian police, as aliens and German nationals. They were not allowed home, so Grossi, who lived with them, had no idea what had happened to them. They were sent from one transit camp to another, until, after the fall of France, they finished up where they now were. Most of the women were released but the men were kept in internment where they were treated reasonably well by the French.

Heinz's wife Susi was missing, believed killed by a bomb on May 10th. After searching for her for several days Heinz was also arrested and sent to France, as was Uncle Ernst, but he was in a different camp.

I was so relieved when I finally heard from my parents and we corresponded with them and sent parcels to them for the next two years. Grossi was not arrested because she was over sixty five. She was allowed to stay on in their flat, where Hans found her when Belgium was liberated. All of my parents jewellery and money, which had been in the flat had been confiscated by the Gestapo and by the German swindlers posing as Gestapo.

Hans was still in college and came to stay with us during vacations. During the summer vacation of 1940 he was arrested by the police and interned on The Isle Of Man. Eventually he was sent to Australia on the infamous ship "Dunera" where refugees and Nazi prisoners were mixed and several refugees committed suicide. Hans was returned to England in 1942, and he joined the British Army and rose to become a sergeant.

After the fall of France and with the invasion of Britain looking imminent many panic actions which had been triggered by the "Fifth Columnists" of France and Belgium were initiated. Most German or Austrian refugees were interned. To many, who had escaped to England directly from a concentration camp, it was a bitter blow and some committed suicide. I was not interned because the country was desperately short of skilled engineers and I was working for the British War Effort making planes.

The air raids were frequent now, day and night. They always seemed to come when I was in the bath on Sunday morning. I felt helpless, sitting there with nothing on and the bombers overhead. I remember thinking that I hoped they would not find me like that. I had a lucky escape one Friday night. The pub that I usually went to on Fridays received a direct hit. Thirty five people including the landlord were killed. I had worked late that evening and stayed home. And then —it was not a bomb—but another blow fell. Again my life was to completely change.

The firm I worked for began highly secretive work and felt that they could not take the chance of employing a foreigner (and one of "German" origin) any longer, so I lost my job. We had to move because we could no longer afford the flat. We moved into one room again in a house in Beulah Hill.

I was receiving dole (unemployment) money, which was one pound per week for a married couple and child. I had to walk to the Labour Exchange twice a week. This was about three miles away in Brixton but I could not afford bus fare. Then came the day when I was informed that, because I was not working, I would be interned within two days and sent to The Isle Of Man. To crown it all, F was pregnant again. It was, indeed, one of the darkest periods of my life. And then —the reprieve. I think they did not want to provide transport for one refugee to the Isle Of Man. They said that I would not be interned but I could attend a job interview. There were about fifty men interviewed and I got the job.

It was with Dunlop and I was to work at their shadow factory in Hinckley. I had never heard of the place.

On February 2nd 1941 we left for Hinckley. I had been out of work for six months. I vowed that if I could help it, I would never be out of work again –and I never was.

THE NEXT THREE YEARS

It was almost two years to the day after I had arrived in London when I left it to start a new life and a new job. We arrived in Hinckley about mid-day on February 2nd 1941 and I must admit it was very strange for me to settle down in a small town as I had lived in capital cities for all of my life until then. The population of Hinckley, at that time, was about 35,000. It is nearly double that figure now. We had been found lodgings by the firm that I was to work for. After depositing our luggage in the small room that was to be our new home, we had a look around the town.

It all seemed so small and old-fashioned compared with London and it took me a long time to settle in, but I did eventually and today, after all these years, I rather like being here.

I started my job the next morning and I was engaged in the building of the Beaufighter Aircraft. There were two hundred employees, out of which about one hundred and fifty were women, as most of the men had been called up for military service. We worked two shifts. Day shift was from eight o'clock in the morning until six o'clock in the evening and the night shift did the same hours at night. Everybody changed over shifts each fortnight and everyone worked seven days a week with a day off in rotation, so if your day off was Monday your next free day would be Tuesday of the following week (after working for seven days). When your free day was Saturday you did get two days off, Saturday and Sunday, because Sunday started the week. We worked these hours until the end of the war.

When I drew my first week's wages it was about thirteen pounds. I had never seen so much money. When on night shift we were paid an extra two pounds for having to work "unsociable hours", so my average pay was about fourteen pounds per week. I had to go on night shift after my first week because I started work in the middle of the shift rotation –and that was when our problems regarding our accommodation started. As we only had one room it was impossible for me to get any rest because there was nowhere else for F and Ralph to go. We began to look for alternative lodgings and we were lucky to find an elderly gentleman and his daughter, who let us part of their house.

We moved into our new home at the end of February and stayed there for about fifteen months until we acquired the first house of our own. On March 24th 1941 F gave birth to our second child. It was another boy and we named him Peter.

It was in May of the following year, 1942, that we were given the opportunity to move into a home of our own. My firm was allocated a number of prefabricated bungalows and I was lucky enough to move into one of the first ones to be completed.

We went shopping and bought some furniture, nothing very luxurious, just everything that we needed. As we had no money we had to buy most of it on hire purchase. A bit later we managed to buy carpet for the living room, but at first it was just linoleum on the floors, but what did it matter. It was our home. We had privacy at last and everything seemed to be perfect.

I heard from my parents quite frequently and we sent parcels to them as often as we could.

And then came that letter in August of that year! It was a letter that was to change everything for me, although I did not realise this at the time. It was a letter from my parents, dated August 8th 1942 and in it my father told me that they were being transported to the "East". At first I did not comprehend it. Did he mean to the east of France or to Russia or to Poland? I did not understand. I only knew that I had a foreboding of something terrible happening to them. My mother closed the letter with the words: "Look after each other and may God help us to see each other again one day". That was the last letter that I ever received from them. It was almost two years later when I heard the truth of what really happened, when I heard for the first time, the name Auschwitz.

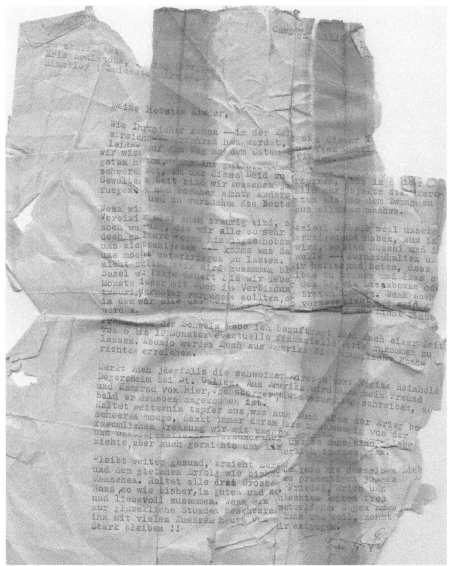

Original last letter to Eric from his parents

Photocopy of Eric's last letter from his parents

Fritz Lewinsohn

Camp les Mill 7.8.1942

zu senden an:
Eric Lewinsohn, 19 King Georgesway
Hinckley (Leicestershire England)

Meine liebsten Kinder,

Wie Ihr sicher schon --- in der Zei
erreicht--- erfahren haben werdet, bis dieser Brief Euch
leider auf dem Weg nach dem Osten uerften Mutti und ich uns
befinden.
Wir wissen, dass Ihr geliebte ...
getan habt, um uns dieses Leid zu ... baumoeglit he
schweren Zeit sind wir Menschen ja rsparen, aber in dieser
Gewalten und koennen nichts andere lle nur Objekte staerkerer
fuegen, und zu versuchen das Beste tun als um dem Zwang zu
aus allem zu machen.

Wenn wir also auch traurig sind, s esiell deshalb,weil unsere
Vereinigung, die wir alle so sehr rbeigesehnt haben, nun in
noch weitere Ferne hinausgeschoben wird, so sind Muschi und ich
doch entschlossen --- komme was da wolle --- durchzuhalten und
uns nicht unterkriegen zu lassen. ir hoffen und beten, dass es
uns moeglich sein wird, zusammen bl iben und denken und dass es
nicht zu lange dauert, bis wir uebe den Weg via Lissabonne ode
Basel wieder mit Euch in Verbindun treten ...en. Wenn /
Monate darueber vergehen sollten,s vergagt nicht ...d s
traurig, es ... ... im dem wir alle uns befinden wir ... ...
werden.

Freunde in der Schweiz habe ich beauftragt Euch nach einer Zei
von 6 bis 12 Monaten eventuelle finanzielle Werte zukommen zu
lassen. Ebenso werden Euch aus Amerika dieslezuegliche Nach=
richten erreichen.

Merkt Euch jdenfalls die schweizer Adresse vor: Regime Reinhold
Degersheim bei St. Gallen. Aus Amerika wird Euch mein Freund
und Kamerad von hier, Jochsberger, die sbezueglich schreiben, so=
bald er drueben angekommen ist.
Haltet weiterhin tapfer aus,was auch Euch allen der Krieg be=
scheeren moege, denkt immer daran,dass unabhaengig von der
raeumlichen Trennung wir mit unseren ... unsere Liebe
und unsere seelischem Verbundenheit uns so nahe sind, dass
nichts, aber auch garnichts uns innerlich trennen kann.

Bleibt weiter gesund, erzieht Eure Jungens mit derselben Liebe
und dem gleichen Erfolg wie bisher zu praechtigen jungen
Menschen. Haltet alle drei Grossen, Friedel, Erich und
Hans so wie bisher,in guten und schlechten Zeiten treu
und liebevoll zusammen. Wenn ein vaeterlicher Segen Euch
nur glueckliche Stunden bescheeren kann und soll, nehmt
ihm mit vielen Kuessen heute von mir entgegen.
Stark bleiben !!

English Translation of Eric's last letter from his parents

FRITZ LEWINSOHN

To SEND TO
ERIC LEWINSON
19 KING GEORGESWAY
HINKLEY (LEICESTERSHIRE ENGLAND)

MY DEAR CHILDREN,
You probably already know by the time this letter
reaches you, that your ellum & I are on our way to
the East.

— We know that you tried to spare us from any
sorrow, but stronger forces are forcing us to go
along ~~and make~~ but we will try and make the best
of this situation.

— We are also sad that our reunion that we were all
hoping for has now been even put further away, but
your ellum & I are braving the odds until we get
via LISABONNE OR BASEL which might take month
before we can get in contact again.

— Friends in Switzerland have been instructed
after a time of 6 to 12 Month any financial works
to come to you, also from America you should
be receiving the same news.

— Remember the Swiss Address from REGINE REINHOL
(DEGERSHEIM) near ST GALLE ~~via~~ A friend of mine from
~~America~~ hier with me JOCHSBERGER, (AMERICA)
will write to you as soon as he arrives OVER ~~there~~.
In the meantime hold together no matter what
the near may bring, we will always be together
in our thoughts.

— Stay well, bring up your children with love and
practical advise. Let the older ones FRIEDEL, ERICH &
HANS be loving and trusting to each other.
LOVE & KISSES. your DAD   — BE STRONG.

But I am digressing. Let me go back to those Autumn days of 1942. We were working very hard. Sometimes we did not even get our day off because Britain was fighting for her very existence and everyone who was not in the armed forces was required in the factories to build the planes and tanks and the weapons needed to rid the world of the curse of the Nazis. Britain was no longer alone. Hitler had invaded Russia in the summer of 1941 and the Japanese had brought the U.S.A. into the war with their attack on Pearl Harbor.

Our little town was swarming with soldiers and airmen of all nationalities but mostly with Americans (yanks) who were stationed at our local dance hall. There was also a garrison of British soldiers stationed here and about five miles away was Bramcote which housed the Fleet Air Arm.

F and I made friends with a work colleague of mine and his wife and occasionally we all went out for a drink together.

It must have been very lonely for F because I seemed to be at work all of the time and that probably explains why she began to go out on her own with some girl friends when I was on night shift. She was young, barely twenty one and perhaps easily led. The first I knew that everything was not as it should be was some chance remark made by someone who had seen her in the company of some soldiers and some acquaintances of mine. Then came the morning when I found the "tie".

I came home from night shift. F was still sleeping and there was this red tie in the house. I recognised it as belonging to someone I knew. When I asked F about it, she agreed that J had been at our house the previous night and by all accounts there had been others too. I asked her what was going on and eventually it all came out. There had been parties galore when I had been on night shift. When I pressed her further F admitted that she had been to bed with some of the men. I was dumbfounded. I could not comprehend it. What I could not understand was how light she made of it. To her it was nothing. We could go on in the same way, as long as I allowed her to enjoy herself when I was not home. Looking back after all of these years, I realise that we were both children. I was trapped in a job from which it was impossible to get released. Jokingly F mentioned someone to me who we had met once. According to F this lady had told F that she would like to take me to a dance. F said that she would not mind this. I remember her telling me that a change would do us both good and that we would appreciate each other more after being with someone else.

Was it the war, the crazy war– working about seventy hours a week with no break? Was it that last letter from my parents? Whatever it was– I took up the challenge and it was the beginning of the end of our marriage.

Today, forty years after the break-up, I know that, whilst in those days I thought that I really loved F and that we would spend the rest of our lives together, it was doomed from the start. We were too inexperienced, too lonely and I suppose the things that really kept us together were our similar backgrounds, both coming from Jewish homes and both victims of Nazi persecution. Once that threat had been removed and we were living in a free country our whole attitudes changed. I blame F no more than I blame myself.

We both started going our own ways. I kept the appointment with Elsie and eight months later she was expecting my baby. Elsie already had a son whose father was a married soldier. By the summer of 1943 F decided to leave me. We talked it over sensibly. I kept Ralph and F took Peter and moved back to London. Elsie moved in with me and her son John, who was about eighteen months old, came with her.

As I mentioned earlier, Hans had returned from Australia in 1942. He was in the British army and he spent his leaves with us. He liked Elsie, whilst he had never seemed too fond of F.

Elsie was a complete contrast to F. She was very good with children, she was an excellent cook and she was very good with anything practical such as sewing, knitting, crocheting and gardening. She was a perfectionist in many ways and by that I mean that whatever she put her hand to it had to be right and therefore she could be rather critical of other people's work. She did not share some of my interests such as classical music and my writing aspirations. However we seemed to match each other in many ways, possibly because fundamentally we were so different. We came from such different backgrounds. She was, of course, not Jewish. She had grown up in a small community in the Midlands. Her mother was a widow. Elsie had never known her father. He died when she was six months old in a flu epidemic and her mother had to struggle to bring Elsie up on her own. Elsie went to work in a factory when she was fourteen. Her mother did not approve of her living with me. She thought that "these foreigners" were all the same and that at the end of the war I would leave Elsie and go back to Germany. Poor soul, she did not understand. However Elsie was very headstrong, and if she had made up her mind to live with me, that was it.

In a way Elsie broke all ties with her family when she decided to live with me. Her uncle was a manufacturer and later town mayor and several of her relations were prominent people in the town. None of them approved of me so they cold shouldered her too.

I soon settled into my new way of life with Elsie. She treated Ralph as if he were her own son and I did the same with John. Our neighbours accepted her. The neighbours never tired of telling me about the parties F gave whilst I was at work and about all of the men who came to the house when I was not there. With typical small town minds, they did not see anything wrong with Elsie living with me and expecting my child or perhaps they were discussing us behind our backs.

Myself, I began to change completely. I was doing jobs around the house, jobs that I would never have dreamed of doing before. I even attempted to dig the wilderness at the back of our prefab and I turned it into the semblance of a garden. Yes, I was changing from being a heavy handed person into a practical one.

F started divorce proceedings on the grounds of my adultery with Elsie. I agreed to this, although I suppose I could have sued her because she committed adultery long before I did. Nothing seemed to matter. A part of me was dead– I think it died the day I received that last letter from my parents.

And then– something happened that brought me back to life. Our baby was expected late in November and we had booked a midwife. I was called out of work at two am. I rushed home. Elsie was in labour. I hurried around to the midwife only to find that she was ill in bed. I had to walk three miles to get a relief midwife, and then when we called on her colleague we found that she was ill too so I had to assist at the birth. I know that today it is quite a common practice to watch one's child being born, but in those days to be asked to roll up one's sleeves and be the doctor was very rare and something that I had not bargained for. I must have done all right because within half an hour, and with me boiling the water, I saw my baby being born. It was a girl– I have always wanted girls. We named her Peggy. The date was November 27th 1943 and I was the happiest father in Hinckley.

TOMORROW IS
ANOTHER DAY

The first time I had the "dream" was shortly after my daughter Peggy was born. Somehow I was on a railway station and there was a train standing there but it did not have ordinary carriages, it was more like a goods train. There were many people about, some in uniform and some not in uniform. The people in uniform were shoving and pushing the others onto the train. They had whips in their hands and they were using these frequently on their victims. As soon as one compartment was full the doors were bolted on these unfortunate people. I noticed that there were no windows nor air ventilation at all. What struck me as odd was how many people were being pushed into each compartment, they must have been packed as tightly as sardines in a tin, yet they were still pushing in more and more people. I could hear the muffled cries of those inside and then– I saw her. I saw my mother. She was running along the platform, looking and searching. She was running along the train from carriage to carriage, looking and searching, and I realised that she was looking for my father. I began to run too, but the faster I ran, the faster she seemed to run, so the distance between us never varied. I seemed to call her, shout her name, but she never heard me. Eventually two big uniformed men caught hold of her and dragged her into one of the carriages. Just before she disappeared she turned and looked at me– smiled, then she was gone.

I had the same dream for the next twenty years at various intervals. Sometimes it would occur at least once a week, sometimes only once or twice a year, but it stayed with me for a very long time.

Shortly after I had the dream for the first time, I heard the name "Auschwitz".

I met someone who I knew vaguely from when I was at school in Berlin. We recognised each other and he asked me to have a drink with him because he had something important to tell me. After we settled down he began to give me some details about my parents and – Auschwitz.

This man had been in the same camp as my father, but when he was told that he was to be moved East he realised that he only had one chance and that was to try to escape. My cousin Heinz, who you may remember was a doctor, joined him and there were one or two more, mostly young men. He told me that, as far as he knew, Heinz had tried to persuade my father to go with them, but my father, for reasons of his own, would not go. Probably he did not want to leave my mother. Their escape was successful and they joined the Maquis, which was the French underground movement, where Heinz, as a doctor, was more than welcome. He said that the rest of the inmates of the camp were taken to Chalons, from where they were put into cattle trucks and transported to a camp in Poland. A camp by the name of Auschwitz.

These trucks, which each normally held ten cattle at the most, were filled with between one hundred and fifty and two hundred people each. The doors were shut on them. There was no ventilation except for a small hole in the ceiling. There were no toilets nor sanitation and many people died on the transport, from typhoid and other causes. Those who survived were gassed at Auschwitz. When I asked him what he meant, he said that he had heard that up to ten thousand people a day were being put into gas chambers and then their bodies burnt. Only the young and fit ones survived for a little while.

He must have noticed the look of disbelief and astonishment on my face and he hurried to add that it was only what he had heard and, like me, he hoped that it was exaggerated. History, of course, has proved that he was right, and so was my dream.

I think, at the time, I did not believe him and was hoping against hope that it was not true. It was, however, the next piece of news he gave me, which although it came as no surprise to me, was the worst of all.

He told me that my mother volunteered to go on the transport with my father, although she need not have gone. As she was free and living in Marseilles at the time, there would have been a good chance of her being able to stay there and perhaps eventually escaping into Spain. However, she made the ultimate sacrifice of love and chose to stay with my father to the end and share his fate. The diabolical irony of it is that the probability of them being allowed to stay together is very slim indeed.

Shortly after that meeting with my old acquaintance questions were asked in the British parliament about a camp called "Auschwitz" and what was rumoured to be going on there. Questions about Auschwitz were also asked in the USA, but it was all swept under the carpet. It was even suggested that the allies bomb Auschwitz, which would have been a great deal kinder to the inmates, even if some of them had been killed. At least their guards would have shared the same fate and these scourges of human depravity would have been wiped off the face of the Earth.

However, at the time, it was thought prudent for "humanitarian reasons" that doing that was not feasible, and of course, at the time, there were far more strategic plans that were of greater importance for the bombers.

So, once again, the free world just looked on. I am making this point here to stress that our statesmen and politicians knew a great many things about Auschwitz nearly two years before it was finally liberated and the rest of the world learned about its gruesome details– yet nothing was done about it.

As far as I was concerned it intensified my great hate for the Germans. A hate, I have to admit, that has lasted for forty years and which, if anything, became worse as more and more details of Auschwitz became known after the war and as I grew older.

It certainly changed my religious views. I had been a reasonable believer but I became an atheist. I just could not believe that if there was a God he could allow for such monstrosities to happen and not punish the people who committed them.

An incident occurred at work that also stopped me from practising the Jewish religion. As I have said before, I was not brought up as an orthodox Jew, but we always kept and celebrated the Jewish High Holidays. The Highest one of these is the "Day of Atonement" or "Jom Kippur" when one does not have any food or drink for twenty four hours. Due to the war I had to work on that day but I still observed the fasting. On the Jom Kippur of 1944 I cut myself badly on a piece of metal on my machine and I was taken to hospital.

The cut was only on my hand and although it was very deep, under normal circumstances I would have been quite all right once it was stitched. On this day however, due to the fact that I had eaten nothing since the previous evening, I fainted and I was taken home in an ambulance. When I came to, I broke with tradition and had some food. I decided then that, if I was required to work on Jum Kippur, I might as well not observe it and I have not done so since.

Somewhere a chime struck two o'clock. I have been sitting here contemplating and looking back on the first twenty years of my life since eight o'clock. I noticed that I was the only person left in the lounge and the staff were patiently waiting for me to leave.

I finished my drink, left a tip for the waiter and made my way to our room. Tomorrow was Tuesday. Tomorrow I would start looking up all the old places of memory, if they were still there. Tomorrow I would start at the beginning. By that I mean from the first house that I lived in after I first came to Berlin, to the first school, to my grammar school, to my place of work, the parks I played in, the woods and lakes where I did my courting, the cinemas, theatres and opera house where I first acquired my taste for culture right up to the last places I stayed before I had to leave it all. Tomorrow I want to try to recall those happy, carefree days. Tomorrow I want to think of only the nice things and the pleasures of youth. Tomorrow I will meet Gerhard, the son of my first boss. Gerhard, who went to evening classes at technical college with me. Gerhard, who, after telling me his story, perhaps may convince me that there were some good Germans too. Gerhard, who in his own way may be able to help me to forget my hate and come to terms with the German people at last. Tomorrow will only be the first of the seven days that I am to spend here. As each day of this short time goes by no doubt I will compare it with my life since the end of my first twenty years up to the present day.

I shall have to go to that lounge again, perhaps not tomorrow night but possibly the night after. I will have seen many places by then. I will be able to think and talk about my feelings on that day and again reminisce about the years which followed the first twenty.

I am looking forward to tomorrow. Tomorrow is another day.

PAST AND PRESENT

I believe it was Winston Churchill who said in his memoirs that, on the day the King sent for him and asked him to become Prime Minister, he felt that all of his previous life had just been a preparation for that day. That was how I felt when I was invited to return to Berlin. Just as Churchill felt that he was walking with destiny, I could not help thinking that my whole life was bound up in that journey.

I think, therefore, that the best way to continue my story is to write about the past and the present side by side. I hope the reader will excuse me if, at the same time I tell you about the intervening years from 1944 to 1983 and also about each day of that unforgettable week in Berlin because, to me, they are inseparable from one another.

As my life unfolds to you and me from the time I was twenty five years old, it will be clear that the next years were very important in every way. My family increased, grew up and had families of their own. Whilst enjoying this part of my life very much, I always felt that there was a vacuum since my childhood and adolescent years which, somehow, I was unable to fill.

It is only lately that I believe this has been achieved. I have been helped greatly by making new friends, who have, in their own way, made their contribution towards me finding what I was looking for. That is the reason why the journey to Berlin and to my past was so very important to me.

Looking back at it now as I write this, six months after I returned from Berlin, I feel that I made the right decision in going. It gave me what I hoped it might, namely peace of mind. I can no more separate the journey to Berlin from the rest of my life than I could be without those who helped me to fill the vacuum.

If all of this sounds rather complicated to you, the reader, I am sure that you will come to understand as I continue with my story. I hope you will. Please excuse me if I leap from one thing to another, to me they are all one, and the seven days that I spent in Berlin gave me the solutions to many questions that I had been asking myself for years.

BERLIN – DAY ONE

In my introduction to Chapter One I may have given the impression that I was travelling to Berlin alone. This was not the case. The invitation included my wife Elsie, and the reason that I did not mention this at the beginning was that I felt that it would have spoilt for the reader of Part One what was to come.

As I said at the end of Part One it was just after two o'clock when I finally went to bed.

We were woken up when the telephone rang. I picked up the receiver sleepily but I was soon wide awake as it was Gerhard. He apologised for phoning so early. He said that he would pick us up at our hotel at nine thirty if that was all right. He said that had brought his car to Berlin with him and he would be delighted to take us anywhere that we wanted to go.

We dressed quickly and went for an excellent cold table, continental breakfast. Gerhard arrived punctually at nine thirty and, after a big hug and introducing him to my wife, he asked me where we would like to go. As we had an appointment at the Lord Mayor's office at eleven o'clock we had just about an hour and a half to spare and Gerhard suggested that we should go to the street where his father had had his workshop in the old days and where I got my first instructions in engineering.

It was only about a ten minute drive by car from our hotel and on the journey I marvelled at how little Berlin had changed in those forty years since I had left.

Later I was to learn that this was not true of course, because forty per cent of West Berlin and eighty per cent of East Berlin had been destroyed during the war, but in some uncanny way the Germans had rebuilt West Berlin in the same way as it was before wherever possible. That meant that practically all of the streets that I knew so many years ago were in exactly the same places. Later that week we had a good laugh because I often had to direct Gerhard to various places, as he used to live in what is now East Berlin and he was not very familiar with the City.

We arrived at Prinzregentenstrasse, where I first started work, and although some of the houses looked different, I recognised it immediately. A feeling of nostalgia came over me as I remembered Karl Murawski, Gerhard's father, who had now been dead for five years. He was eighty three when he died and, according to his son, he had not been in good health for some years before that.

Gerhard showed me the spot where, in 1944, his father had dragged his machines into the street when his workshop was on fire after a raid. Luckily he had managed to save most of them. I listened to Gerhard with mixed feelings. Obviously those machines had been used for the German war effort and must have been responsible for the loss of some British lives, but I was determined not to say anything at this stage as I was curious to hear Gerhard's story, both during and after the war.

It was now time for us to go to the Lord Mayor's office and Gerhard took us there. He stayed in the foyer whilst we were called into the office of the Deputy Mayor. He greeted us warmly and, for the sake of my wife, he spoke in English. He asked if we were satisfied with our hotel and then proceeded to acquaint us with the programme planned for our visit. There would be a trip round Berlin the next afternoon and tickets to a show, the ballet or the opera. We chose the ballet and the opera. The ballet was "Giselle", my wife's favourite and the opera was "Carmen" performed by international stars from The Scala Milan and Metropolitan New York companies. The tickets for these were the best in the house and to round off the week there was to be a farewell lunch given in our honour at the Hotel Berlin, one of the largest and best hotels in the city.

Eric's first workplace showing war damage. Circa 1944

I had expected some of this after the marvelous suite we had in our hotel, but I must admit that I was astonished. There was no doubt that they were treating us like royalty and certainly, in their own way, they tried to make our stay as perfect as possible. I suppose one could say that they were making amends for what had been inflicted upon us by their people forty years ago. I was not prepared to concede anything. My hatred for the Germans was too deep-rooted for me to be deceived by all the glitter and glamour. I thanked him politely and we took our leave, after he had given us further advice about visiting East Berlin, warned us about the vandalism in West Berlin and assured us that his office was at our disposal at any time. He finished by giving us the equivalent of fifty pounds each to spend and apologized for not giving us more.

We returned to Gerhard and I felt like I needed some fresh air, so when Gerhard asked us where we would like to go to next, I suggested the lakes, to which he readily agreed.

Berlin is surrounded by beautiful lakes and woods and it only takes about twenty minutes to get there from the city centre.

It was a beautiful day, the temperature was in the 80s farenheit, and when we arrived at Lake Wannsee we decided to have lunch at an open air inn overlooking the water. After a beautiful lunch of trout cooked the German way, washed down with a bottle of Moselle, we had one of their big pastries covered in whipped cream followed by coffee. I noticed that the prices in the restaurants seemed cheaper than ours in England and the portions were about twice as large as ours.

After lunch we took the steamer to the Pfaneninsel or Peacock Island, where we walked among the peacocks for an hour or two. During the walk Gerhard began to tell us about himself and his life.

When war broke out he was enlisted immediately. This meant that he had to cut short his apprenticeship as a machine tool builder. In those days the apprenticeship for a skilled engineer was seven years. As he was only nineteen when war began he lost the last two years of his apprenticeship. He was sent to Vienna to complete a course which trained him as an explosives disposal expert. After completion of his training his job was just that, to dispose of any ammunition that had not been exploded, such as grenades, mines etc. When I interrupted him to ask if this was not a very dangerous job, he laughed and answered that, as long as one knew what to do it "could" be quite safe, and that in any case, in war one had a good chance of getting killed one way or another.

I let him continue with his story and I learned that in 1941 he was sent to the Eastern front, where he was wounded twice. Once he was even paralysed for some months, but apparently he recovered well enough to be sent back to the front again. In 1943 he was taken prisoner just outside of Stalingrad and for him the war was over. According to him that was the best thing that could have happened to him, as he hated being a soldier right from the start. However, he had not reckoned on where he would be sent to for the rest of the war, and it turned out to be Siberia.

He then began to tell me about the prisoners' treatment by the Russians. To be fair, he admitted, he could not blame them for what they did to the Germans, because of all the atrocities that the Germans inflicted on the Russians. Her told me that, in the first three months of his captivity, ten thousand German prisoners died, mostly of the cold and the conditions they were living in. For eighteen months the Russians would not speak to them, after that things improved. However, he did not get repatriated until 1947 and on his return to Berlin he lived with his father for some time.

I must explain here that Gerhard's father and mother got divorced when he was three years old and he was brought up by his grand-parents, spending the odd weekend with either his father or his mother in turn. He therefore did not feel any great attachment to either of his parents.

During one of his leaves in 1944, he married a girl who he had known for some time and who had been unfortunate enough to have a child by someone else. Gerhard felt that he was sufficiently enough in love with her to marry her and give the child a name. On his return to Berlin he found that his wife, who lived in East Berlin, had become deeply involved with the communist ideology and had been offered a scholarship in Russia. For him this was the last straw. He gave her the alternative of either remaining married to him and starting a new life in West Berlin or getting a divorce. She chose the divorce.

Gerhard described to us what Berlin looked like in those days. He said that it was one big mass of debris and very often it took a long time to reach what used to be a certain nearby street. He could not find any work and he felt guilty being a burden on his father, so when the blockade started in 1948 he decided to leave Berlin. He was lucky enough to get a ride in a British plane which took him to Hamburg. From there he begged further rides until he finished up in Fichtelge-birge, which is a beautiful strip of land consisting of forests and mountains near to the Czechoslovakian border, and about forty miles from Bayreuth.

Although Gerhard was born in Berlin, he had always preferred the countryside and open spaces, and this is where he finally settled down and where he still lives today.

He found a job, managed to rise in his trade, became foreman, married a local girl and built his own house in the middle of a wood. He and his wife have one daughter who is a ward sister in a hospital and he is very contented with his present life. He showed us some photographs of his house and it certainly is very beautiful. He goes to Berlin about once every five years and he is always happy to return home to his beloved "Wauldhaus" (wood house) as he calls it.

We had been walking for about an hour and we sat down in a beautiful spot to watch the peacocks and enjoy the lovely countryside.

It was now my turn to tell Gerhard about myself and my life. I went into some detail about our escape and the fate of my parents. I then told him briefly about my years in England up to the present.

Gerhard was full of condemnation of Hitler and his regime. However, when I questioned him closely about his feelings of guilt for what had happened–for six million Jews murdered, for countless Russians butchered, for all of the atrocities throughout the occupied countries– I found something that I was going to find over and over again with the Germans of my generation. There was an uneasiness, yes, but there was always an excuse. In Gerhard's case, he started listing all of the bad things that have happened since 1945. He mentioned Korea and Vietnam, the Lebanon and Afghanistan. In fact he tried his hardest to compare Hitler's atrocities with those of today. And then, of course, there was the excuse that they all made– that they did not realise what was going on.

I let him continue to talk. I said nothing. I made a mental note of everything. He was a nice chap and he had never been a Nazi. He might have been what one would call a "good German", but like so many, many others he would not have been prepared to do anything about it.

He was only the first. During my week in Berlin I was to encounter the same attitude from everyone I spoke to who was of my age.

I was very quiet on the journey back to our hotel. Something had happened to my relationship with Gerhard. He was a good man who would do anything to help me during my stay in Berlin, but he was a German first and foremost, and I was a Jew, and British too. At that moment I felt very proud to be British. Before we reached our hotel, I asked Gerhard to drive slowly through Motzstrasse where I had lived, up to Victoria Luise Platz where I used to play as a boy. It was all there, Victoria Luise Platz, just as I remembered it.

We then walked the few steps along Munchenerstrasse to where my old school, The Werner-Siemans School used to be, and there I got the biggest surprise so far.

The whole street was different, every house in it was new, but there, on the corner of Munchenerstrasse and Hohenstaufenstrasse stood my school, undamaged, the same as it had been fifty years ago when had I left it. I could not believe my eyes and a peculiar feeling feeling rose in my chest. It was late and the school was closed for the day, but I was determined to revisit it the next day and also to take another good look at the house where I had lived for many years– only I knew that I had to be on my own to do this.

99

It is perhaps difficult for me to explain, but neither Gerhard nor my wife were a part of this. This was between me as I am now and the person that I was all those years ago, and I just knew that I had to be alone.

Gerhard asked me what we were doing the following morning as he was visiting some relatives in East Berlin in the afternoon. This suited us because we were going on the conducted tour of Berlin in the afternoon, so we were free in the morning.

I asked him if he would mind taking me back to the school again the next morning and he replied that he would be only too pleased to do so. Encouraged by his generosity I then asked him and Elsie if they would mind if I left them for an hour or so whilst I looked at some of the old places. I think they both understood and I felt grateful to them for this. Gerhard joked that he might run off with Elsie and we all laughed at that.

We said goodbye at the hotel. Elsie and I had a very good dinner at a restaurant opposite the hotel and then Elsie asked to be excused as she was feeling very tired. I said that I would follow her soon and made my way to the bar for a nightcap– and to be alone with my thoughts.

HINCKLEY
(1944 – 1947)

The night of June 5th 1944 seemed like any other. I was on night shift and had just returned to check if Elsie was all right as there had been several raids on Hinckley lately. Our home was only a ten minutes walk from my place of work. As we had a one hour break at midnight I could easily go home, have something to eat and return to work within that hour. At about four thirty in the morning we could hear the planes roaring overhead. There were so many of them that we could hear them above the noise of the machines–and they were ours. We all knew what that meant. For many weeks we had been waiting for the invasion of the European mainland and surely this was it. And it was! When I arrived home at eight o'clock that morning it was on the B.B.C. news. At last it was the beginning of the end for Hitler and his monsters.

As the days went by, the Germans were pushed back and a few weeks later the allies were in Paris.

My brother Hans, who held the rank of sergeant in the British army, was sent over to France within the first week of D-Day. His name had been changed by the authorities to Lewis, in case he was captured by the Germans, as they would have treated him as a traitor and shot him. This is rather ironical as we lost our German citizenship on Kristallnacht, and as far as the Germans were concerned we were stateless. After the fall of France, Hans went with the army into Belgium and two months later I received a letter from him with the good news that he had found Grossi. She was still living in our parents' flat. Apart from a slight injury to her leg that she had received during a British air raid in 1943, she was very well and over the moon to know that we were all right. Because she was now sixty eight years of age she had not suffered too much at the hands of the Nazis, except for the fact that, shortly after the German occupation of Belgium in

101

1940, the Gestapo had relieved her of any money and valuables that she had, and they also confiscated bank books and valuables belonging to our parents. This meant that everything she had was gone and she was penniless and often went hungry or had to rely on friends to help her. Hans provided her with some money and food. On the question of our parents' fate, she knew less than we did. Hans told her very gently that there was very little hope that they would still be alive. At this she broke down and cried. Hans promised her that, as soon as the war was over, she would come to England to live with us.

Towards the end of that year Elsie found that she was expecting another baby. This time we hoped for a boy, who would be a little brother for Peggy who was our delight.

The new year brought further victories for the Allies. Then came the day when I heard that the biggest monster the world has ever known, Hitler, was dead. I suppose I should have felt elated, but I felt nothing. A part of me was dead and remained so for many years, until the day when I found a new purpose in my life.

During those last few weeks of the war in 1945, many concentration camps were liberated, and the pictures of them, and what the allied troops found are now well known and too sickening to describe.

Then came the day when they entered Auschwitz. I do not want to go into detail. We all know of the misery and death that confronted the liberators.

I have since spoken with people who were there when the troops entered. British soldiers who wept openly at what they saw, who just could not believe that human beings were capable of such inhumanities and in those days many of them felt like I did,– that the only good German was a dead German.

On May 8th 1945, the war in Europe, which had lasted for nearly six years was over, and the hunt for the criminals who did this to the world and inflicted the atrocities was on.

Many of the these criminals were, consequently, brought to trial at Nuremburg and hanged. As far as their execution is concerned I have always felt that it was made far too easy for them. I believe that they should have been made to suffer as they made their victims suffer. However many of them escaped the punishment that they deserved, either because they were given lighter sentences or because they were never caught.

Let me return to life in England and to my own family. On July 21st, which is my own birthday, Elsie gave birth to a healthy boy. We named him Stuart. He was a lovely boy, always laughing and smiling.

Shortly after Stuart's birth Hans came home on leave and we discussed, in detail, our plans to bring Grossi to England.

Hans was now stationed in Herlohn in Westphalia. He was in charge of de-Nazifying the Germans and finding work for them in clearing up the mess that their cities were. He told me that the stench of dead bodies was everywhere and was almost insufferable. As far as the de-Nazifying was concerned, he said that it made him feel physically sick, as no-one would admit to any allegiance to Hitler. He said that he thought that if it were not so tragic it would have been almost laughable. The Germans all claimed to be good citizens who did not like Hitler and the Nazis. What a farce! We knew better as we had lived in Germany. Hans said that he treated them accordingly.

Early in August the Allies released two Atom bombs over Japan and the Japanese surrendered.

With the end of the war proper my job at Dunlop ended. Although they offered me a job at their main factory in Coventry, at very reduced pay, I decided that I would look for a job more local to my home. I was lucky to find a job immediately, again only ten minutes walk from home. It was still two shifts, changing over each fortnight, but at least I was working a normal working week and was able to have my weekends at home.

Early in 1946 I went to Dover to meet Grossi. It was a very emotional moment after all those years and with the memory of my parents deep in our thoughts. We arrived in Hinckley at about midnight. Grossi immediately took the children to her heart, especially young Stuart, who remained her favourite for the rest of her life. She was to live with us and was to spend several weeks a year with her brother who lived in the north of England.

We were still living in the prefab. It was becoming very crowded as there were six of us plus Grossi. In the beginning everything seemed to be all right, but it was not long before there was friction between Grossi and Elsie. I found myself in a very difficult position. I felt sorry for Grossi, but loyalty to Elsie and my family told me that I had to take their side. It was with a sigh of relief that I greeted the announcement from Grossi that she was going to stay with her brother for some time.

However, the respite was short-lived. Apparently the same situation arose there and Grossi did not get on too well with Nelly (her sister-in-law). The result was that, within six weeks, Grossi was back with us again.

As the children were getting bigger and we were so cramped for space, Grossi decided to take a room in Hinckley to sleep in and she spent the daytime with us. This seemed to work better. Grossi started to pick up a few words of English and Elsie a little German. They both managed to know what each other meant at any rate.

At the beginning of 1947, Hans informed me that he was getting married to a German girl who was half Jewish. He had met her in his office. He was also hoping to get discharged from the forces later that year, which I heard with great relief.

At the end of 1946 my firm had moved back to Coventry and I had gone with them. This meant that I spent less time at home and consequently, relations between Elsie and Grossi had deteriorated again. I feel that some of the troubles arose because Grossi was so old-fashioned in many ways and in her ideas, and there was bound to be a clash of personalities.

When Hans finally arrived home with his new bride, Ruth, he and I discussed this problem and we came to an agreed arrangement. Hans had been able to purchase a cheap terraced house in Sutton, Surrey. He now had a job in London with an export firm. We agreed that Grossi would spend six months of the year with him and the other six months with us.

In the autumn of 1947 my divorce from my first wife finally came through and Elsie and I made arrangements to be married on December 13th.

The Council was building some houses in the street next to where we lived and I applied for one of these on the grounds of overcrowding.

During the last week in November I received a letter from the Council informing me that I had been allocated one of the new houses. We moved in on December 6th 1947, one week before our marriage. We are still living in the same house today, thirty six years later. I was now able to tell Hans that Grossi could sleep at our house when it was our turn to look after her for six months.

That Christmas was one of the happiest that I have ever known.

Two days later I received a letter from the Red Cross informing me that records showed that my parents were transported from Drancy in France to Auschwitz in August 1942. Extensive enquiries had been made, as it had been known for people to lose their memory and to wander about in the Eastern zone after their liberation from Auschwitz. However they prepared me to accept the fact that my parents were either gassed or had died on the transport. There was only a slim chance of anything else.

It was no more than I had expected.

My place was here with my children, my family, to ensure that they never had to know hate and discrimination as I had witnessed it. I determined to bring them up to be tolerant of everyone.

BERLIN – DAY TWO

On Wednesday August 22nd, which was our second day in Berlin, Gerhard called for us punctually at nine thirty. Again it was a glorious day with the sun shining brightly and the promise of another warm afternoon.

He drove us to Victoria Luise Platz and there I took my leave from him and my wife. I left them sitting on a bench facing the fountain, my wife knitting and Gerhard reading the morning newspaper.

First I went to my school which was only about two hundred metres from the park. I was admitted to an office where a very nice lady asked me to sit down. She was the secretary of the director of the school.

I explained to her that I was a former pupil of the school from fifty years ago and I told her how surprised I was that the school was still there. I went on to tell her why I was in Berlin and how I had escaped so many years ago. I said that I would love to look around the old school although I expected that there had been many changes.

She was delighted and she told me that I was not the first one to seek out the school. Several former pupils, who now lived in various parts of the world, had visited them over the years. She apologized saying that the director was away that day, but made an appointment for me to return in two days time, when she felt sure that he would be delighted to talk with me and to show me around.

While she was talking to me I happened to glance through the window of her office and there was the courtyard where we used to play games, fight, and tell one another our first secrets about love and sex. It was still there. It was exactly the same as it had been over fifty years ago. In my mind I saw all of my old friends. It was just as if it was yesterday, and that funny tight feeling was there in my chest again.

I turned to the secretary and mentioned the courtyard. She said that she was not surprised that I recognised it easily because the school was, by some miracle, one of the few buildings in Berlin that was never hit by a bomb, in spite of it being a big imposing building that towered over the other buildings in the area.

We spent another few minutes chatting and then I took my leave, promising to return at eleven o'clock on Friday.

I walked along Hohenstaufenstrasse, down Martin Lutherstrasse and turned into Motzstrasse. I walked past the house on the corner of Eisenacherastrasse, where I had lived with my Aunt Ella, Uncle Leo and my cousins Heinz, Max and Kurt. I paused for a moment to think about Aunt Ella who had been like a second mother to me whilst my parents were still in Vienna. She had died from cancer many years ago in England. Both she and Uncle Leo had managed to escape by being accepted as a domestic couple working for a rich man in Hertford-shire. Heinz, as I told you earlier, escaped from the same camp that my father was in. Heinz joined the French Marquis as a doctor and married a girl he met in the Marquis (his first wife, Susi, was killed by the Germans on the day that Belgium was invaded). He was now living and working as a doctor in Vienna. I met with him a few years ago, but more of that later.

Max, who was the person who first got me interested in classical music, was living in New York. He was a conductor and teacher of music. He had gone to Prague in 1937 to study music. Whilst he was there a member of the Hearst family heard him play and paid for him to go to America. He married a sculptress and now has a family. I have not seen him since 1938, but Hans has met him several times.

My thoughts turned to Kurt, who died so tragically at the age of thirteen. Kurt, who had been my closest friend and whom I missed so very much for a long time.

I gave a sigh and looked across the road to No.11, the house where we used to live. It seemed the same– and yet it didn't.

I walked past the house, past the Hotel Sachsenhof, which was there in those early days, down to Nollendorfplatz, which looked completely unchanged to me. I went into the Marmorhouse, which used to be a first class cinema and where I had seen the original Ben Hur with Ramon Navarro. It was now a dance hall and discotheque.

Slowly I walked past the Hotel Sachsenhof again and past what I thought must have been our old house. I was still not sure so I decided to make enquiries at the Hotel Sachsenhof. I went in and asked the man at the reception desk if the hotel had been rebuilt since the war. He retorted that it had been there for over fifty years. Encouraged by his reply, I continued to prod him about the houses around, especially No.11. He looked at me suspiciously and wanted to know why I was asking all of these questions. He was a young man of about thirty five, and I did not feel the need to confide in him. After making some excuse and thanking him I left. I could feel him watching me. He probably thought that I was a spy.

I finally plucked up enough courage and entered No.11.

I must explain that most homes in Berlin, now and all those years ago, are apartment houses, four or five storeys high. Behind this building is a courtyard and then what is called the "hinterhaus" (the backhouse) which has as many apartments.

We used to live in the front house on the third floor. I did not recognise the front of the house, obviously it had been rebuilt. I entered the courtyard and that was it. There was no hinterhaus, only weeds growing wild where the hinterhaus used to be. The courtyard was still there. It looked just the same as when the organ grinder used to play there and we children threw pfennings (coins) to him. Sometimes we would go down to the courtyard and the organ grinder would pick us up and sit us on top of the organ.

I stood there in the courtyard, now desolate and depressing, where the sun hardly ever shines because of the houses all around it. All of a sudden something mysterious and beautiful happened. Somehow the sun shone down on me. The whole place was lit up as if by lightening,– and they were here with me. My father and my mother, there they stood in front of me, hand in hand, and they were smiling.

I am not even going to try to explain this unique experience, because I know I can't. Cynics will say that I dreamed it up. Perhaps I did. I do not know. All I know is that we were together once more after all those years and I was glad that I had come alone. I closed my eyes. I could feel the tears and I cried unashamedly, something that I had not been able to do for many years. When I opened my eyes again I promised myself that I would return here, perhaps not tomorrow, but the day after, and certainly on the last day, before I left Berlin.

I looked at my watch. It was almost twelve thirty. That meant that I had been away from my wife and Gerhard for nearly two hours, much longer than I had anticipated.

I hurried and rejoined them within a few minutes. I apologized for being so long, but Gerhard said that it was all right. They had been to a nearby cafe where they had coffee and lovely cream cakes and they had not noticed the time.

We had a small lunch of Bockwurst (jumbo sausage) and salad, and after that Gerhard left to visit his aunt in East Berlin. Elsie and I made our way to the Lord Mayor's office to join the coach party for our tour around West Berlin.

We were a mixed group on that journey. We were all Jewish and we were all there by invitation, every one of us. Yet– I was the only one who had lost their nearest and dearest. I had lost them to the gas chambers.

There were about twenty five of us and we drifted into conversation with each other. It transpired that, without exception, they had all managed to leave Germany well before Kristallnacht, and they all survived because they went far enough away. Some were from Israel, others from the USA and a few from some South American countries, Australia and New Zealand.

The tour was very interesting. I found the wall at the Brandenburg Gate rather depressing, with the crosses and the names of those who had died trying to reach the West and freedom. To add to this desolate picture, there were the high sentry boxes with the Russian or East German guards, and the vast, desert-like wilderness on the other side of the Gate, where nothing except weeds seemed to grow, until the houses started again. I was going to see a lot more of the Berlin Wall the following day when we were due to go to East Berlin ourselves, but more of that later.

A very moving close to our tour was when we called at Plotzensee, where those people who had dared to oppose Hitler were executed. It was most interesting and reminded me that there were some people who, like me, felt that the world must rid itself of the Nazi monsters at all costs. What a pity there were only so few, compared with the sixty million Germans who were quite prepared to go along with Hitler's ideas, and the rest of the world looked on, feeling that it had nothing to do with them. Silently I saluted the brave men and women who had paid for their courage with their lives.

We returned to our hotel. We were rather tired. We had a meal around the corner on the Ku-Damm and then we retired early. However, I lay awake for a long time, thinking of all that had happened that day. Then my thoughts turned to my family, some of them 15,000 miles away. I remembered my children being small and I remembered watching them growing up.

That is the end of the autobiography written by my father Eric Lewinsohn.

THE REST OF THE STORY
(WRITTEN BY PEGGY)

Dear Peggy and Family,

At long last the promised part of my autobiography that I have written up to now. It is almost a year since I last put pen to paper, not because I have run out of ideas or memories, but simply because I have not had the time to do so.

No doubt one day it will be finished, although since starting to write it two years ago at Xmas 1982, my life has so dramatically changed. Although I am a good deal older and poorer, I have acquired knowledge and new friends, which helped me greatly to gain five "O" levels and two "A" levels, which I would have never thought possible and which have helped me greatly in my new life as a part time lecturer, this being the first time in my life that I am really enjoying what I am doing.

Please forgive me for being so long in sending this. I hope you enjoy reading it.

Although I have had no success with publishers here, maybe someone will come along one day and take a chance with it. Until then, remember, I love you all.

Dad and Grandad

X X X

The letter above, dated November 16th 1984 was sent to me by my father when he sent me the manuscript of his life story, "The Journey Back". It seems that he never did resume writing his autobiography. This is sad in one way, as it means that he never wrote down, in his

111

own words, his thoughts and feelings about the final five days spent in Germany on that traumatic journey back in 1982, and about the effects that journey had on the rest of his life. However, I believe that Dad became so busy fulfilling personal dreams that he never thought would be possible that he simply did not have time to continue to write more about his experiences, thoughts and feelings. I would have liked to have read Dad's life story to the end in his own words, but I think it preferable that he was able to achieve what he thought were unachievable dreams, even if that meant that he did not finish putting his story down on paper.

This chapter, "The Rest Of The Story", has been written by me. It gives a brief overview of what Dad experienced after 1947, which is really where he finished telling us about his personal life, until the end of his "Journey Back" to Berlin in 1982

As already mentioned by Dad, in 1947 we moved from a prefab into a house newly built by the local council. My parents both lived in this house for the rest of their lives. This house was in a street situated just one street away from and parallel to where we had lived in the prefab, so Dad lived in these two neighbouring streets from 1942 until his death in 2006, a total of sixty four years.

In September 1950 Dad became a British citizen. I can only imagine how proud and happy he would have felt on that day. He always, throughout his life, said that England was the best country in the world.

My parents second daughter, Deryn, was born in January 1951, and this was obviously a wonderful time for both of them. I am sure that Dad would have been overjoyed to have another little girl.

It was at about this time that Dad's brother Hans, known to us as Jack, and from now on I will refer to him as Uncle Jack, (in spite of the fact that, after his name was changed for safety reasons when he was in the British Army during the war, his name became Harry, we always knew him as Jack), and his wife decided to emigrate to Canada. This decision was probably a difficult one and painful for both Dad and Jack as, other than their grandmother Grossi, they were the only two members of their nuclear family still alive and they would be so far apart. They must have wondered whether they would ever see each other again. International travel was not a common occurrence in those days.

The reader might remember that Grossi had been living with us for part of the year and with Uncle Jack for part of the year. At some time in the early 1950s Grossi moved into a nursing home in Leicester. I do not know exactly when this was. I am purely speculating now when I wonder if her move had anything to do with the fact that Uncle Jack and his family moved to Canada and my parents had a new baby in the house and, therefore, space was at a premium as there was now my parents, three boys and two girls in a three bedroom house. Both I and my younger brother remember regularly visiting Grossi at the home. It was a lovely building set in beautiful gardens. I remember the elderly people living there and the staff as being warm, kind and friendly. Grossi lived in this home until her death in the mid 1950's.

In November 1954 Mum gave birth to their last child, another little girl who they named Angela Marye. The birth was not an easy one and Angela was diagnosed as a Down Syndrome baby. She also had a hole in her heart. My parents' joy in the birth of their new daughter must have been mixed with concern and worry for her future. It must be remembered that this was the 1950's and medical science was not nearly as advanced as it is now. Angela was loved and adored but sadly she died in March 1956. Her death had a terrible effect on both of my parents.

Life went on. Dad continued to work in the motor car industry and after Angela's death and Deryn had started school Mum began to work outside of home in a factory. Up until then she had been an "outworker", having hosiery work delivered to and picked up from our home.

At some time during the 1950s Peter, Dad's second son, who had been in the custody of his mother since she and Dad had separated, came to stay with us. I imagine that Dad was very happy to be renewing contact with Peter but he only stayed with us for a short time, soon returning to his former life in London. In later years, during the 1990s Dad and Peter did interact and meet on several occasions.

We always went on an annual two weeks holiday to the seaside. We were lucky as many families who went away went for one week only. Dad would take a day trip on the train to the chosen destination a few weeks before the holiday dates and walk from door to door in order to get affordable suitable accommodation.

The household reduced in size in 1960 when both John and myself married. Stuart also left home shortly after this to take up a job in a Holiday Camp and soon after this he also married.

Dad continued to work. By this time he was working at second and sometimes third part-time jobs as well as his full-time job in the factory as is explained in the later chapter devoted to his work.

My parents now only had one dependent child and they began to venture overseas to Europe for their annual holiday. Something they both enjoyed.

I know it was a sad day for my parents when my husband and I, together with our four children, emigrated to Australia in 1972. Did Dad feel that he was losing yet another family member? When we left England none of us thought that we would see each other again, but we did, both in Australia and in England.

In the late 1960s Deryn left home to go to university in London. She has lived in the London area ever since then.

Dad's eldest son Ralph remained living at home for many years. He got married later in his life. Ralph had suffered from mental health issues from the time he was a teenager and sadly he died during the late 1980s, I believe it was in 1988. Although this chapter is about events up until 1982 Ralph's death is too important not to mention here. It was an extremely traumatic time for both Dad and Mum as they had always treated all of the children in the family as "their" children.

At the end of 1979 Dad accepted a redundancy package from Standard Triumph (British Leyland) in Coventry after working there for almost twenty six years. I don't know whether he intended to retire from full-time work at this time as he was sixty years old or whether he intended to look for another full-time job. He did work in a factory again later at Carnall Precision Engineering in Barwell.

After his redundancy Dad began to explore the possibilities of taking further education classes at Hinckley College of Further Education, which he did on a part-time basis. This led to him making new friends, as he spoke about in his letter to me and going on to achieve academic success at levels far above his expectations.

As we all know, in 1982 Dad returned to Germany at the invitation of the German Government. This was his first visit back to Berlin, and in fact his first visit back to Germany since his family had escaped the fear, horrors and persecution of the Nazi regime in December 1938.

Dad's autobiography finishes whilst he is talking about this trip back to Germany. I have not been able to find out a lot more detailed information about how Dad spent his time and what he did during the remainder of this week in Berlin but I will share what I do know. Dad sent me tapes of a talk he gave after his return from this trip and from these tapes I have been able to learn more about this week. The German Government had organised a coach trip of West Berlin and this is the last thing that Dad wrote about participating in during this journey back to Berlin.

On day three of this week in Berlin, the day after the tour of West Berlin, my parents went on a tour of East Berlin which they had organised themselves. It must be remembered that, at this time, Berlin was divided into two, West Berlin and East Berlin, by the Berlin Wall. East Berlin was under the control of Communist Russia

Dad said that when the coach arrived at the checkpoint the driver from West Berlin was replaced by a driver from East Berlin. Every passenger's passport was stamped and each person was given a number. Dad was number 19. Each person entering the East from the West had to take twenty five marks into the East and they had to spend this money in the East or it was confiscated when they left East Berlin.

According to Dad the atmosphere in East Berlin was very different from that in West Berlin. He said that the look on the faces of people in the East was one of sadness and despair and that the communists exported as much as they could and, possibly as a result of this, the shops shelves were quite empty and there were queues of people trying to get goods.

He also said that at that time a couple both working in East Berlin would only earn about half as much as one person earned in West Berlin. Rents were extremely cheap in the East, only about 10% of what they were in the West. However everything else seemed to be far more expensive in East Berlin compared to West Berlin. Food cost twice as much in the East as it did in the West, and, as already mentioned, choice and availability of food was scarce as the shops were virtually empty.

Television and radio were not officially allowed in East Berlin at this time.

Dad was surprised that people living in East and West Berlin were allowed to cross the border for work. I don't understand and wonder how they were able to obtain these cross-border jobs?

By the time he was there, in 1982, Dad said the East had been well rebuilt and there was a huge memorial in East Berlin in memory of the Russians who had died in the war.

From Dad's tapes I think that, on the day after the tour of East Berlin more time was spent at the beautiful Wannsee Lake. Dad must have really had a fondness for this lake as, when we visited Berlin with my parents in 1996, we spent time at Wannsee Lake as Dad wanted to take us there.

During their week in Berlin my parents also attended two theatre performances. They saw the opera Carmen and the ballet Giselle.

Tickets for these had been provided by the German government and Dad rated both performances as excellent.

As arranged, on the Friday Dad returned to his old school. He spent time there with the headmaster and was shown around the school. He was introduced to students as a past pupil and was able to find textbooks that were used when he was there as a child. I wonder how this visit made him feel? Did it bring back memories of how his school life changed from one of carefree days, as schooldays should be, to days of sadness, confusion and fear as they became under Hitler's Nazi regime?

After this return to Berlin, his first return to Germany since his family fled from there in December 1938, and after talking with German people in Germany, Dad came to the conclusion that the German people of his generation, the older Germans who had experienced Germany during Hitler's Nazi regime both before and during the war, generally either didn't want to talk about the atrocities that had occurred or they were in denial and refused to accept that they had happened.

He found that the younger generation, those born after the war, generally accepted the truth of the horrors that had occurred during the Nazi regime both before and during the war and they couldn't understand how people could have allowed such horrendous things to happen.

On the tapes Dad did state that since this first return to Berlin he felt better about the German people than he had before. He said that the trip gave him solutions to questions that he had been asking himself for years. It is good to know that this first return to the city where he had spent his vital growing years, the city where he had witnessed atrocious cruelties and from where he had been been forced to escape, this journey back there had a positive effect on Dad emotionally.

Dad could not understand why Hitler was never stopped. As he said, countries knew that inhumane atrocities were occurring during the Hitler regime. Hitler could have been stopped in 1933/1934.

Governments knew, but too often people are too reluctant to interfere in the business and politics of others. When the facts about Auschwitz became known it was suggested that bombs should be dropped on Auschwitz but such a plan was rejected. Six and a half million people died in Auschwitz. Bombing Auschwitz would have meant that many people died a possibly easier death than they did die and the bombs would have killed many of their cruel guards, as well as ensuring that the Nazis would no longer have this extermination camp available for them to use for the murder of so-called "inferior" people.

During 1996 Dad spent four weeks in Europe and during this time he visited Auschwitz. He did this after much soul searching and with much trepidation as he was concerned about how this visit would affect him emotionally and how he would cope. Whilst there he made enquiries regarding the fate of his parents. In October of that year he received documentation from Auschwitz informing him that their archives contained a record of his parents being on transport 20 from Drancy to Auschwitz-Birkenau. The transport arrived at Auschwitz-Birkenau on August 19th 1942. 997 prisoners survived the journey. It is assumed that Dad's parents were among the 897 who were murdered by being gassed immediately on arrival.

The perimeter fence at Auschwitz

118

The Rest of the Story (Written by Peggy)

Above: Entry gate to Auschwitz

Below: Railway track at Auschwitz

Above: Eric at Auschwitz
Below: Auschwitz

The Rest of the Story (Written by Peggy)

Eric leaves a note for his parents at a ruined crematorium.

After he returned home from this visit to Europe Dad sent me the following letter which is dated August 10th 1996.

Dear Peggy and Bill,

As I promised on the phone, I am now sending you various items, newspaper cuttings and some stuff from Auschwitz. Auschwitz was very harrowing for me. It seems to have a delayed action effect, I keep dreaming almost every night about it. As you know, I went twice, on the Sunday (my birthday) with a conducted tour and on Monday by myself, when I spent seven hours there. I saw lots of documents relating to my parents' transport and also obtained forms to fill in from the archive dept. for them to conduct a search. They have, apparently, records of about half a million people. It was far worse than Satchenhausen, as all the original buildings are still there exactly as they were when the camp was liberated. Birkenau, that's Auschwitz II was the worst. That's where the arrivals and immediate gassings took place and I walked along the railway ramp my parents must have

121

walked to the gas chambers. These were partly destroyed by the Nazis but I lit a candle and left a note under some of the debris as curiously they have not got a book of remembrance where you can record your name.

Since I came back, I don't know whether I did right to go there, as it has opened it all up again, and yet in another way I am glad I did.

My four weeks in Germany were very interesting. I saw many places and I went to France, Czechoslovakia, Luxemburg and Poland. Krakow is a beautiful city but I was not impressed with Poland itself, very dirty, poor and backward, beggars everywhere, but it's a very cheap place, one simply can't spend one's money. In Germany I also went to Hamburg (beautiful), Nuremburg, Regensburg and of course Bayreuth from where I sent you a card.

Well I have to read nine books before the start of my last year at the University, the end of September. My results in the summer were very good, two firsts and two 2/1s so hopefully I should finish up with a 2-1 which is a very good result.

Hope you are all well.

Love to all.

XXX Dad and Mum

The Rest of the Story (Written by Peggy)

To conclude this chapter of my father's life and to conclude "The Journey Back" I will share a tribute that Dad wrote to and about his parents:

LEST WE FORGET

"In the beautiful Rose Gardens of Beth Shalom Holocaust Centre in Nottinghamshire there is a white rose with a plaque which bears the following inscription:

Fritz Lewinsohn aged 49

Blanka Lewinsohn aged 42

gassed at Auschwitz 19 August 1942

In everlasting love

Your son Eric and family

This rose is dedicated at the Beth Shalom Memorial Rose Garden and these are my parents who never had the chance to know my family and their grandchildren never had the privilege of knowing them.

After Kristallnacht when my father who was a chartered accountant was no longer allowed to work in Germany, we escaped from Berlin in the only way possible to us, by entering Belgium illegally. We were smuggled into Belgium by being locked into a double-panelled lorry. Had we been discovered by the Belgian authorities, we would have been sent back to Germany and immediate imprisonment in a concentration camp.

Because of the shortage of skilled labour in England, I was able to enter this country six weeks after our arrival in Belgium and my brother, who was still at school, could then follow because I was already in the UK.

My parents remained in Brussels as illegal immigrants until May 10th 1940 when the Germans invaded Belgium and they were arrested by the Belgian authorities while travelling on a tram and imprisoned because they could show no valid papers.

After the surrender of Belgium and France, they were moved to the south of France to various internment camps, Gurs, St Cyprien and Les Milles. My mother was freed after a few weeks and took up residence in Marseilles and gave German lessons as she spoke fluent French. She was able to visit my father in those camps periodically until August 1942, when Pierre Laval, the Prime Minister of the Petain regime, agreed to have all Jews who entered France after 1919 transported back to the East.

Because we were a very close family, my mother decided to join my father on this transport, although she had not been arrested.

They left France on 17th August 1942 and arrived in Auschwitz on August 19th, where out of a total of more than 900 people, 100 were selected for work and the rest gassed immediately on arrival.

The following is a translation of the last letter I received from my father. By the time I received it my parents were no longer alive.

"Fritz Lewinsohn Camp de Milles 7.8. 1942

to send to

Eric Lewinsohn

19 King Georges Way,

Hinckley (Leicestershire, England)

My dearest children,

As you probably know- by the time this letter reaches you your mother and I will be unfortunately on our way to the East. We know that you our beloved ones would have done everything possible to spare us this sorrow. But in these difficult times people are only objects of stronger forces and we can do no other.

Please stick together whatever the war may face you with, always remember no matter how far we are apart, in love and thoughts we are always near you and nothing and nobody can separate us from each other.

The Rest of the Story (Written by Peggy)

Stay healthy, bring up your children with the same love and success so they will grow up to be splendid young people. If a fatherly blessing can wish you only happy hours please accept it from us with many kisses. Remain strong.

Your Dad."

When they died my mother was 42 and my father was 49. They were never politically active. Their only crime was that they happened to be Jewish".

End of tribute "Lest We Forget" written by Eric Lewinsohn.

Lewinsohn Family plaque at Beth Shalom

Left and above: at Beth Shalom, a pillar naming the six death camps with its plaque.
Below and bottom: at Beth Shalom, stones collected in memory of murdered children.

THE JOURNEY ONWARDS

A Biography by Peggy

PREFACE

Dad's story does not end with his trip back to Berlin in 1982.

Far from it.

The reader may recall that, in his preface to "The Journey Back" Dad spoke about the difficulty he had in deciding upon a title for his autobiography. He said that he felt that by naming his story "The Journey Back" he was travelling back in time and looking at his life from it's beginning up to 1982 when he began to write his story. He wondered whether, at his age, it was the "Beginning of the End" and hoped that it was the "End of the Beginning".

He got what he hoped for. In retirement Dad found a whole new world. He looked for and grasped with both hands opportunities to participate and excel in academia, an area of great importance to him and one that he had thought unattainable. These opportunities opened up a whole new world for him and, after the "End of the Beginning" Dad ventured into a new phase of life which, with my sister Deryn's agreeance has been named "The Journey Onwards".

In "The Journey Onwards" I have tried to show what kind of a man my father, Eric Lewinsohn was by writing about various different aspects of his life.

"The Journey Onwards" has its emphasis on Dad's life after he "retired" in 1979. However it also includes memories of him before this time including as a family man and father.

My writing is supported by testimonials and memories written by people who knew and interacted with Dad. These tributes support my belief that my father was a very special man who had such a positive effect on people that they will always remember him with fondness and respect.

Following my contact with the social media page of William Bradford Community College and after having a letter printed in the

Leicester Mercury and the Hinckley Times I was both surprised and overjoyed to receive feedback from so many people.

Not only did these people remember Eric Lewinsohn.

They wanted to write about their memories of him.

I ask the reader to accept that each individual will perceive and remember every incident differently, and that, over time, memories can become blurred. Every person who has shared their memories in this book has shared them as they remember them. None of them knew that about fifteen years after my father's death they would be asked to share the effect he had on them

I know very few of the people who have shared their memories of my father. Most of them I have never met nor had I heard of them before they contacted me.

Every one of the testimonials has touched me emotionally.

I always knew that my father was a very special man.

The testimonials that people have written for inclusion in this book are an indication of just how special a man he was and the lasting positive effect he had on people.

ERIC – THE WORKER

MARCH 1934 to MID SUMMER 1938– In Berlin, Germany.

Apprentice to Karl Murawski, Photo Mechanical Workshop, Prinzregentstrasse 53, Berlin- Wilmersdorf.

It is very probable that this workshop had connections to the cameras that were used to show the 1936 Olympic Games in the cinema newsreels in Germany. In 1938 the proprietor, Herr Murawski, was told that he had to terminate Dad's employment as the workshop was going to be doing highly secretive work (armaments) and because Dad was Jewish the Germans did not consider him to be trustworthy.

MID 1938 to LATE 1938.

Full time student at a Jewish School of Engineering in Berlin.

———— ◆ ————

Left Germany December 1938. Arrived in England February 7th 1939.

———— ◆ ————

FEBRUARY 12th 1939 to FEBRUARY 2nd 1941.

Lathe operator and mechanic at Churchill Engineering, Croyden, Surrey, England.

This employment was terminated because of the war work that was being done in the factory. Dad was classed as an alien or enemy. This must have seemed like "deja vu" to Dad as it really was a repeat of what had happened in Berlin when his apprenticeship to Herr Murawski was terminated. As a result of this termination Dad was forced to accept a job in Hinckley. His reaction was: "Where is Hinckley"? He had never heard of the place. He only knew the area around London.

FEBRUARY 10th 1941 to SEPTEMBER 1st 1945.

Lathe operator at Dunlop Rim and Wheel, Hinckley, Leicestershire, England.

A shadow factory of Dunlop in Coventry. This shadow factory in Hinckley was assumed to be more protected from air raids than the main factory in Coventry.

SEPTEMBER 3rd 1945 to FEBRUARY 1st 1954.

Lathe operator at British Piston Ring Company, Coventry, England.

FEBRUARY 4th 1954 to DECEMBER 20th 1979.

Lathe operator, machinist and mechanic at Standard-Triumph (British Leyland), Coventry, England. This employment came to an end when the plant was closed.

DECEMBER 20th 1979 to JUNE 9th 1980.

Unemployed. Wasn't this supposed to be retirement?

JUNE 9th 1980 to MAY 14th 1982.

Lathe operator at Carnall Precision Engineering, Barwell, Leicestershire, England.

MAY14th 1982 onwards.

Retired.

Politically Dad was a Labour man and for many years he was a shop steward of the union at his place of employment.

At this point I am inserting a testimonial written by Martin Dunn who worked with Dad:

"I worked with Eric Lewinsohn at British Leyland Standard Triumph from 1977 until about 1980 when the plant was closed by the Thatcher Government. We both travelled from Hinckley. Eric was the shop steward for the Machine Shop which was located in the same building and adjacent to the axle welding gang where I worked. The whole facility covered a very large area. It was about the size of the Hollycroft Estate (for those who know Hinckley). Vehicles that we were involved in the production of were the Triumph TR7, Dolomite and Spitfire as well as the SD1 Rover.

The shop steward of the axle welding gang (where I worked) was a fiery Scotsman named John. He was in constant dispute with management and I can recall several differences of opinion between John and Eric regarding procedure with management. These differences of opinion occurred on a regular basis due to the fact that Eric was more diplomatic in his approach than John.

One stand out occasion occurred when we arrived one very cold winter's Monday morning to find that there was no heating in the building. After a quick gang meeting, in which it was decided that a joint delegation should confront management, John went to talk with Eric who gave his support. Eric said that he would tell his people and that he and John would go to management together. John went around the welding bays and borrowed a load of coats from the lads and by the time he had dressed himself up, in an effort to exaggerate the cold conditions, he looked like the "michelin man", complete with scarves and a woolly hat. Without waiting for Eric, John went marching off to confront the managers and Eric followed him about five minutes later. When they came back John was cursing and calling Eric "a wee doltage of a man", which, as I understand it, is some sort of idiot. As John was confronting the management about the unworkable conditions in the factory, dressed looking like an arctic explorer, Eric walked in to the meeting wearing just a t-shirt and sucking his pipe!

As shop steward one is required to stand for re-election every twelve months. This involves being proposed and seconded. For my part I was asked by Malcolm, a senior member of our gang, to stand against the then deputy as he had advised John to stand down as a result of other run-ins and issues. At this time John was on a final warning and in danger of losing his job. I agreed and was proposed by John and seconded by Malcolm. They told me that the deputy steward was not popular with many of the work gang and that they expected me to receive sixteen votes for and nine against. After the votes were counted I got fifteen for and nine against as there was one man absent that day.

Now we come to Eric's vote at the same time. A strange thing happened that had never been heard of before. Eric represented about one hundred and fifty machinists and after nominations he had two people standing against him. When the votes were counted Eric, who was well-liked, won the vote with a sizeable majority over the man who came second. However the third person actually received zero votes, which meant that neither his proposer nor his seconder had voted for him, but strangest of all, he hadn't voted for himself. Was it that they thought that the vote was going to be closer than it turned out to be and they had decided to vote for Eric?

It was as a result of this election that both Eric and I served on the Joint Shop Stewards Committee together. This was during the time of the Derek Robinson dispute and the eventual closure of the plant.

As I hadn't got much service time I left before the final redundancies but I am pretty sure that Eric was one of the last to leave.

Coming from Hinckley Eric and I, as well as other "Hinckleyites", were labelled knicker stitchers or woolly backs by the "Coventry kids" as they called themselves. There were quite a few people who travelled from Hinckley to Coventry to work so they got together and organised a bus to transport them to and from work. Eric travelled on this bus. However towards the end of our time there, because of the dwindling numbers using the bus as a result of the lay-offs in the industry, they were unable to keep the bus running as it was not financially viable. People began to use their cars to get to work and, to reduce their costs, they would charge to carry regular passengers to and from work. Eric travelled as a paying passenger and I remember that he would change lifts if he heard that someone had a spare seat and was charging less, even if it meant that he had to walk from one side of Hinckley to the other to catch his ride to work".

Written by Martin Dunn (2020).

Another story about Dad's negotiating skills as a shop steward that has come to light whilst I have been researching material is the following:

The workers wanted to receive an allowance for washing their dirty work clothes including their underwear. As shop steward it was Dad's job to negotiate with management regarding this allowance. I have been told that Dad took a pair of his dirty underpants with him to use as a bargaining tool when he discussed this allowance with management. We can only hope that the only dirt on the underpants was work dust and fumes!! I have been assured that he was successful in negotiating the desired laundry allowance.

The humorous way in which Dad negotiated in his role as a shop steward (union representative) is indicative of Dad's sense of humour. He generally tried to see the funny side of a situation even if it meant that he made himself the brunt of the joke. He would always laugh with other people even if it was him that was being laughed at.

The reader may have noticed that Dad was employed at Standard-Triumph for almost twenty six years. After twenty five years of service he received the traditional gold watch at a presentation ceremony.

In Britain in the late 1970s, there was a government scheme which allowed for workers over the age of sixty to draw part of their state pension if they were made redundant. Dad asked to be made redundant from Standard Triumph (British Leyland) under this scheme and he was successful in this request.

Family members agree that it was probably during the six months that Dad was unemployed following his redundancy that he first began to explore the idea of further education for himself and that this is when he began to study at Hinckley College.

In June 1980 Dad began working at Carnall Precision Engineering. He said that he got this job because of his knowledge of the metric system of measurement which he had used during his youth in Europe. Until this time Britain had used the imperial system of measurement but was forced to adopt the metric system to be in keeping with the rules of the EU (European Union).

Although Dad had grown up using the metric system he said that he was so used to using the imperial system since being in England that he had forgotten how to think in metric. He must have managed quite well as it seems he was highly thought of, as indicated in the following testimonial written by Simon Carnall.

From Simon Carnall:

"I have fond memories of Eric from when he used to be a Precision Engineer working at my father's company in Barwell, Leicestershire (R&D Carnall Precision Engineers). His skill was turning on a lathe machine working to high tolerances and he was damn good at it.

However, even though he was an excellent engineer, that's not how I remember Eric...... I remember the humble, kind hearted gentleman, short in height in his oversize all-in-one boiler suit, smoking or holding his pipe. Oh, that pipe and Eric were inseparable. He loved that pipe.

The other thing that I recall about Eric was his openness to studying. He was a very very clever man. At the time that I knew him he was attending college as a mature age student...... he soaked up knowledge like a sponge.

Eric was one of those gentlemen that you loved being around. He had one of those kinds of faces that you never forget. I can picture his smiling face now as he told many of his life stories, telling them with passion and honesty.

I am a better man for having the privilege of working alongside Eric and I am thankful that I had the opportunity to meet him.

I often thought to myself that one day this man should write a book and it now looks like, with help, he will achieve it".

Written by Simon Carnall (2020).

Dad was a keen worker. In addition to working full-time in a factory he often had a second and sometimes a third job too, generally because of financial necessity. He worked part-time as a barman at various pubs and clubs over many years and from about the 1960s until almost the end of the century both he and Mum were the local "pools collectors", distributing and collecting Littlewoods football pools coupons and monies to and from regular customers. In addition to these regular part-time jobs Dad also did other irregular jobs such as painting etc.

I think that our parents' enthusiastic work ethic rubbed off on to their children as we have all had extremely good employment records and we have all always been willing to accept any available job. We have all always given of our best in every working situation that we have found ourselves.

ERIC – THE STUDENT AND THE TEACHER

Pre 1928.   Primary school in Vienna, Austria.

1929 – 1934.   Attended Werner-Siemens Grammar School in Berlin.

Mid to late 1838. Full time student at a Jewish School Of Engineering in Berlin.

———————•———————

Early 1980s -1984. Attended Hinckley College. Gained 5 "O" Levels and 2"A" Levels.

1985.   Qualified as a teacher of languages to adults.

1985 – 1999.   Taught German at the North Warwickshire and Hinckley College.

1987.   Achieved a distinction in the Institute of Linguists' Advanced Level.

1989.   Passed Institute of Linguists' International Diploma.

1989.   Became an Associate Member of the Institute of Linguists.

1989.   Commenced part-time studies at Leicester University reading History, Politics and German.

1997.   Graduated from Leicester University.

1998.   Commenced a Master of Philosophy in Holocaust Studies at Leicester University.

137

2001.   Graduated from Leicester University with a Masters
             Degree in Philosophy.

2001.   Recipient of Achievement Award from Hinckley and
             Bosworth Borough Council.

Dad liked to be active and busy. After "retiring" in December 1979 when Standard Triumph closed down he began to consider the idea of taking a course at Hinckley College of Further Education to keep himself occupied. Initially he thought that he might participate in a course in woodwork, something that he had always been interested in. However he did not enrol in woodwork. Instead he enrolled in an Alternative Programme being ran by Ava Farrington. This programme was designed to encourage people to expand their skills and knowledge in many various areas and Dad became an active member of the programme. It was during his time at this College that he achieved his first academic success in England by completing the GCSE in five O levels and two A levels subjects.

This success made Dad want more. He had a thirst for learning and he enjoyed quenching this thirst. He wanted to achieve a university degree. He wanted to do this not only to achieve for himself but also to honour the memory of his parents. He knew that, if Hitler and his Nazi regime had not occurred, his parents would have expected him to remain at school and go on to higher education. By returning to formal academic education he was showing that, in spite of the traumas his family had suffered and the murder of his parents in Auschwitz, he could achieve the academic goals that his parents would have wanted him to. I think he did this and more.

He applied for enrolment at Leicester University. His application was successful and, in 1989, at the age of seventy he commenced study as a part-time student at the university.

Above: BA graduation. Eric with his family and friends

Right: Eric's BA graduation

During the time that he was at this university studying for his B.A. Dad was the oldest student there, a title which he enjoyed My husband and I travelled to England to be present at his graduation ceremony in 1997. It was a very proud moment for me when my father received his Degree and, needless to say, he was beaming with pride at what he had achieved for himself and in memory of his parents.

After graduating Dad decided that he wanted to continue on to a Master's Degree but he was concerned that he would not be able to as he could not afford the fees. Upon hearing about Dad's plight a grateful ex-student of his, Mr Clive Walley, sponsored Dad by giving him a cheque for 1000 pounds, enough to cover the cost of the first year's part-time study fees. This is an example of the profound effect that Dad had on people who were his students. Clive Walley has written a tribute to Dad which can be read later in this chapter.

By the time Dad graduated as a Master Of Philosophy he had lost the title of being the oldest student at Leicester University. He did say that he might just continue to study until he regained this position but obviously he was not serious about this. He had achieved what he set out to achieve and far more.

Professor Aubrey Newman, Founding Director of Stanley Burton Centre for Holocaust Studies at Leicester University remembers my father and he has written the following testimonial for inclusion in this book:

"I remember Eric Lewinsohn as an enthusiastic student, keen on his studies and determined to make the most of them. He was enrolled as a student in Combined Studies, a degree course which did not go as deep into individual subjects but very demanding in the breadth of subjects which students had to undertake. At that stage I was already teaching the History of the Holocaust, a detailed analysis intended for specialists in History. Strictly speaking, Combined Studies students could not enrol in such Special Subjects, but he was very keen to be allowed to sit in on the classes and to undertake the same study commitments as the others.

He had come late to academic studies, but he coped well with its demands on him, and amongst the work he did was a study of the problems of leadership in the special "show-ghetto" established by the Nazis in Terezin (TheresianStadt) in order to suggest to the International Red Cross that statements about ill-treatment of German Jews were ill-founded. Some of the leaders of the ghetto collaborated while others resisted as best they could; it was an appalling dilemma with which they were faced. His analysis was extremely interesting, and a number of his conclusions have been borne out by subsequent evidence.

I certainly benefited from having been involved with him, and I know that he had a great impact upon his much younger fellow students. After he graduated he kept in touch, and I was always impressed by seeing reports in the local newspapers about his various talks to schools in Leicester and Leicestershire where he spoke about the Holocaust and about his own experiences as an example of German official antisemitism. It was a pleasure and a privilege to have taught him"

Written by Professor Aubrey Newman, Founding Director, Stanley Burton Centre for Holocaust Studies at Leicester University (2020)

Clare Taylor was Head of Student Welfare at Leicester University from 1990 to 2013. She got to know Dad during the time he was a student at the University and she has written the following kind words for inclusion in this book:

"I came to know Mr Eric Lewinsohn whilst he was studying for his first degree at the University of Leicester in the mid 1990s; he graduated with a Batchelor of Arts at the age of 77, then went on to gain a Master's degree.

I was Head of Student Welfare at that time, and recall that he visited our office quite often; sometimes to introduce students who he felt would benefit from our input, occasionally just to have a chat and, perhaps, escape from the mayhem which can be a feature of University life. My guess is that he would have spent a great deal of time between the Stanley Burton Centre for Holocaust and Genocide studies resource room, the Mature Students' common Room and the main library.

Mr Lewinsohn's presence at the University would have been invaluable for fellow Historical Studies students, He was a living primary source. He had witnessed the birth of the Nazi regime and escaped Berlin in 1938 at the age of 19; (the same age as many of his contemporary students in Leicester). The young Eric would have witnessed first-hand the raw anti-Semitism and discrimination which the Nazis wrought upon Jewish people and minority groups across Europe at that time. The slow erosion of freedoms which occurred during Eric's formative teenage years, leading to the sudden deportations which would have prompted Eric's escape from Germany. Tragically, his mother and father, Blanka and Fritz Lewinsohn, perished in the Auschwitz death camp in 1942.

For his Mphil, Mr Lewinsohn visited Prague and Terezin; he built up many contacts across Europe. He continued to practice the German language, therefore would have been equipped to access primary documents. His research remains available to scholars. His supervisor Professor Aubrey Newman, of the Stanley Burton Centre for Holocaust Studies at the University, praised Mr Lewinsohn's academic work. Eric certainly made a valuable contribution to the understanding of this challenging subject, from a very personal perspective.

My team and I were fortunate to have known such an interesting and inspiring man.

Written by Clare Taylor, Head of Student Welfare,
University of Leicester (1990-2013) (2020).

I did not get to England to attend Dad's final University Graduation in 2001 when he was awarded his Masters Degree. At this time Dad was eighty two years of age. One family member who was at the ceremony has told me the following story of a verbal encounter he had on this day with a man he had never met before. I am writing this in the same words as it was told to me.

The family member said the following to me:

"A guy next to me said: "It's a proud day when your son or daughter graduates". Looking at me he then said: "In your case I expect it's a grandchild".

"No", I replied, "it's my Dad".

"You're taking the mickey" the man replied. (Taking the mickey means teasing, joking).

"No, I'm not, and he also got remarried last week".

"Now I know you're taking the mickey" the man replied.

His academic record shows Dad's thirst for academic learning. He loved to learn and to achieve success in academia. Was this because he had been forced to leave school early as a consequence of the Nazi regime? Perhaps this experience did have something to do with Dad's insatiable thirst for learning in his later life. I know it was his way of honouring his parents as he stated that "everything I do today as far as education is done in honour of these two people. If they can see me today they will be pleased with what I have done". He knew that his parents had not planned for him to leave school early and work in a factory throughout his working life. Whatever the reasons Dad held formal academic learning in very high esteem.

Right: Family and friends at Eric's Masters graduation.

Left: Eric's MPhil graduation with Clive Walley

Although this could and should be applauded, I personally do not think that academic achievement is any more important or valuable than other sorts of learning and achievement. I think that people who have manual skills, artistic skills or any other type of skills, knowledge and achievement are just as praiseworthy and brilliant as those with academic achievements, whereas I think that Dad thought that academic ability was "better" than ability in other areas. Although Dad always maintained that all human beings were equal this is one area where his equality beliefs could possibly be questioned.

Dad's academic achievements did not go unnoticed. In September 2001 Dad was recognised by Hinckley and Bosworth Borough Council when he was the recipient of an Achievement Award at the Borough's first ever Achievement Award Ceremony. These awards were given to people who had helped to put Hinckley "on the map" and were a sign of the Borough's appreciation of what the recipients had done for the Borough.

More than forty of the seventy Award winners were present at the ceremony and they each received well earned applause. However, it has been stated that the biggest applause of the evening was given to my father. He would, quite justifiably, have been very proud.

We should remember that when Dad was a young child he had enjoyed playing schools with himself as the teacher and his younger brother Hans (Jack) as the student. In his later years Dad not only satisfied his desire to learn but he also enjoyed passing on knowledge and skills to others.

He began to teach German during the 1980s. Students would go to my parents' home for their lessons. He later taught classes at North Warwickshire and Hinckley College whilst still continuing to give private lessons at home.

One lecturer at Hinckley College maintained that "one always knew when Eric had used the copier. It never worked for the next person"!!

Teaching gave Dad great pleasure. He took great pride in the achievements of his students. His students enjoyed his interactive method of teaching and learning and many of them remember him with pride and fondness to this day. Some of Dad's ex-students and others who knew him as a student or teacher have contacted me and I am proud to include testimonials that they have written about their time spent with him. These testimonials are not printed in any chronological order nor in any order of preference. I have tried to group them together using the criteria of where the people knew Dad from.

Clive Walley became a friend of my father. It was a financial donation from Clive enabled Dad to begin his Master's Degree.

Testimonial from Clive Walley:

A Tribute to the Late Eric Lewinsohn, a Scholar, Teacher and Friend.

"It is an honour to have been invited to contribute a piece to the biography of the late Eric Lewinsohn and a pleasure to do so.

I first met Eric when I joined his German Language evening classes at Nuneaton College in or about September 1997. I had attended this college several times to study "A" Level Law and also Japanese to help me communicate better with my Japanese customers. I owned and ran Flowtronics Systems Ltd., an electronics assembly company, manufacturing a wide range of products including Defence Equipment for international and NATO countries and companies, with a workforce varying between 50 and 100 men and women.

For me, doing some evening studies was a break from routine and I managed to acquire an "A" Level Law Certificate in less than a year which was a bonus. I had failed my German GSE in 1959 so I was hoping to refresh my German and sit the exam again.

When I saw Eric for the first time, I saw in him a man of character and purpose. He was a respectable elderly gentleman with energy and determination. I was very happy to join this class! Eric liked his students to work with the language, using it as much as possible in the classroom to help them grow in confidence and competence.

I was hardly surprised that when he caught a youngish student using an electronic, handheld translation device the student was immediately discharged from the class! I'm afraid that I couldn't contain myself and I burst out laughing as did one or two others.

I think Eric was pleased to see an endorsement of his strictness and purpose. After all, what is the point of going to night school, paying for it and cheating in class practice by using a personal translator? I actually noticed something of a smile from Eric as he clocked up his victory over deceit!

I was the only person in the class anywhere near Eric's age and that was with a 23-year age difference. The class was mostly comprised of teenagers who were either using the night school work to complement daytime schooling or who were, like me, doing a resit although mine was after 39 years. In addition there were a few others of ages between 30 and 50.

Eric could sometimes be just a little bit stern and on such occasions I would try to break the ice a bit without offending him. He was a great teacher beyond doubt and I enjoyed his lessons and made good progress with my German.

Sometimes funny situations arose and it was good to see him enjoy them despite his seriousness. Eric introduced us to a game called "Herz Drei". It was a card game which trained us to use the German language to interact with each other.

On one occasion when we were playing this game a young lady of about 30ish asked me for a particular card which I did not have. I didn't have it, but she still thought that I did and asked me yet again so, using language I had acquired from general chatter, I replied to her

147

by saying: "nein meine chatz, ich habe es nicht". For readers not familiar with the language "meine chatz" means "my kitten".

Eric burst out laughing and asked me where I got the word from since he didn't teach familiarities in his class room. I told him jokingly that I got the word from the dismissed guy's electronic translator which made him laugh even more. Such a small incident but one that was enjoyed by all and, in particular by the recipient of the affectionate words from me!

One evening, as the class emptied out, Eric asked me if I was going anywhere near Hinckley because his usual lift wasn't available. I told him it was no problem and I drove him to his home. Along the way he started to tell me the gut-wrenching facts about his life. He told me how his parents had helped him escape Nazi Germany when he was 19 and how his parents had perished in the Auschwitz Concentration Camp in 1942, – the year I was born.

I could see that he carried a horrendous memory of his earlier life as so many Jewish people did. I had read and heard so much about all this even from a tender age in England after World War 2 ended and although I had later suffered the loss of my 19-year old brother at the hands of a hit and run drunk driver in 1965, which has haunted me for all of my life, I wondered how he had managed to cope with the knowledge of knowing what had been done to his parents.

Eric told me that, in a year or two, he was hoping to go back to Leicester University where he got his BA and study for a Master's Degree in Holocaust Studies to honour and remember his parents. He was already 78/79 but determined to do this for his Mum and Dad. He won my fullest respect for his intentions.

I knew he received only a pittance for his teaching work and my company was doing well so I offered to help him by sponsoring him through Flowtronics. He was amazed at my offer and thanked me over and over again. It was my intention to sponsor him for two years but sadly my company, which had been running since 1981, went through a very rough patch in the second year so I was unable to cover that year, but when that happened he told me not to worry and that he would get some help from the family. I felt very sad about that but I was pleased that I had been able to help this very great guy for at least one year to get him started.

I often gave Eric a ride home. It was no problem for me and I liked to chat with him We called in at a pub a couple of times on the way and I noticed that he liked a drop of whisky, as I did, so when we broke up for Christmas I presented him with a bottle of the stuff. He was delighted and called me a "goodun".

In the New Year things in the class were moving at a fast pace. Eric was constantly reminding us that the exams would be upon us before we knew it and so, rightly, he drove us hard.

When June arrived we not only had to take a written exam but also a spoken one. When I took mine it was being done by Eric and another teacher. They sat me down at a small table in the store room and told me that I had to act out a scene where I was supposed to be in a restaurant and that I should call the waiter and tell him, in German of course, what food I would like.

I thought "well that's not too difficult", but pride comes before a fall!

I called out "Herr Obst" and two adult men collapsed in a fit of laughter! I didn't know what I had done wrong at that moment then, interlaced with more fits of laughter, they tried to explain.

"What you should have said was "Herr Ober" but you said "Herr Obst" which means "Mr Fruit" not "Waiter".

Now I could understand the hilarity and they then apologised for taking my test time up but assured me that I would have extra time.

I passed my GCSE with flying colours although, of course, the GCSE is not as difficult as the old GSE.

Eric enjoyed pulling my leg (teasing in a friendly manner) about it for a long time.

In September I continued in Eric's class as he was running an AO programme. This was quite difficult and we had to learn to read magazines, newspapers and books like "Der Teufel General" ("The Devil's General") and "Die Tagebucher von Anne Frank" ("The Diary of Anne Frank").

For those who do not know, Anne Frank was a young 14 year old Jewish girl who, with her family, hid from the Nazis in the attic of her father's business premises. She kept a diary until 1944 when she was caught in occupied Holland. She and her sister died of Typhus in Bergen-Belson Concentration Camp in 1945. Her diary was published in about 1947.

I didn't stay in the course for very long because the work load was too great and took too much of my time away from running the business. I kept in contact with Eric and on one occasion, when my former German teacher came up from Walton on Thames in Surrey to visit my factory, I invited Eric along too and was able to introduce Eric to Ralph Fletcher. We had a meal together in a local pub and they were able to joke about the man who took 39 years to get his German Language Certificate.

When I used to take Eric home at night he used to like to puff on his pipe but I had to tell him that I had been registered as having COPD and I had given up smoking in 1986. He understood and snuffed out his pipe and put it in his jacket pocket. I asked him several times if he was sure that his pipe was totally out and he said, "oh yes, it's ok, don't worry".

On a later occasion he told me that he had burned his house down! When I asked him how he managed to do that he said that he had put his pipe in his jacket pocket and put his jacket upstairs but half an hour later flames were roaring down the staircase!

It was, of course, a serious situation, but Eric was cool and relaxed, and his matter-of-fact way of telling me made me roar with laughter. Obviously he was ok and nobody got injured or anything and the insurance company had been very kind and helpful and given him alternative accommodation whilst all of the repairs were carried out. What a comedian!!

During his university programme Eric had to go to the Czech Republic as a part of the course and he sent me a card to let me know that he hadn't forgotten me. That's the kind of man he was.

Eric with his pipe.

One day in 2001 he called me to tell me that he was going to be presented with his Degree and that he had reserved a place for me in the seating area. He said he was only allowed one non family supporter so I had better show up because he had booked the seat for me.

It was a great day and an honour to see my friend walk up to receive his Degree Certificate and to meet his wife. She was a charming lady and I could see the love in her eyes for him and vice versa.

In that same year my 12,000 square foot modern factory was ripped apart by a tornado, resulting in severe damage which took over 6 months to repair and, unfortunately, in that time I lost a number of major contracts. I tried to save the company but, sadly, the losses were too great and I had to liquidate the company in 2002. I had been supported by so many youngsters who had joined me in the 1980s and who had trained well and become very skilled. It was a heartbreaking day which felt more like a funeral than anything else.

In 2004 I gathered my things together and from my private pension I bought a small villa in Spain where, 17 years later, I still live. Eric and I still kept in touch but then one day he went off the radar and I later found out that one of my best friends ever had passed.

From time to time I still think about him and our experiences. Eric was a lovely guy, kind of heart and straight as a dye. I am sure that this good man looks down and smiles on us all every day. God bless you Eric".

Written by Clive Walley. (1st February 2021).

Testimonials from other people who knew Dad from North Warwickshire and Hinckley Colleges of Further Education.

From Suz Moreton:

"In the 1980s I attended an English Literature Course run by an aspiring teacher Annie Boylan. There were three adult students, Eric, myself and another lady. The rest were 16/17 year olds, girls I think, doing it as part of a full-time course. Eric was a very quick and able student and he was willing to answer and talk at length on whatever question Annie put out to us. Once he'd got "the bit between the teeth" there was no stopping him. One lesson, a few weeks into the course, one of the girls was moved to write a verse about Eric and his erudition, which she read out to the class to much hilarity. Thankfully dear Eric took it all in good part and laughed along with everyone. Thankfully he was not abashed and continued with his studies, amazing man! Thinking of Eric I have the memory of a brave kindly, determined gentleman who I am proud to have known".

Written by Suz Moreton(2020).

From Andrew Brown:

"My mother, Elsie Brown, had enrolled in an English "0" Level evening class from September 1982 until July 1983 and following this she continued to take courses at the Hinckley Further Education College. She had been influenced to enrol by me as I was studying French and English "0" Levels there in the evening during the same academic year.

She consequently enrolled in a course set up in 1984 by Ava Farrington called "The Alternative Programme". This course was designed to offer occupational classes for people who had been affected by the changing economic landscape and its resulting redundancies and unemployment. Eric Lewinsohn was heavily involved in the implementation of this educational programme. The course attracted people from a wide age range and there were several retired people enrolled in it too. At the time, from 1983 to 1986, I was attending college full-time, first in Nuneaton and then in Leicester, but, during the summer holidays I accompanied my mother to many of these Alternative Programme sessions where I met other attendees, including Eric.

The Alternative Programme was a great programme and it ran from Mondays to Thursdays. There were some fantastic topics covered and there were also educational day trips to various parts of the Midlands. Ava also occasionally invited guest speakers to speak with us and she showcased several thought-provoking films.

One such film that I remember watching in one of the sessions was "Sophie's Choice". The next day there was a discussion about the film and the Holocaust. I remember that there was often a fracas between Eric and another man named Albert. Albert was very keen on giving an alternative view on everything and he often ruffled quite a few feathers. Albert walked out of a session once due to a disagreement. Eric said that he had tried to tell Ava that Albert was toxic to the group and that he should be banned, but Ava disagreed, saying that he was good for the group. Of course Albert stayed as the group had to be inclusive and he continued to give "alternative" views.

My mother enrolled in a daytime German class in 1984. I don't know whether Ava was the primary teacher, with Eric acting as Ava's language assistant, or whether it was just Eric as the teacher, as he did teach German at Hinckley College. She then often bumped into Eric around town as she went shopping in Hinckley most days and she regularly worked on a market stall on Mondays. She told me that Eric was German and taught at the college.

My mother and Eric became friends and I think she had a lot of respect for him. When a German friend of hers gave her a few books to help her to learn German, she took these books to show Eric.

I remember Eric as a very active person and very accommodating of all those he met. I moved to London in 1986 and lost contact with many people in Hinckley, including Eric".

Written by Andrew Brown (2020).

Eric with Ava Farrington during Hinckley College days

From Robert William Irving:

"I knew Eric in the mid 1980s during the time when I did some work for Joyce Loftus with a Special Needs Group at Hinckley College of Further Education. I supervised the group for activities twice a week. At this time I also studied in a group called the "Alternative Programme". I was aged around 20 at the time and I met Eric in the General Studies O/A Level course, which Ava Farrington, the coordinator of the "Alternative Programme" taught.

Eric was a mature student, probably the oldest in the college. He was a kind and helpful man and incredibly full of knowledge and passion about his specialised subject, his family's experience of the Holocaust and escaping Nazi Germany.

Eric had a great rapport with Ava Farrington, who had had similar life experiences as Eric. Her father was a German artist who had refused to paint Hitler.

Eric became a familiar figure and much loved gentleman on the college campus and he went on to great success with his studies".

Written by Robert Irving,
former activities organiser and student at
Hinckley College of Further Education (2020).

From Phil and Carole Herbert:

"We both remember Eric very well. In a class he once said that he had a major disagreement with Adolf Hitler and that's why he ended up in England. He made light of it but we all knew that he had had a very narrow escape and could easily have ended up in a concentration camp.

One of the endearing things about Eric was that, although he had been in England for such a long time, he couldn't pronounce the letter "V". He used to be giving us an insight into the structure of sentences in German, in particular the past tense. He always said that you must put the werb (verb) at the end of the sentence. We all tried to keep a straight face and not to laugh, as we all knew how concerned he was to teach us the correct way of speaking.

We both enjoyed the class immensely, having continued our lessons with Eric after our previous teacher passed away suddenly".

Written by Phil and Carole Herbert(2020).

I have assured Phil and Carole that they need not have been too concerned about keeping a straight face as Dad would have laughed with them about this. He had an amazing ability to laugh at himself.

From Kath Morton:

"Eric taught me German at Hinckley College. It was a long time ago. I remember him as a kind, gentle man".

Written by Kath Morton (2020).

From Hazel Herbert.

"I attended Hinckley Grammar School. In fact I was in the same year level as Eric's younger daughter. I studied German whilst at the Grammar School, but I did not study German at "A" Level. I went on to study French and Russian at Southampton University. After graduating from university I worked in France, Switzerland and Brussels after which I came home to England and had various jobs using my French.

In 1990 I got a job in Leicester with an American-owned Textile machinery company. They had offices in the US, UK, Germany and Italy. I decided to take evening classes in Italian and German. This is where I met Eric as he was the teacher of the German class. I told him that I had been at school with his daughter. He was a wonderful teacher and I learned so much. I went on to take GCSE. I have kept all of the books from the lessons and keep meaning to revise a bit now that I'm retired, but I never do, although I do watch foreign films and still travel to German-speaking countries.

Eric was a lovely man and a wonderful teacher. I am so glad that I met him".

Written by Hazel Herbert (2020).

From Charlotte Towe:

"I was a student of Mr Lewinsohn at North Warwickshire and Hinckley College when he taught German night classes there. It was in about 1996 (I can't remember the exact year). I remember that I really enjoyed the lessons. His passion and enthusiasm for the German language were infectious and really helped it to come alive. I loved going to the lessons and loved German too. Thinking back, to inspire a 15/16 year old girl to want to attend night school is no mean feat and this is the effect Eric had on me".

Written by Charlotte Towe (2020).

From Lis Walton:

"I first met Eric in the late 80's when I joined an evening class at the local college to brush up on my German language. Eric was the teacher.

It was a very enjoyable class which I always looked forward to and which I rarely missed (unusual for me at that time). He treated each of us with interest and respect. As the class progressed and we all got to feel more at ease with each other, Eric would occasionally refer to his life in 1930's Nazi Germany.

As well as being a very good language class, we would also benefit from hearing Eric's recollections of his life at this deeply disturbing time. I remember him telling the class how, under Hitler, babes' first words, rather than being mummy or daddy, were instead "Heil Hitler". As a German Jew whose parents and other family members were killed by the Nazis at Auschwitz, these memories of his youth must have been weighted with suffering and tragedy, but Eric was able to recount them with fortitude and great dignity without diminishing the inhumanity of the regime or his loss at its hands. His ability to teach the language and the history of Germany resulted in classes that were instructive, lively and never dull.

About 5 years after leaving the class, I got to know Eric again when I rang the number on an advert offering German tuition. To my surprise it was Eric and he remembered me! I would go round to his house for weekly hour long lessons. Again these classes were extremely enjoyable and I came to count Eric as a good friend. Again, my German improved – so much so that after I'd had a serious accident in which I sustained a head injury, my first spoken words were in German! Eric had written me a card in German and it had refreshed my language skills.

Despite his increasing age, he maintained his vigour and curiosity, achieving a postgraduate degree in Holocaust Studies in his 80's, when he also got married again! His lust for life was infectious and still is an inspiration.

Eric smoked a pipe, liked red wine and was a lively, entertaining and respectful friend. He was never boring and always had plenty to say. Me and my then husband had many enjoyable nights out with him when conversation would flow, along with the wine. And Eric would be smoking his pipe. I remember his mischievous twinkling eyes and chuckle. I feel proud to have known him as a friend: he enriched my understanding and appreciation of life. He was well liked and respected by many, and used his experiences of Nazi atrocity to educate and enlighten, while remaining someone who, it seemed, regarded himself as no better and not worse than others".

Written by Lis Walton (2020).

Testimonials from people who knew Dad from his teaching from home.

From Serena Baker (nee Russell) and her brother Dean Russell.

"Eric taught my brother and I privately from age 11 to age 18, over 25 years ago. We visited his house every Saturday for lessons, and he helped us to prepare for our GCSE and A-Levels at Hinckley College.

He was quick witted with a keen sense of humour, but always got down to the business of teaching. We remember the plumes of tobacco smoke, glint in his eye and him cackling with laughter. Right from the very beginning he made learning a new language fun and never a burden.

He used to make us tapes when we first started, to use at home in our own time with study books. These tapes could be an hour or two in length, and what was surprising was that he used to call us by our names in the recordings. He had made the tapes specially for us. It goes to show the lengths he went to in order to help us develop our German skills. Eric would never dream of increasing his teaching price/hour. Our parents had to insist on it every year!

That initial interest into German grew for the both of us. I now work for Aldi UK and my brother works for a German firm in Coventry.

Certain things trigger memories of Eric: the sound of opening a front garden gate, the smell of tobacco, or stollen and gluhwein at Christmas.

Always in our thoughts. We were lucky to know him".

Written by Serena Baker (nee Russell) and Dean Russell (2021).

From Andrea Shires:

"Eric Lewinsohn taught German to my mum when she was in her 70/80s. I know mum got a lot from it and continued through two exams. He also taught German to our daughter when she was studying for her "A" Levels. Our daughter went on to do a Degree in International Business with German and when she came back from Germany Eric could tell which area she had been in.

Eric was also an enthusiastic student in the same English class as me in the 1980s".

Written by Andrea Shires (2020).

From Zoe Shires (daughter of Andrea Shires):

"I was introduced to Eric Lewinsohn by my grandma as he taught her German. When I was studying for my "A" Levels I was struggling a bit with the level of German (it was Faust, who wouldn't be?). I must have spent six months or so (probably longer) going to Eric for help.

He used to teach me on a Saturday morning. I remember that I used to ride my bike over to his house as it was on the other side of town and we used to sit at a small square table in his kitchen. I remember Eric being calm and patient. I never did like speaking German in front of a native, it used to make me feel shy, but he was always friendly and supportive".

Written by Zoe Shires (2020).

From Laura Shipley:

"I was 16 when I first met Eric. I had private German lessons with him. I used to go to his house and we would sit around the kitchen table with a coffee. Eric was one of the most fascinating and gentle men I had ever met. He didn't talk much about his past with me, but he did tell me that he and Hitler didn't get on, so he left! I have such fond memories of the time I spent with him, and he inspired me to take a German language module whilst at university".

Written by Laura Shipley (2020)

From Wendy Prince:

"Eric gave me private German lessons for two years. I found he was very easy to talk to. I was in my late 20's at the time and I was attending lessons because my employer at the time felt it would help me in my job. I admit to being there under duress, and I attended many lessons with a hangover! Eric used to jokingly tell me off, but showed me no mercy when it came to learning. The worse the hangover the greater the likely-hood that for the entire hour we would speak only German. He did have a sense of humour and thought it quite funny when I asked him to teach me to swear in German!

I did quite well with my lessons and Eric wanted me to take the GCSE but I was content to just learn the language without the added pressure of preparing for an exam. I think the removal of a set syllabus made the content of my lessons more interesting and real as I learned more than how to book a hotel or order food and drink. We had a lot more interesting conversations in German.

At work I had a German speaking colleague who used to spend a lot of time on the phone, claiming that he was talking with engineers. He didn't know that I could understand quite a bit of his conversations. I used to tell Eric what I had heard and ask him to translate bits that I couldn't understand. Some of it was quite juicy gossip which used to make him laugh!

After my lessons ended I didn't see Eric again. He was a private but interesting man, a very good and patient teacher with great intelligence and a great sense of humour to match".

Written by Wendy Prince (2020).

From Ruth Drake:

"My son and I first met Eric in 1984 when David (my son) first began to learn German as a hobby. He was 8 at the time so Eric adapted his lessons to suit this younger student but he soon found that the rules and structure of the language suited David and David made good progress.

Eric began to encourage David to translate children's stories such as Snow White or Cinderella and to read them in German and within a few months he was interested to find David's progress in his Saturday morning lessons was at least comparable with the progress that Eric's college students made. He suggested that David could be entered for his GCSE "O" Level exam, usually taken by 16 year olds, in 1986 when David would be 10.

Eric was an enthusiastic teacher, patient but uncompromising, expecting the same attention to accuracy from David as he expected from older students. He was also very generous with his time and talents, spending a lot of time finding subjects to talk about during lessons that would interest a young boy yet still satisfy the syllabus meant for teenagers.

When he took holidays in Australia and Europe he was kind enough to bring back souvenirs for David and when we took a family holiday in Germany he prepared David for some of the situations he would be likely to meet and encouraged him to keep a holiday diary. Since David, then almost 9, was the only German speaker on that family holiday we relied on him to book train tickets, pay entrance fees and to order from menus. We ate a lot of "frikadellen" during that week.

We remember Eric with gratitude and affection. His pride and interest in David was easy to see and his enthusiasm for teaching him German and seeing and appreciating David's skill was kind. He took no personal credit for David's success and he told us that he had wanted to be a teacher when he was younger, but the necessity of caring for his family meant that, in the years following the war, giving up his job and re-training for teaching was not practical. I'm so pleased that he was able to teach in his later years. He was very good at it".

Written by Ruth Drake (2020).

*Frikadellen is a pan fried meat patty.

From David Drake (Son of Ruth Drake):

"I was probably about 7 years old when I met Eric. I was a young black boy who had been adopted by very loving parents 6 years earlier. I had a younger sister who was also adopted but from another family. This is relevant to my memories of Eric as when I reflect on

163

how he was as a person, it was his warmth, kindness and patience that stand out. All attributes that for me at that time were probably more important than I realised then and I don't think I would've succeeded in my learning of German as a young boy (and more remarkably, continued to learn it for as long as I did, through moving from primary school to high school and dealing with my adoptive parents' separation) adapting to the challenges of being visibly different not only to my friends but also to my family. (My adoptive parents were white and I was the only black person in the town where we lived).

I'll come back to Eric's nature and those tributes later, but for now let me explain how I came to meet Eric!

My adoptive father was a probation officer and my adoptive mother was a teacher. My mother was the main reason I met Eric. She passionately believed in the value of learning and also saw no boundaries in terms of what could be achieved through learning and hard work. For this reason she thought it would be great for me to learn a language outside of those I would learn at school. With French guaranteed to be part of the curriculum when I got older and went to high school, she decided that German would be a good language for me to learn. It would be potentially useful in later life as well as a good hobby to keep me occupied and learning.

I don't now how we found Eric but I do remember going to his house to meet him for the first time along with my mother. It was in a part of town that I did not really know and the house itself was a small semi-detached built in local authority style. I remember going in and, as well as being nervous about meeting a new adult, I also remember the smell. Eric liked to smoke a pipe and that leaves a particular smell around a house. I came from a non-smoking household and so to me it was quite pungent. In fact if it had been based on the smell, I probably wouldn't have gone back! We sat in the small but comfortable lounge and I don't know what we discussed but I do remember my memories of Eric being that he had a warm smile that twinkled with kindness and with a hint of conspiratorial fun.

Eric and I bonded quickly and, over the years to come, I spent an hour every week in that lounge room learning German. One of the things that I remember about Eric as a teacher was that his teaching ranged from the more prosaic aspects of language (umlauts, prepositions etc.) through to German culture. One example of this (which also gives an insight into that "conspiratorial fun" element of his personality) would be that one of the early phrases I remember learning was "Ich mochte eine dunkel bier bitte" (I'd like a dark beer please). I recall Eric explaining to me that Germans liked dark beer and light beer and I can remember having a real visual image of what these beers were like. Another example of Eric teaching me German culture as well as German language was that I remember him introducing me to Stollen, the German cake that's eaten at Xmas time. I think that his wife had cooked it. It wasn't my favourite to be honest, but it was another example of the way the teaching went wide and the way that I was made to feel really comfortable and welcome as a student.

I said I'd come back to Eric's nature and attributes of warmth, kindness and patience and now seems a good time to do so.....

Eric made me feel warm, and at a time when I was starting to be conscious of being different (i.e. a black child brought up in a white culture, not quite belonging with white people because my skin colour was different, but not quite belonging with black people because of my accent and cultural upbringing). Eric was someone outside of my family that made me feel that I belonged and was just me.... It's hard to describe but this was a stage in my life where I started to become conscious of being treated differently due to the colour of my skin. It's not something that people do consciously or even deliberately but it's often an unconscious bias that, as a black person, you feel. That feeling was so noticeable in its absolute, 100% absence in Eric and that was what I felt when I entered his home and when I studied with him. I wonder, on reflection, whether it came from his own experiences with the things he must have experienced in Germany, the things that brought him to England from Germany as a person of Jewish heritage during the atrocities of the war. Whatever it was though, it was palable, and it made this young boy, who should not really have enjoyed spending his after school time learning a foreign language, feel comfortable and engaged.

After a little while of Eric's teaching, he suggested that I could probably do an "O" Level qualification if I wanted to. It didn't seem strange to me and I thought that if Eric thought I could do it then why not?

It also gave us something to aim for and I quite liked that. Eric worked with me to prepare for the exam and when I look back, the way he prepared me was amazing – I don't remember any anxiety or stress in preparing (this may have helped me in future exams actually) and I was really well prepared and went through the whole experience just enjoying it. That was Eric's way. He made it all feel natural and there was no pressure at all, it was just an experience to enjoy. I don't really even remember thinking about what grade I might get!

I was 9 years old at the time I took the exam, and when I got the result, a grade C, it caused a bit of a stir as I was the youngest person in the country to do a German"O"Level. National and local newspapers did reports and came to take pictures of Eric and me at his home. Now you hear about pushy coaches who seem as focused on their own success as on the success of the people they are coaching. Whilst I don't really remember the interviews what I do remember is that, for Eric, it was all about me and my achievements and that was definitely a reflection of his kindness and his nature. He was just a good man. For a few months it was quite exciting, culminating in Jon Craven coming to my house to film Newsround – quite a few curtains were twitching in our street on that day!

After the excitement had subsided, Eric and I discussed what we'd do next and if I wanted to continue learning German. I did and I enjoyed learning with Eric so we decided to do a Diploma. Eric thought that would be better for me than an "A" Level at my age as he felt the "A" Level might put too much pressure on me and not be enjoyable enough to learn as a now 10 year old. The diploma meant learning about German culture as opposed to more language and I also felt that this would be more enjoyable.

Eric taught me about aspects as obscure as brief histories of smaller German towns and cities as the exam would require me to write short essays about these things and I would not know which part of German culture would come up until I got into the exam. It was interesting, as he had promised, and I enjoyed finding out more about places like Leipzig and the background of the Lorelei mermaid statue on the River Rhine.

Sadly when it came to the exam, this aspect of it proved one step too far for an 11 year old. I passed all modules except for the German knowledge one – to pass a diploma you had to pass all of the modules.

A short while later, with my family life changing as my adoptive parents separated, school life changing as I went to high school and the normal challenges of early teens, I decided to stop the German lessons and, naturally, that meant that my relationship with Eric also ended. It was a time of a lot of changes for me and, although I went through a lot in the following 10-15 years, I didn't forget about Eric. I remember meeting with him once after that and he had the same warmth and kindness that I always remembered him for. He was certainly someone that, without either of us realising it, had a subtle but significant impact on my early years and my life".

Written by David Duke (2020).

ERIC – THE HOLOCAUST EDUCATOR

After Dad retired and commenced his life of study and teaching I think he became aware that his life experiences could and should be shared to help people to realise the terrible truth of Hitler's Nazi regime and to warn people about the dangers of racial prejudice, inequality and popularism. I think he wanted people to know what had happened, and could easily happen again, if people allowed one person's ideals and opinions to influence their own thoughts and behaviour.

He became quite actively involved within the local Leicestershire community sharing his life experiences with local clubs, schools and other groups.

In 1999 when Dad became aware that the British Government was planning to mark January 27th (the day that Auschwitz was liberated by the Russians) each year as Holocaust Remembrance Day he voiced his opinions about this publicly in the local newpapers. He thought that there were two points of view. He felt that anything that reminded people of the Holocaust was good but he did not want Holocaust victims to be seen as martyrs. He said that he preferred to see the Holocaust taught in schools as a part of the history syllabus.

The first National Holocaust Memorial Day in England was held on January 27th 2001. Dad was involved in the planning and presention of a service on this day and he continued to do this for the few years left in his life.

Simon Lake, a former curator at Leicester Museum and Art Gallery, remembers my father giving a talk in the Leicester Museum on Holocaust Day and he has written the following testimonial.

Email to me from Simon Lake, former Curator of Art at Leicester Museum and Art Gallery:

"Dear Peggy,

Thank you for your email regarding your father Eric Lewinsohn, with my apologies for this delayed reply. I had met him through Ava Farrington I think, around 2001, during, or shortly after the art exhibition about the life and art of Ava's father, Johannes Koelz. I was the Curator of Art at the time, based at the Leicester Museum and Art Gallery. I also remember a visit he made to the Leicester Museum (then called the New Walk Museum), on Holocaust Memorial Day – January 2002 I think. I caught part of a talk he gave on the Holocaust to a party of schoolchildren. He was seated in a chair in the middle of the Victorian Gallery, and the children and a number of adult visitors were there. He spoke slowly but clearly, and the gallery was pin-drop quiet during the talk. I was moved that he felt strongly that the Holocaust should not be forgotten, and how important it was that the message should reach young people in particular.

After his death, this prompted me to write to the Mercury, and I described him as a passionate communicator, which is what he was, as I remember him, from the occasion I heard him speak at the museum. I felt it was important to acknowledge, and I'm glad the Mercury published my letter".

Written by Simon Lake, former Curator of Art at Leicester Museum and Art Gallery (2020).

The letter that Simon wrote to the Mercury after Dad's death can be found in the final chapter of this book.

I think Dad felt that it was very important to educate the young, as these people would be the adults and decision makers of the next generation. Perhaps they could encourage the world to become less biased against groups of people who were perceived to be different and to realise that we all belong to the same race, the human race, and that, whatever the colour of a person's skin or whatever their beliefs, there are good and bad individuals in every colour and creed.

He became particularly involved with William Bradford Community College in Earl Shilton, Leicestershire, as it was called then (now Heath Lane Academy). He visited this school on a fairly regular basis, becoming known and liked by students and staff alike.

He gave talks there to senior students in years 10 and 11, telling them the true personal story of his life in Austria and Germany and the effects that Hitler and his Nazi regime had had on the life of his family.

He showed them original photographs and papers that were relevant to his talks and he let the students handle these precious photographs and documents. These talks had quite a profound effect on both students and staff. I have managed to contact just a few of the ex students and staff who attended these talks and remember Dad from his visits to this school (his last visit was more than 15 years ago as Dad died in 2006) and each has written a testimonial about their inter- action with Dad for inclusion in this book.

Dad was keen to educate the students about The Holocaust and also, as was his way, he wanted them to aim for excellence in their education and in the work that they produced. To encourage the students in their studies of The Holocaust he set up an award. This was known as the Eric Lewinsohn Holocaust Award. This award was presented annually to five students. Details of the criteria for the award were as follows:

THE ERIC LEWINSOHN HOLOCAUST AWARD

- Students studying Humanities and History have the opportunity to enter a competition.

- The five chosen winners will each receive a special certificate and a ten pound gift voucher, kindly donated by Eric Lewinsohn.

- The task for students is to represent ideas on Hitler's persecution of the Jews.

- A variety of approaches could be used:

    - Poetry.

    - Music.

    - Drama.

    - An imaginative account, eg diary, letter.

    - An essay.

    - Art work.

- The work must be original and of no more than 1500 words in length.

- It can refer to the Lewinsohn family experience or be of a general nature.

Many ideas were given to the students for the presentation of and themes for their work.

Dad obviously felt that this award was valuable educationally as he left a sum of money in his will to allow the award to continue.

Holly Beasley (now Holly Barnes) who was an award winner has kindly agreed to have her award winning work included in this book. She has also written the following words about the effect that Dad's involvement in her education had on her whilst she was studying the Holocaust.

From Holly Barnes (nee Beasley):

"As a teenager in school, learning about something such as The Holocaust, that was so awful and so far removed from your present day experiences, it would have been easy to disengage or not really take it in. Hearing about Eric and his personal, family stories made it all hit home, that it was real, and made our learning so much more meaningful. I won the Eric Lewinsohn Award that year for my "Guard's Recount Of Auschwitz" work, and met Eric in person to receive the certificate. I think it was a wonderful thing that he got involved with the school like this and brought our learning to life".

Written by Holly Barnes (formerly Holly Beasley) (2020).

Holly Beasley receiving the Eric Lewinsohn Holocaust Award

Here is the winning essay that Holly wrote:

A GUARD'S ACCOUNT OF AUSCHWITZ

by Holly Beasley.

"As an SS member in Nazi Germany I was in 1943 sent away from my friends and family, to the suburbs of the Polish city Oswiecim. Oswiecim in the second world war, had been taken over by Nazi rule and renamed Auschwitz, this also became the name of the death camp there to which I was sent. I had no real idea of the horrors that were to meet my eyes as I arrived at Auschwitz, no-one did, it was all kept fairly hushed, other SS members as well as myself left blindly for the camp merely as an order from Hitler. When we arrived we met three main parts of the camp; Auschwitz 1, Auschwitz 2-Birkenau and Auschwitz 3-Monowitz. The camp also had 40+ sub camps. We discovered that Poles, Soviet prisoners of war, gypsies and prisoners of other nationalities had been imprisoned and died or were killed there, mid 1942 was when the mass systematic killing of Europe's Jewish population began. The air was thick with the stench of death. Some SS members like me were disgusted and sickened but there were other guards of higher authority or more anti-semitist guards watching over us, we were also ordered straight into work, constant imports of Jews were coming into the camp by train and most would be killed within two hours of arriving if they had not died on the much overloaded train journey. The camp was all of a rush. I suppose we didn't really oppose because we didn't dare stand up to the other guards nor have time to think. I was in complete shock and more terrified than most now could ever imagine. I was not an anti-semitist person myself; I was an SS member because at home this was seen as a noble and respected thing to do. Germany loved Hitler. At first my first job was that I was made to actually determine which of the people imported were well enough to work for a few days before they were killed, this was terrible, I didn't want any to work in helping to kill their friends and relatives nor did I want any to be just sent off to die. I cannot begin to express in any way how this felt to me, these were real live people in front and all around me and I had to determine their either way morbid future. After a while I was moved to work at the gas chambers where I saw for myself and assisted in the end of those whom I had sent here. The Jews on arrival to the Birkenau gas chambers were told they were to be showered and de-loused. They were made to remove all of their clothing, regardless of no privacy or their dignity, jewellery and other such-like items, these were then taken away. I was made to shave them, this hair was collected too, it was sold for mattresses and pillows. They were then sent to "the shower rooms" where they would be gassed. The gas was called "Zyclon-B". Some harsher colder anti-semitist guards watched the death of these people through a peep hole in the door, the worst part of this for me was having to hide my emotion, if I did not I feared a future like that of the ones dying. When the room was opened they were dead. Dead but still standing as they were so overcrowded that there was no room to fall to the floor, sometimes people would be laying across the heads of the bodies, they had attempted to climb to the top of the room for air. I worked there for the rest of my time at Auschwitz. Sometimes also I had to remove the bodies from and clean the chambers after use. I was also although very rarely made to spend a couple of days in the nearing to the end of the war in the crematoria. At the end of the war, in an effort to cover up the extent of the crimes, myself and the other also low authority guards were ordered by the higher authority guards, most who then left, to dismantle the gas chambers, crematoria and other significant buildings and also burn documentation. After this effort I fled, back to Germany to my family whom I could not look in the face for six months. Only last year did I actually share with my closest family the experience, the one who does not remember history is bound to live through it again".

Written by Holly Beasley when she was a student in Year10
at William Bradford Community College.

In March 2003 the work that Dad did at the school was acknowledged at a school assembly during which he was presented with a memorial folder "in grateful recognition of his services to William Bradford Community College". Lorraine McClintock, the then Head of Humanities, read the following:

TRIBUTE GIVEN TO ERIC LEWINSOHN
AT COLLEGE ASSEMBLY MARCH 2003
BY LORRAINE McCLINTOCK– HEAD OF HUMANITIES.

As Mr Roberts has indicated, Mr Lewinsohn or Eric, as he likes to be called, has for many years volunteered his German Language skills to help post 16 and Yr 11 students prepare for their speaking exams. Eric is always patient and supportive and encourages all students to do their best. This work in promoting foreign language learning is very much appreciated by students and teachers alike.

The other valuable input Eric has made to the College curriculum is in History and Humanities lessons, where he has given us a thought provoking insight into the disastrous effects of prejudice and racism.

Eric's personal testimony is a vivid account of the Jewish family experience of Antisemitism under the Nazis. His accounts are extremely moving and students are absolutely captivated by his story of growing up in Berlin, his escape to England and his parents death in Auschwitz Concentration Camp.

Eric is a very special man with his own brand of charisma. During his talks, which are always delivered with great humility, clarity and care, all students have been generally moved and engaged by his personal story.

It is a rare thing in teaching to witness an entire class spellbound for an hour. His talks are extraordinary experiences, deeply respected and appreciated by our students.

I know that students here this morning in Years 11, 12 and 13 can testify to the insight given and emotional impact of his talks. Over the years students have volunteered to write letters of thanks to Eric.

I will end by reading two such letters.

Firstly from a student now in Year 12:

"Dear Eric,

I would like to take this opportunity to thank you for the inspiring talk you shared with my History class. Your delighted account has given us an insight into how Jewish families suffered severely under the Nazis. The courage of your family is a strong example of how many people had to make sacrifices.

From your educational talk you have made many of us reconsider first how fortunate our generation is and how important it is to overcome prejudice in our society.

Once more I would like to give our sincere thanks to you on behalf of the class."

And finally from a Year 11 Humanities Student:

"Dear Eric,

I am writing to tell you that I was very touched to hear the story you told about your life as a Jew in Nazi Germany. Personally I think we were all honoured to have such a great man like you visiting us. I found it very interesting. You even brought tears to my eyes: it touched me deep down.

You are a very brave man to go through so much and still tell the story. It was terrible to hear what they did to you and your parents. But what makes you so brave and special is that you still smile.

I really appreciated you coming into William Bradford, thank you very much."

Above: Eric receiving the award
from William Bradford Community College.

PRESENTED TO

ERIC LEWINSOHN

IN GRATEFUL RECOGNITION
OF HIS SERVICES
TO
WILLIAM BRADFORD
COMMUNITY COLLEGE

"TO THE MEMORY OF HIS PARENTS
BLANKA & FRITZ LEWINSOHN"

Pictures copied, digitally modified and
reprinted from original photographs & documents by
John O'Donovan
1st March 2003

"LEST WE FORGET"

The award from William Bradford Community College.

I have been fortunate in that I have made contact with Lorraine and she has written the following testimonial for inclusion into this book.

From Lorrainne McClintock (former head of Humanities and History Faculty):

"I knew Eric for several years. He firstly joined my A Level European History lessons but unfortunately I can't remember the exact dates. Although there was a huge gap in age between Eric and 17-18 year olds, his warm, friendly manner and cheerful disposition bridged the years and he was well liked by his classmates.

When Eric's compelling and poignant family story from Nazi Germany became known, I asked him if he would be willing to give talks about his family's treatment to 14/15 year old students studying Humanities and History. (As well as teaching History and Humanities since 1978 at the then called Earl Shilton Community College, I managed the wider Humanities group of subjects as Head of Faculty until 2007).

For several year Eric spoke to spellbound teenagers of his childhood and schooldays in prewar Berlin. Eric's quiet but memorising voice entranced his audience, some of whom would not usually be so attentive! When he recounted how he and his brother escaped from the Nazi regime, the students were amazed at their daring and relieved that they were not captured. However, the very sad ending of his talk and the reading of his father's final letter to him brought a tear to many eyes. Eric always stressed the parallels with modern day prejudice and its negative effects, and urged the young people to remember that we are all part of the human race. His talks, illustrated by a slide show including family photos produced by the Head of Maths John O'Donovan, a keen photographer, were always a highlight of the school year, as were his assemblies for Holocaust Day.

Eric also donated one thousand pounds to William Bradford Community College to be used over years as "prize money" for empathetic work about the effects of Nazi Jewish persecution. Students, inspired by Eric, were keen to get involved and produced an impressive range of work including moving poems, diaries and artwork.

Each year, Eric presented his "Award" to the winning students at a school assembly. His last appearance was for a Holocaust Memorial Day. We had noticed Eric's increased frailty but still felt shock and great sadness at the news of his death in March 2006. I attended Eric's funeral with the Principal of William Bradford College, Mrs Mary Neate, who gave a tribute at the service.

In my final years at the school I continued to give Holocaust Day assemblies, with the help of John O'Donovan, based on Eric's story, and organised his "Award" work. My last academic year at William Bradford was 2006-2007. The school then had a new principal, GCSE Humanities was dropped from the curriculum and I do not know how the Eric Lewinsohn Award fared. The Head of History may have continued the work. Since then there have been many changes at the school including another change of name. I taught part time in three other Leicestershire schools, was based in Northern Ireland for two years and moved to live in the south of England in 2013.

Eric had a very special charisma and moral courage to present his personal family story to teenagers from a very different generation and culture. His contribution to widening their world view and encouraging a greater understanding of the destruction caused by prejudice was considerable and hopefully long lasting. A powerful legacy".

Written by Lorraine McClintock (former Head of Humanities at William Bradford Community College) (2021).

Following are more testimonials written by people who knew Dad from his involvement with William Bradford College.

From Hannah Webb (nee Bates):

"I remember Mr Lewinsohn coming in to William Bradford Community College and talking to us, in both History and German lessons about his experiences during the war. He was always so calm when reciting such extraordinarily horrific events (which I'm sure had been sugar-coated for our little ears!). One thought which always comes to mind is how he would be so happy, polite and truly pleasant to be around. It was as though the life he was sharing with us was not his own, for how could a person have seen such horrific things and still be so happy. Mr Lewinsohn is such an inspiration of how to value each moment and aim forward. A true gentleman and I will always be grateful for the lessons he taught me, in History, German and life".

Written by Hannah Webb (nee Bates) (2020).

From Stephanie Brentnall (nee Taylor):

"Eric totally inspired me as a High School student of German with his passion for the German language and its grammar. He used to lend me novels to read. Despite the despicable way Germany had treated him and his family, Eric never lost his faith in his native country and his love for German literature and customs. I remember thinking, even as a naive 17 year old, what an amazing strength of character Eric possessed to remain a proud German.

Today I live and teach in a High School in Germany myself and Eric is often mentioned in my lessons as a shining example of the power of forgiveness. It was definitely Eric's passion and my interactions with him that inspired me to study German at university. His memory and story live on in my classroom in Neuss, Germany".

Written by Stephanie Brentnall (nee Taylor) (2020).

From Deborah Abbott:

"I remember Eric Lewinsohn coming into William Bradford Community College to talk to the students about the Holocaust. He was a very interesting man and the kids loved him"

Written by Deborah Abbott (2020).

From Chris Hopkins, previous Head of History at William Bradford Community College, Earl Shilton Leicestershire UK:

"Eric contacted me in the 1990s, offering to speak to History students at William Bradford about his personal experiences of the Holocaust. Our students studied the rise of the Nazi Party as part of their History GCSE syllabus therefore we knew that Eric's input could be invaluable to their education. As a teacher it is straightforward to teach facts, viewing a historical era from a personal perspective is often achieved through contemporary writings: letters, diaries poetry, etc. To actually have someone in the classroom who had, first hand, experienced the tragedies of the Holocaust was of inestimable value.

The students were aged between 14 and 16, some wanted to learn, some were indifferent; Eric's presence affected them all. He would tell them a little about what it was like to be a Jewish schoolchild in the 1930s when he began to experience State driven bigotry and discrimination. He remembered clearly the Nuremburg Laws and Kristallnacht, and being ordered to comply with new laws. He could relate the effects this gradual erosion of freedom had on his family and friends. He explained his escape from Germany and how devastating it was to eventually leave his beloved parents. He attempted to describe the degradation of Concentration Camps and how his mother and father had died in Auschwitz; innocent victims of a totalitarian regime. I clearly recall him reading aloud the final letter he had received from his father, most of our young students were quietly sobbing and obviously deeply affected. I am certain that the memory of Eric's visits will stay with these young people for ever. He gave them a glimpse into the devastating consequences of hatred and ignorance. Moreover, he made a very important contribution in the fight against Holocaust deniers.

I had huge respect for Eric Lewinsohn. He was a very brave man; where many would have attempted to blank out the horrors of their formative years, he was determined to use his experiences to inform young people and give an insight into the dreadful times he lived through. He gave us an awareness that can never be learned just from the written page. I will always be grateful for his input; as will my colleagues and those students who were privileged to receive his wisdom".

Written by Chris Hopkins, former Head of History
at William Bradford Community College (2020).

From Sarah Fell, school librarian:

Eric Lewinsohn – A Memory

"I have been the librarian at Heath Lane Academy (formerly William Bradford Academy) for just over 30 years. In that time, as you can imagine, there has been much change and many memories made. A memory that is very clear in my mind is Eric Lewinsohn's association with the college and the impact that he had on both staff and students.

I first met Eric in the 1990s when he came to the college at the behest of the Head of Humanities. Eric had been invited to come and speak to the students about his Holocaust experience. He came to the library to wait before the first of these lectures and was introduced to me. My first impression was of a modest, very polite, smiling man who was interested in everything and everyone. I had no idea of his past struggles and asked if I could go and listen to him speak.

The college lecture theatre was full of Year 10 and 11 students, at least 200 of them. Eric was introduced and he walked onto the stage with no props, no prompt cards, just a single piece of old folded paper. As he began to speak, all the shuffling and fidgeting from the students stopped as they listened with rapt attention, as Eric told his story of escaping across Europe in the wake of the Nazi oppression of the Jews. Then, as he was nearing the end of his lecture, he unfolded the piece of paper in his hand and began to read the last letter that he received from his father, telling him to live a good life and to become a good man. The silence in the room was palpable, the students hung on every word and many were visibly moved. His lecture bought the past alive for them. It was no longer a page in the history books, but real events that happened to real people. Over a number of years Eric repeated these lectures on an annual basis and the effect was always the same. He was an involving, moving speaker who told his story in a straight forward but passionate way.

As part of his work with the students Eric also endowed the 'Eric Lewinsohn' award. This was a prize given across years groups, for the best creative piece of work commemorating the Holocaust. This Award continued for many years under Eric's patronage and even for a number of years after he sadly passed away, such was the impact that he made on the college. As the college librarian, it was my privilege to assist students and staff with research materials for the award, which became a major part of the curriculum. Students put an immense amount of effort and ingenuity into producing a piece for the Award. They wrote poems, produced diaries artfully aged by liquid coffee, they researched individual histories and on one memorable occasion, produced a scaled down model of Auschwitz concentration camp. All this combined, for many years, to do what Eric had hoped that it would, it kept the memory of the awful events of the Holocaust in the minds of young people so that it, and the millions it affected, would not be forgotten.

As time went on Eric became more and more interested in studying. He moved effortlessly from teacher to student, joining A level classes as a mature student. I often saw him and had conversations with him during this period of his life as he came to the library often and loved spending time amongst the books. From there, in his eighties, he became a university student and there was much celebrating at the college when we learned of his qualifications!

Looking back on this time now, it is apparent how much a part of the college Eric became, how much a part of the lives of many of our staff and students. Eric was passionate that his story and the story of millions of others who suffered in the Holocaust should be kept alive and that future generations should remember so that it never happened again. In one school, in one part of the world, Eric did that. Even though the years have gone by, I will personally never forget the looks on the faces of those students when Eric gave his lectures. It was a privilege to have known him and a privilege to write about him now".

Written by Sarah Fell. (28/02/2021)

From John O'Donovan (former Head of Maths at William Bradford Community College):

"I became aware of Eric Lewinsohn while I was a teacher at William Bradford Community College. This 14-18 comprehensive school is situated in the small town of Earl Shilton in rural Leicestershire. Now I'm retired, and Eric has passed away, though my memories of him still make me smile with affection. Then I was head of the mathematics department and Eric a not infrequent visitor to the school. I knew he spoke to groups of students in Years 10 and 11. Eric was not so different in age to my own father who was in the Royal Navy for the duration of the Second World War. Eric, I gathered, was talking about his escape from Nazi Germany and of the Holocaust. I was interested, so I asked if I could attend one of his sessions.

Before I continue, a small caveat. This account of my interactions with Eric are as I remember them. And I remember with that imperfect memory of which we all partake. If I knew then I would be writing of these events some twenty years later, I would have paid more attention. I may even have made notes but I doubt it. Looking back on my relationship with Eric, my friendship I like to think, I still see his diminutive figure, but mostly I see his ready and sparkling smile. A smile behind which lay memories. Memories that would embitter most of us, but for him they seemed a well of inner strength to draw upon. He was passionate that by conveying his personal memories, young people of today would learn of those dreadful years of Nazi atrocities. To learn, but not to reciprocate the hatred that he and his family endured. Rather to learn, "Lest We Forget", of the very worst that mankind is capable, and hoping beyond hope, that we dare not follow the path that culminated, for his parents, in the Gas Chambers of Auschwitz Birkenau.

I watched Eric as he spoke to the children. I watched the 14 and 15 year-olds as they listened to him. I don't know what you think of teenagers, but these were good. Good in all the best senses of the word. I saw that they felt they were touching history. And they respected all they saw and heard from this small, old, Jewish guy. Here was a man whose heart must be so much heavier than theirs, but who spoke calmly and with no trace of rancour. How could he do it I wondered? He would even smile. He told of his escape from Germany into Belgium with his parents. Like in a film, they hid in a secret compartment of the lorry, knowing that the slightest sound could betray them to the vicious border guards. In Belgium they applied for asylum in England. Eric and his brother were light engineers, and we wanted those. His father, I believe was an accountant. He was not needed, so his parents had to remain in Belgium and await the coming German invasion. They were captured and transported to a French concentration camp, and from there to their ultimate destination, Auschwitz Birkenau. As he engaged with the class, he passed round

186

photographs and papers, some of which confirmed the death of his parents. I was dismayed. I knew that such precious memorabilia would all too soon further deteriorate by being handed from one student to the next. After the lesson I approached Eric and conveyed my misgivings. He nodded slightly and smiled as I explained what I thought I could do. He readily agreed that I could digitise all his resources. I said I could print them and protect them for classroom use. Most importantly that I could make a PowerPoint Presentation for projecting his resources onto a large whiteboard. He was not so sure with this, claiming no competence with technology. I promised that I or a technician would always be on hand to help.

At home with Eric's pictures and papers I felt a great sense of responsibility. Just as I do now as I type these words. Then there were no smartphones and thus no easy way to copy the photos. Luckily, I had a copy stand to which I attached my Canon SLR camera. I used my usual Fuji slide film and then a transparency scanner to get the images into my computer. I had some editing digital software, but I had not really used it much before. And most of the images needed "corrections" from the ravages of time and the classroom. Strangely, or maybe not, I found the whole process of editing quite emotional. All the photos had creases or other blemishes. Manipulating the images, I recall revealing the freshness of the young smiling faces of Eric's parents, Blanka and Fritz, a year before their marriage. She just 17, he 7 years the senior. But now they were dead, most cruelly killed over sixty years before. How pointless is this! How important is this I felt, as tears came to my eyes. With each image I was forced to reflect upon the enormity of the tragedy encapsulated before me. I kept recalling scraps of words remembered from his classroom presentations or gleaned from him over coffee in the staffroom. Occasionally I might smile. Fritz having the same birthday as my Dad. I noticed that their wedding day 17th March 1918, was only months before the end of the First World War; optimism amid chaos. And their love was strong, with Fritz phoning Blanka every day from his workplace just to say, "I love you". "Many times a day", Eric added. And for two Jews, how ironic to me that the wedding was on St. Patrick's Day. Resonant too as I had a Jewish uncle, not a real uncle, but when you're a kid what is an uncle anyhow. We called him Uncle Solly and he owned a corner sweet shop in the East End of London where we lived. We were a Catholic family but, to use the euphemism of the day, he was friendly with my Aunt Esther. And as I was later told, they would not marry because of their differing religions. But it did not stop him providing a yearly Christmas party for us kids. Plenty of sweets of course.

I remember editing the picture of Eric and his brother, arm in arm with their parents as they strolled down a High Street in Berlin. They were all smiling. Eric and his Mum linked together smiling the most. In the background I could see flags adorning the shop fronts. Swastikas! I guess they had no inkling then of what we all know now. No portent of just how horrific was their imminent fate. And the picture of Eric's bombed out workplace had a familiarity for me. The photo, taken in 1948, was the year I was born. The scene not so different from parts of London I saw a few years later.

As I now look at the picture of Eric with his classmates and schoolmaster, I recall Eric's account of his return to Berlin long after the war. He did not want to go. He had been urged to return to be feted by the Germans. Though he was an old man, he told me his feelings were still too raw. However, he did go, and he was made something of a celebrity there but found the apparent warmth of his former classmates difficult to accept. He remembered their former selves too well. The teacher in the picture may have been the one instrumental in his school expulsion. The class had to sing several nationalistic songs. In one they would sing of the killing of Jews and of the spurting out of their Jewish blood. Eric would not join in and was sent home. His Dad was concerned by the premature ending of his education. The two of them returned to discuss the situation with the headmaster. They were told that the matter would be overlooked if Eric would not refuse to sing again. He was just a teenager at the time, but he said no and thus his schooling was over.

Probably the most poignant, and saddest moments I found was when I was enhancing the last letter to Eric and his brother from their Dad, Fritz. It was sent from the Camp des Milles, on the outskirts of

Aix-en-Provence, France. Here is a link to its website, and the camp is now a memorial centre that can be visited. It's Wikipedia entry is interesting too.

link http://guyboutin.free.fr/lesmilles/campdesmilles/camp.htm

My Dearest Children,

As you may probably know, by the time this letter reaches you, your mother and I will unfortunately be on the way to the East. We know that you, our beloved ones, would have done everything possible to spare us this sorrow, but in these difficult times people are only objects of stronger forces and we can do no other than obey those forces and try to make the best of it. If we are therefore so sad that our reunion for which we are longing so very much, has been again postponed, we are determined come what may, to stick it out and hope that mother and I can stay together. We hope and pray that it won't be too long before we can get in touch with you again. Please stick together whatever the war may face you with, always remember no matter how far we are apart, in love and thoughts we are always near you and nothing and nobody can separate us from each other. Stay healthy bring up your children with the same love and success, so they will grow up to be splendid young people. If a fatherly blessing can wish you only happy hours, please accept it from us with many kisses. Remain strong.

Your Dad

Reading this again I'm struck by a huge moral conundrum. This letter was from a concentration camp in France, in the middle of the war, and it was sent to the small town of Hinckley in England. That sounds like a difficult but humanitarian thing to do. Yet just ten days later Eric's parents were put on a train bound for Auschwitz Birkenau. How could they do both? If you go on Google Earth, you can still see the train track right next to the Camp des Milles where Blanka and Fritz boarded a cattle truck. Two days later on 19th August 1942, they arrived at their final destination. Later the same day they were gassed to death.

Once, while we were looking through his photos Eric told me of the promise he had made to them, saying to his parents he would "return to them". In the photo you can see Eric next to the Gas Chamber. He writes a simple note and tucks it into the ruins, "I've Come Back".

I have many fond memories of Eric, his instant warmth and ready smile. Animated conversation around my home dinner table. His light-hearted chatting as we prepared the equipment for his presentation or more talk over coffee in the staff room. He would tell me of his ongoing university studies. In fact, he gained a BA degree from Leicester University when he was 77 and continued to his Master's when aged 82. He said his research, which related to the Jewish organisation within concentration camps, took him across Europe. Remarkable at such an age I always felt. My culminating memory was of the full school assembly held to thank Eric for the years he had given us with his reflections and insights. I made the final speech and spoke forthrightly to the students regarding the continuing curse of Holocaust denial. Standing shoulder to shoulder with Eric I said, "You will hear some people say that the Holocaust has been exaggerated or that it did not happen. But you, and I, have heard from Eric. I have looked into his eyes and I know who I believe". Rapturous applause erupted.

Thank you Eric, I feel I'm a better person for having known you. I'm certain there are many of us".

Written by John O'Donovan (former Head of Maths

at William Bradford Community College) (2021).

From Tom Waugh, former teacher at William Bradford Community College:

"I first came across Eric when I took up my first teaching post at William Bradford Community College in Earl Shilton, a small rural village in Leicestershire. As a new teacher fresh out of University I'd spent many years being "taught the Holocaust", the reasoning behind it's horrors, the concentration camps and the numbers murdered by the Nazi regime. As far as I was concerned this was a piece of history to be studied, reflected upon and explained as an almost abstract concept. I'm sure that as historical events such as the Holocaust fade from living history and fewer and fewer people that experienced them are here to tell us about their lives we can forget that behind the numbers are real people, families and individuals who all have a story to tell.

I distinctly remember how Eric came to change that world view and give many hundreds of students and dozens of staff a new perspective, one that I have carried with me ever since. Within our curriculum we taught the Holocaust and we had been told that a local man who had lived in Nazi Germany was willing to come and talk to our students about his experiences, his escape and the destiny of his family members. Little did I know what Eric would reveal to us.

For our students, the Holocaust, the Second World War and even events that have happened much more recently were difficult to grasp, it was hard to explain just how close to them these events really were. Eric arrived clutching a folder of documents, some of which would be passed around to students as Eric talked, some to be projected for the whole class to see. The talk was always around an hour. Eric would describe his childhood with his parents and brother, a family so similar to the ones our students lived in, with their hopes and expectations for the future, but as the story unfolded Eric would slowly reveal that their futures would not be the ones they envisaged as a family. Eric was extremely generous with the students, allowing them to handle precious family documents, photographs and even letters that he had carried with him his entire life. It was always a worry as a teacher to see students casually passing these between each other, documents from the 1930s being handed from one student to the next. Eric was

191

clearly proud to show these to students and rather than seeing them as historical documents they were simply photographs from his childhood and letters from loving family members.

As the talk continued to his family's departure from Germany and escape to Belgium the mood among staff and students clearly shifted. Eric told them of the events in a way that clearly signposted their destinies long before Eric revealed the conclusion of their journey. Students would be listening intensely to his every word, enthralled to hear the next stage in Eric's family journey. When Eric revealed their eventual fate, many staff and students simply wept, some sat motionless and some closed their eyes in an attempt to take in the tragic end to the talk.

It's fair to say the impact of the talks would be long lasting on those who listened to Eric. As a school it became central to our year, more and more students were able to hear the talk and staff from around the school would come to the Humanities Department to hear first-hand the events surrounding Eric's family. Very quickly we moved from classes with around 30 students in them to whole year groups of 200 students, so that every single student (and staff) was given an opportunity to have this experience with Eric. One of the most memorable features of Eric's talk were his touches of humour. His talk had a heartbreaking conclusion but Eric shared the love and experiences in such a warm way. He was never visibly upset recalling events and it was always clear to me that his legacy was about human-ising some of the inconceivable number of victims. Eric didn't talk in the millions, he talked about Fritz and Blanka, two loving parents and their children, Eric and Hans (Jack).

It was an honour to work alongside Eric and I was always delighted when he came back year after year to tell our students about the events of his life. The talks changed our students and staff for the better, giving them an insight into history but also an insight into what life was like for individuals exactly like them; real people experi-encing real suffering under the Nazi regime. Students would always warmly applaud Eric at the conclusion of his talk, and they would be discussing it long after. Many would enter a competition about the Holocaust and this continued after Eric passed.

I'm sure I speak for hundreds of people when I say Eric changed our worldviews with his talk. When new films or books are released or when Holocaust Memorial Day comes around it takes me straight back to my experiences with Eric, his family and the fate of his parents. This little old, kind, warm, funny and charming man had experienced such tragedy and was determined to ensure this was shared with future generations. I was proud to call him my friend.

I'm sure that the many hundreds of students and staff that listened to Eric have never forgotten the day that this man in his late 70s sat down to tell them the events of his life and I'm certain that none of them have forgotten the lessons within it. I certainly carry those lessons forward with me, they've made me a better teacher but also a better human being".

Written by Tom Waugh, former teacher
at William Bradford Community College (2020).

The next testimonial has been written by Cori MacGregor who met Dad when he spoke of his life experiences to a class at Hinckley College.

From Cori MacGregor:

"In 1993 I was a student at Hinckley College doing an Access to Higher Education course. History was a part of the course and we were studying World War 2. Eric came to give us a talk on his experiences. His talk was moving. By halfway through a lot of us were crying as he told us about losing his family and the dangers of extremism. It is something that I still think of to this day as I think of our political situation and the way that Muslim people are being treated in the UK, the growth of Islamophobia.

But with humour Eric sent us away laughing. He said that he had been proud of being the oldest student at Leicester University but had recently been beaten by an older woman. He said that he would have the last laugh because he would do course after course until he regained his title".

Written by Cori Macgregor (2020).

The final two testimonials in this chapter are written by mothers whose children heard Dad tell his story at other schools.

From Sheena Lewinsohn-Marston:

"Our girls remember him fondly coming into their schools to talk about his life during the war. Talks in which he was determined to document the struggle of the Jewish population. A lesson that needs to be told over and over".

Written by Sheena Marston-Lewinsohn (2020).

From Janine Yarwood:

"When my grandparents lived on King Georges Way Eric Lewinsohn collected the football coupons from them on Friday evenings. My grandfather, father and Eric were all friends.

Both my daughter and son attended Westfield School and they were present when Eric gave talks about the Holocaust and about his childhood experiences. When he came home on the day of the talks my son quite rightly said that he had met a war hero called Mr Lewinsohn.

Whatever Eric said in his talks will remain with the children forever and is a true statement to Eric's courage and resilience. He was a very brave man to be able to turn his horrific experiences into something positive by teaching the children a very important, though harrowing, part of history. What happened must never happen again and those who suffered deserve to be heard. I and many others in Hinckley will always remember Eric Lewinsohn".

Written by Janine Yarwood (2020).

In the late 1990s Dad was asked what message he would give to young people today. His reply was:

"If you make up your mind to do something, do it. Don't let anyone stop you. In my case, in spite of everything I wouldn't have wanted to be born at any other time. Do whatever you want".

Dad went on to say:

"Never ever think someone is worse or look down on someone because of their religion, colour of skin or anything like that".

As far as I'm concerned I hate it when people talk about the German race, the English race. There is no such thing as race. There is only one race, that's the human race. There's no such a thing that you can talk about different races of people because when it all boils down to it whether you are a black man or a white man or a Japanese or a Chinese or whatever, if you cut yourself the colour of your blood is the same. It's not green or blue or anything like that. I think one of the main problems in this world is that people have this superiority complex, such as "I come from this such and such country. We are more educated and superior to you". There's no such thing.

I think it's getting a lot better. Young people realise that they must work together and there is no such thing as different Races or one person superior to another. That's what's caused all the trouble in the past.

Never look down on anyone. Take everyone as you find them. Of course there are good and bad in all sorts of people. Take everyone as you find them no matter the colour of their skin or their religion or nationality. They are all equal. They have all been put into this world for a purpose and the sooner people of the world realise that then the better it will be for them to work together"

End of statement made by Eric Lewinsohn.

I will now add another statement made by my father. This, in my opinion, sums up how the planned extermination of so-called "subhuman" people was carried out during Hitler's Nazi regime.

Dad said:

"The Holocaust is beyond anyone's understanding. Not just the numbers killed or the way they were killed. Since the Holocaust as many have been killed around the world in Ethiopia, Bosnia, Vietnam, Angola.

The Holocaust was different because of its beaurocratic precision. It was carried out from behind what the Germans called "schriebema-chine" that is with desk precision. Faceless grey people sitting behind a desk signed hundreds/ thousands of people to death. Not only Jews. There were gypsies, homosexuals etc. Anyone who, in their eyes, was inferior or subhuman.

It is difficult to understand how these people could sit and do this. Some didn't even hate Jews. It was just a job, they never thought of the people.

I just cannot comprehend the Holocaust.

Here is my message to deniers. If it didn't happen why did my family not come back? Where did they go to?

To say it didn't happen is just an insult to people like myself who experienced it.

In Germany denial is a punishable offence. Deniers can be imprisoned. The same has been suggested for other countries, for England. I don't know about this.

This is a democratic country, the UK. If a person can be locked up for stating an opinion where is the freedom of speech that England is known for.

I feel strongly that all perpetrators should stand trial however long ago it was. Too old? Can't remember? They should still stand trial. They should know that they are being hunted, to feel scared and hunted. They should know the feeling of being hunted. They are living freely in many countries including England. They should be prosecuted".

End of statement made by Eric Lewinsohn.

It must be remembered that during his youth Dad had experienced firsthand the boycott of Jewish shops in 1933, the Burning of the Books in 1934, the Nurembureg Laws (Racial Laws) in 1935 and Kristallnacht in 1938 as well as the daily ongoing fear of the Nazi monsters. After Kristallnacht no Jew was allowed to work. How could they feed their families? 80% - 90% of Germans wanted Hitler as he was very good for the economy. Six million unemployed became employed building autobahns etc..

In 1997 Dad said that he was still suspicious of Germans of his age. He always wondered: "What did they do during the war?"

Personally, I think that no action or behaviour, however small, can stand alone and not have an effect on other people. The Holocaust was possibly the most horrific event that has occurred in the history of mankind, therefore it seems obvious that the emotional effects will last for a very long time. This is sad and traumatic for those whose lives have been affected, and in some cases are still being affected by the Holocaust, but we must not allow the world to ever forget the events of the Holocaust. By remembering perhaps the people of this world will try to ensure that such an atrocity is never allowed to happen again. Is education the key? If Holocaust Studies were a compulsory part of secondary school education every young person would at least know that the Holocaust had occurred and know a little about what happened during this time of persecution. This knowledge might help to prevent young people from becoming swept up and involved in activities that are harmful to others. The planet Earth has only one race of people, the human race. Let us all be tolerant of one another and embrace our varying cultures, customs and beliefs. As Dad used to say:

"If I cut myself my blood is red,

If a black man cuts himself his blood is red.

There is only one race,

The human race".

ERIC – THE MAN

I have spoken about Dad's life as a worker, student, teacher and educator but who was the man Eric Lewinsohn? We all have those habits, quirks, hobbies etc. that are a part of the person we are and obviously Dad was no exception.

It seems that Dad made an impact on most people that he met whether they were adults or children.

He was quite a creature of habit and he always had his hair cut at the same barber's shop close to his home. When I lived at home he would get his hair cut there every second Friday night on his way home from work. After all these years the barber's daughter Diane still remembers him.

From Diane Frost (nee Turner):

"Eric Lewinsohn came to my father's barbers shop to have his hair cut. He had his hair cut fortnightly. I was a child at the time but I remember that, from a child's perspective, he was a very nice man".

Written by Diane Frost (nee Turner) (2020).

Some people who have contacted me remember Dad not as a student nor an educator but as a neighbour/ friend's parent/ parent's friend etc.

From Margaret Wilson (nee Fletcher):

"I lived next door to the Lewinsohn family from about 1957 to 1963. I was friendly with Deryn Lewinsohn. I remember that when we were playing in the garden, whatever we were playing, Deryn's Dad, Eric Lewinsohn would join in. He would come down to our level and play with us. He was my second dad. He was always available to talk to any child. In my mind he was a good "pied piper". All the kids in the street knew him. If he was walking in the street and boys were playing football he would join in for a while. Deryn and I used to put on little shows for parents and I remember that he would make me personally feel like a film star. He would whoop and clap. I just have very happy memories of him".

Written by Margaret Wilson (nee Fletcher) (2020).

From Tina Swift (nee Alcock):

"When I was growing up my family lived four houses away from the Lewinsohn family so we knew one another as neighbours. Eric Lewinsohn used to collect the football pools and coupons from our house on Thursday evening each week. I remember him as being a quiet man and he came over as being a lovely man. I remember that he always carried a briefcase under his arm and I remember him smoking a pipe. I know that he taught German from his home and I remember seeing his students arriving at the door of his house".

Written by Tina Swift (nee Alcock) (2020).

From Malcolm Davison:

"I grew up living five houses away from Mr. Lewinsohn and his family. Eric was a lovely man. He could always be relied on to collect our weekly football pools entry. At one time Eric and his wife used to travel with my brother to Aston Villa to watch the football. My last, and enduring, memory of him was on the day of my mother's funeral. He came to his gate and stood with his head bowed as the cortege moved off from our house and passed him. I thought it was a lovely gesture from a lovely man....RIP Eric".

Written by Malcolm Davison (2020).

From Pat Harris:

"I first met Eric Lewinsohn when we both used to wait for the bus at the same bus stop. He would often be at the bus stop and we would chat about all sorts of things. He was a very interesting man. I met up with him again some years later when I was working at Multi Broadcast (a rental firm). Eric came in one day to pay his television rental fee and he recognised me. From that day on I had the pleasure of having regular monthly chats with him until I changed my job. As I said, he was a very interesting man".

Written by Pat Harris (2020).

From Kay Otter (nee Kareena Clarke):

"Eric befriended my mum, Joan Clarke, who had polio as a child and was crippled in one leg, wore a leg iron and was mostly confined to a wheelchair. In the late 1950s and early 1960s they both used to go out to clubs in Earl Shilton where we lived and in Hinckley where

Eric lived. They enjoyed each other's company. I remember my mum saying that Eric was a kind and gentle soul who knew how to treat a lady. My memories of Eric are that he seemed to be a kind and very clever man who had suffered greatly during his life".

Written by Kay Otter (nee Kareena Clarke) (2020).

The next testimonial has been written by Karen Parkyn and her sister Jane Mayne who worked in their parents cafe:

"My sister and I remember Eric Lewinsohn from when we worked at The Corner Cafe on Coventry Road, Hinckley. He was a small, very polite gentleman who loved to have a talk. He told us that he was writing a book of his life experiences and, to be honest, I was shocked at how matter of fact he was about it. I wouldn't have wanted to recall it. He said he went to libraries. He was also doing a course. I think it was at a college or a university. I can't remember which as this was a long time ago in the period 1976 to 1982 which is when I worked in the cafe. The main thing my sister and I remember is how polite and full of information he was".

Written by Karyn Parkyn (2020).

Istvan Kemeny whose family were tenants of a hotel in Hinckley has written the following:

"Mr Lewinsohn was a gentleman who reminded me of the personalities of my ancestors in Budapest. He had this measured, polite manner so characteristic of my father, my uncles and my lovely grandfather. We were the tenants of the Union Hotel at the time and he was a regular visitor. My father and he had many conversations about the history and politics of Central Europe. My dad was also a smoker, which of course was very much allowed in those days. In fact the room on the right of the entrance was called "Smoke Room". It signified men only, whereas the room opposite was called the Coffee Room, a more genteel place for the ladies. Even the way Mr Lewinsohn smoked his pipe and my father held his cigarette somehow evoked a different era. I do believe his tipple was a half of Pedigree. I also seem to remember that he taught German in the college. In these worrying, turbulent times I look back and long for the civilized era of a past Europe inhabited by gentleman of such scholarly, civilized intelligence".

Written by Istvan Kemeny (2020).

Did Dad have any hobbies? What did he enjoy doing in his spare time?

He was a keen and, I believe, good chess player. He belonged to a chess club for many years, but I have not been able to contact anyone who knew him from there.

For a period of several years (about 1956-1962) he went to watch Aston Villa play football. However, I don't think he was particularly keen on sport. He did stop going to watch them play, although he did continue to take an interest in the team's progress.

He enjoyed dancing. I remember ballroom dancing with Dad on many occasions. He was an average dancer although I'm sure he thought that he was better than he actually was. I enjoyed dancing with him. It always seemed special to me to be dancing with this man. Whether he was at a public dance hall or at a private party if there was music Dad would dance.

Dad was very proud of his "Al Jolson" impersonation. He would go onto his knees to give his rendition of "Mammy" on many occasions, particularly if he thought he had a captive audience.

Music was always very important to Dad. He would put on his earphones and "conduct" intently as he listened to his beloved classical music.

Reading was another thing that he enjoyed. This is to be expected as he was an avid learner.

Dad enjoyed playing Bingo in his later life. He would often play on Saturday evening in a local club.

He also belonged to a German Circle and a fellow member of this German Circle has written about his interaction with Dad.

From Frank Mitchell:

"I met Eric in about 1990 when we were both members of the Cedars German Circle. This was a group of local people who were interested in both speaking German and learning about German speaking countries. Of course Eric became one of the main members as he could talk to the group in German and tell them about his life and experiences in pre-war Germany.

I remember him telling us why he left his school in Berlin and became an apprentice to a camera maker. When the Nazis made their attacks on the Jewish population during Kristallnacht in November 1938 his father decided that the family must leave Germany. Eric told the group about the difficult journey across the border into Belgium at Christmas 1938. They went at Christmas because they thought the border guards would be in good spirits, but they weren't. They had to stop in "no-man's land" between Germany and Belgium. However the family finally reached Antwerp with the help of "people smugglers" as Eric called them. In Belgium the family were officially tolerated but not allowed to settle legally. Before the war started Eric, because of his training as a precision engineer, was able to come to Britain. His brother was also allowed into Britain. His father was an accountant and was not deemed necessary to the war effort. His mother and father, being German, were arrested in Antwerp.

His father was already being held when the Germans took over Belgium and he was sent to a prison in Toulouse in France. His mother was not imprisoned and went to Marseilles. Eric said that when his mother found out that her husband was being sent "to the East" she asked to go with him. They were both murdered in Auschwitz.

When Eric came to work in a factory in Hinckley he said he had a train ticket from London to Hinckley and had to change trains at Nuneaton. Due to wartime conditions trains were often delayed and he had to wait a long time, in cold weather, at Nuneaton Station. When the train eventually came he saw that the journey took only a few minutes and he could have got on a bus and been in Hinckley at his lodgings an hour or more earlier had he known.

After he retired he began teaching German part-time to adults at Hinckley College. At this College he met someone who had a friend who was a policeman in Toulouse. He was able to find paperwork relating to Eric's parents.

In the 1980s Eric was able to make contact with some pre-war friends and colleagues from Berlin. He got in touch with and met up with the son of his first employer. This man had been conscripted into the German Army and had been sent to Stalingrad. He was one of the 10% who returned from there to Germany after the war. I wonder how many people there are in the world who escaped being sent to Auschwitz and also had a friend who returned from Stalingrad. My guess is that Eric was the only one.

When I met Eric he had begun to consider a university degree, but had to take "A" level in German to be accepted into the course that he wanted to do. I had already taken this exam. Another member of the Cedars German Circle was a lady who was a teacher and a German who had married a British ex-serviceman. We both talked with Eric about the work that was necessary.

Eric went to Leicester University and was awarded his degree. I think he was their oldest student and the oldest person to graduate there.

After his wife died Eric remarried.

One incident, and I don't know how widely he told this, is how he set fire to their house. He went to bed and put his pipe into his jacket pocket. The pipe was still alight and he woke in the night to a bedroom full of smoke and the wardrobe on fire. The fire brigade rescued them and they had to be accommodated by the local authority until the house was repaired. Fortunately, coincidentally, the council home that they were taken to was just on the opposite side of the street from where their house was.

After his death all the surviving members of the former Cedars German Circle went to his funeral in the parish church.

In all Eric was liked by those who met him and he is remembered for his straight talking and knowledgeable conversations. Most of all I remember the assistance he gave to those of us trying to improve our spoken German".

Written by Frank Mitchell

(former member of the Cedars German Circle) (2020).

Now seems like an appropriate time to talk about Dad and his pipe. I don't know when he started to smoke nor why he chose a pipe but I don't remember him not being a pipe smoker.

This seems quite innocent enough but Dad was often not careful about ensuring that his pipe was extinguished before he put it down or away and this did cause problems. Not many of Dad's trousers or jackets escaped being burnt after he put his still lit pipe into his pocket. He also managed to put burns into carpets and chairs as well as other things. Dad always had Household Contents Insurance so he made a claim each and every time an item suffered burn damage. As a result of his claims the insurance company would increase his premium. He would complain vehemently about this rise in premium costs and if the matter were not resolved to his satisfaction he would shop around for a better deal!

One day a family member saw Dad in the shopping area of Hinckley. Dad asked this person what he thought of the jacket that he had just bought at a bargain price at the Oxfam shop. The family member asked Dad if it was a "smoking jacket" because the pocket was on fire. Yes, he had put his burning pipe into the pocket of his "new" jacket!!

The most serious "pipe" incident was the one that Frank Mitchell referred to in his testimony. This occurred after my mother had passed away and Dad had remarried.

Dad had put his coat away with a still lit pipe in a pocket and soon the upstairs of the house was on fire. The fire brigade was needed to extinguish the fire and, because the house was uninhabitable, Dad and his wife had to be rehoused whilst the house was repaired. At the time of this fire Dad was in the process of purchasing the house from the local council. However, as the actual building was still owned and insured by the council, the council paid for all of the repairs and redecoration, just before Dad became the owner of the house that he had rented for over fifty five years.

Although he was not brought up as an orthodox Jew Dad's family had always celebrated the Jewish High Holidays. For a period of time during the 1990s Dad became a member of the Synagogue, Neve Shalom, Leicester Jewish Progressive Society and he attended services quite regularly. I did not know this until I was contacted by Michael Gibby who has written the following testimonial:

From Michael Gibby:

"Summer 1995 was a significant time for Leicester Progressive Synagogue. The congregation had just acquired its own permanent building. By this time Eric had made himself known to some of the community by attending services held at a Friends Meeting House, where he had already told his life story on a number of occasions. Having then acquired our own building Eric was invited one Sunday afternoon to lead the first congregational meeting in the grounds of the synagogue. It was a very moving event and was such an important message to us all. Subsequently a flowering cherry tree was planted in the synagogue grounds as a memorial to the victims of the Holocaust.

Eric continued to visit the synagogue from time to time. He was always delightful company and spoke with great interest. Somehow we lost track of him but I can only say that when he was with us it was a pleasure to be in his company".

Written by Michael Gibby (2020).

I don't really know why my father began to attend the synagogue. Did he want to learn more about the traditional religion of his family? Was he searching for reasons as to why the Jews had suffered so much persecution throughout history? Was he trying to find a reason for the Holocaust? Was he trying to find an explanation for antisemitism in general which seems to have always existed up to and including to this day? Was it because his second son, Peter, had been brought up as an orthodox Jew and it was at about this time that Dad was reconnecting with Peter? I don't know. It could have been for one or more of these reasons or it may have been for another reason known only to Dad. Someone at Leicester University had given Dad information about the Progressive Jews. I have recently found evidence that Dad said he felt a need to be involved, he felt a certain allegiance. He said he believed that this had more to do with heritage than religion. It is also on record that Dad said he could not continue with his involvement with the synagogue because of the difficulties of getting to meetings using public transport.

As a Jew in England did Dad suffer from antisemitism? This is a question that I have sometimes asked myself, particularly since beginning to complete this book. I don't remember any antisemitic behaviour being shown towards Dad or any of our family. When I was a child I didn't even know my father was Jewish. In fact I didn't know anything about my father's past history. However, since embarking on this project a few antisemitic occurrences have come to light.

Apparently, shortly after Dad moved to Hinckley, a brick was thrown through the window of his home. This would, obviously, been quite a frightening, unpleasant experience for Dad and his family. Did it remind him of the violence and hate he had left Germany to escape? Did he wonder if he was going to suffer degradation and persecution all over again in England?

I have been told that, even though Dad was liked and highly respected by the people he worked with, in his early working days in Coventry, he did occasionally have to cope with unpleasant comments. Some were anti Jewish, some anti German. These must have been very upsetting for Dad who would have just wanted to fit in and be accepted. Luckily he had made friends with a man named Don who supported him through these unpleasant experiences. Don and Dad remained friends throughout Dad's life. If Don had still been alive now I am sure that he would have had many stories to include in this book.

Over forty years after the war had ended one person who had worked with Dad during the war still referred to him as "Rommell" when she spoke about him. Another example of this type of antisemitism came from a person who had travelled to work in the same car as Dad. This person always referred to Dad as the "Jewboy". Again this still occurred more than forty years after the war ended. We can hope that these people did not do this with any malicious intent to hurt or offend Dad, but it is a warning to us all to be careful of the words we use to describe people, as simple innocent comments can cause pain.

These are the only examples of antisemitism that Dad encountered that I know of. I'm sure there were more but, on the whole, I think Dad worked hard to fit in with the local Hinckley community and he was accepted, liked and respected by most people, as he deserved.

During the years when Dad was studying, teaching and an active Holocaust educator he was interviewed on many occasions including for at least one television report and also by the USC Shoah Foundation for their records. He was also interviewed many times by newspaper reporters and articles about his academic efforts and achievements, his Holocaust experiences and about the time and effort that he put in to ensure that people became more educated about and more aware of the horrors perpetuated by the Nazis appeared in the local newspapers. I believe that this publicity was good because it made people aware of what one can achieve with determination and it also reminded people about the atrocities that the Nazis had perpetrated. I think Dad enjoyed this publicity and enjoyed seeing his achievements recognised.

Shirley Elsby, a former reporter, interviewed my father on several occasions and she has written the following testimonial for this book:

From Shirley Elsby (former reporter for the Leicester Mercury):

"In my job as a reporter I interviewed Eric several times over a few years. I represented his story as faithfully as I could, although governed, always, by constraints of space. What struck me personally was his willingness to recount his memories, these stories, seemingly without rancour, always at pains to remember accurately and tell it as it really happened. He intended to educate people, as many as he could; newspaper readers, college students, whoever he came in contact with, but also, in great part, to honour the memory of his parents.

By taking his Honours and Master's Degrees I think he felt he was repaying a debt to his father. He credited Fritz with great insight, both in allowing him to leave school and arranging for him to pursue an apprenticeship in a practical trade, engineering, and in planning and funding the family escape across the border. I think it would have been quite costly to claim that spot squashed into a hidden compartment behind the cab, much like our modern day refugees paying fortunes to arrive here at great peril in dinghies. Though his parents ultimately ended up being murdered, Eric, his brother, his grandmother and a cousin escaped permanently, I believe.

I'm sure he would have taken an academic route in the normal way if it were not for the Nazi regime. In his 60s he had to start at the 15/16 year olds stage, gaining his GCSEs and A levels first, so it was a long learning journey. It was as if gaining these qualifications so late in life was a way of claiming back, in full, at least one part of his life that the Nazis had stolen, his lost education.

I worked from what was one of five Leicester Mercury offices covering news from the country towns. I was a reporter for Hinckley and District and Eric came up to see me on each occasion, rather than me visiting him. He spoke lucidly even when the experiences were clearly upsetting, even harrowing, for him to relate. I think the trip to Auschwitz was very challenging for him. It meant that he had to recall horrors at a very deep personal level. It took extraordinary courage for him to describe the place and how very clinically and heartlessly the mass murders were performed, not to mention the degradation that took place. He was quite tearful. I'm sure it reawakened the terrible hurt and haunted him thereafter.

Eric struck me as a person of great dignity and certainly great determination. He would also seem to have been a natural teacher. I've met several people who loved his teaching style and found his lessons both highly effective and fun. He evidently had quite a way with words, both in English and in German, and he used this skill in both his language classes and in his Holocaust sessions. I believe he used his skills the best way he could to make the deaths and hardships of his family and fellow Jews to be as meaningful as possible and to serve as a warning that such things should never happen again".

Written by Shirley Elsby
(former reporter for the Leicester Mercury) (2020).

Dad first met Ava Farrington when he embarked on his "retirement" journey of academic education and he became a student in her classroom at Hinckley College of Further Education. Their backgrounds were similar in some aspects. Over the years Dad and Ava developed a close friendship that continued until Dad's death.

The "Harry" referred to in Ava's testimonial is Dad's brother Hans (Jack). His name was legally changed to Harry Lewis.

From Ava Farrington:

"Some thirty years ago, I was meeting a new group of students when I felt that unmistakable awareness of a laser look that was quietly being directed at me from the front row.

Eric.

The moment I heard him speak I knew what his issues with me were.

My family had come to England from Germany and he needed to know my background story. He needed to know what my father was doing in Germany in 1936. This was a question I fully understood as I too asked it, inwardly, of every German I met.

It is the question that every displaced person understands.

It is the question that haunts us when we have been persecuted for our race or our political beliefs.

Our epiphany, the moment when Eric knew with certainty that he could trust me, was when I happened to mention that my father had been interned and sent to Australia on the troop ship Dunera as an enemy alien in 1941. So too had Eric's younger brother.

My father was 47. Harry was 18 and Harry remembered the artist and sculptor.

Over the years that I knew Eric, I grew to have the greatest respect for him. He expected to have to work for everything he wanted. And work he did.

He was passionate about learning, trying to catch up on the opportunities that had been snatched from him in his youth. He followed the standard path to attain his master's degree, starting on a journey when most retirees are simply glad to put their feet up and watch the world go by.

He was passionate about accuracy and honesty, trying to understand the darkest inhuman acts that took place in the name of nationalism and he dedicated his time and energy to ensuring that the suffering endured by millions, had a voice.

He was an excellent communicator able to touch his audience, to break down barriers.

He was passionate about music and would be in the seats behind the orchestra in the De Montfort Hall at every concert, totally enthralled by the sound.

He had the ability to immerse himself completely in the moment and was never afraid to show his joy or sorrow.

He had learnt to be himself, and to remain positive whatever the negative influences around him. This is a mammoth achievement. Not many of us can claim to have done that.

213

Now, I rejoice in his memory. I rejoice in his achievements which gave him such pleasure. I delight in his happiness in his years with Meriel, who was a kindred spirit.

I am grateful to have met Eric and to have had the privilege of sharing many hours in his company.

Thank you Peggy, for completing the story that Eric began and for giving me the chance to become involved in your emotional journey on behalf of your father".

Written by Ava Farrington
(former teacher at Hinckley College of Further Education (2021).

Reginald Cooper met my father when he decided to learn German and someone gave him Dad's details. The two got on very well together. They both enjoyed playing chess which they began to do together. They spent many hours together and became very close friends.

Reg had contacts in France and he was able to find and give to Dad, documents that related to his parents internment in France and their final transport to Auschwitz. Reg has written a detailed tribute to my father including explaining how he was able to help my father learn about his parents' fate.

Testimonial written by Reg Cooper:

My Eric Lewinsohn.

"In 1986, I was talking to a work colleague, I worked for an insurance company at this time, about my interest in languages (she had studied German) and how I would like to learn German. Her name was Lorraine Haskins. She said she had private lessons with a man named Eric and gave me his telephone number. She left me with the intriguing comment that he was, "A very interesting man once you get to know him". I contacted him and we arranged to meet at his house in Hinckley.

For about 2 years, we got to know each other and I had private German lessons with him. The relationship developed from a professional one to a friendship, and we shared a mutual interest in chess (we were about the same standard). I started to spend longer evening with him, first a paid German lesson and then chess. We chatted and I got to know his political inclinations and his activities in the trade union in the Coventry car factory where he had worked. Politically, we shared interests. I can be quite inquisitive when my interest is aroused. He explained to me that he had ended up in Hinckley because of a job at the local Dunlop factory in the early 1940's although he had no idea where Hinckley was. He only spoke German then, and he encountered a lot of anti-German feeling. At some stage, he mentioned his Jewish background and that he had come over in 1939. I sensed that there was some anger which expressed itself in his militant trade union activities. Although guarded about his background, he was clearly a very sociable person and probably craved the sense of belonging that his union activities provided. Later, I learned of his middle class upbringing in Vienna, the son of an accountant, which was a bit of a surprise at first when compared with his apparent working class credentials by 1990. The other aspect to Eric was he was mischievous and, as a result, fun. Or maybe it was the excessive amounts of cafetière coffee which he drank! He liked wine and whisky as well. He went on visits to see and stay with his friend in his caravan in Mablethorpe. No doubt a good drink was had with him!

Eric was an extremely restless man, driven probably by this hidden anger. It gave him great energy, and notwithstanding his prolific smoking habit, he went most places on foot or by bus, but was always up for a trip somewhere, usually a pub, if I was willing to drive. He needed outlets and so I encouraged him to look at his talents, his German-Jewish background and experience, and his longing to study. So he studied. He continued teaching German but also got work translating for a Coventry enterprise that supplied carriages for Deutschesbundesbahn. Together we tried to figure out what these technical, German letters meant! And, whether he was competent enough to translate "How to install an industrial diesel generator". We discussed his thesis on the Theriensenstadt concentration camp not that I was of much help to him, but he was grateful for my contribution and gave me a copy when it was finished. I also visited the camp on a visit to Prague. I attended his undergraduate degree award ceremony, for which invitation I felt privileged. It was now as if another life had presented itself to him and he was going to grasp it with both hands.

Over these first few years, I realised there were two aspects to Eric. To most he was a good chum who liked his Saturday night bingo, his glasses of wine, dare I say, his hard work and no doubt many other typical interests that one can find amongst many persons in a working town like Hinckley. He lived an ordinary life outwardly, modestly in a council house with his wife Elsie. Occasionally, we drank too much at the Hinckley social club where he introduced me as his guest, and we staggered back. I'm not sure Elsie approved.

But there was another Eric. He started to tell me about his other, earlier life in Vienna and Berlin, in the Jewish quarters. About his background of classical music and studiousness. I had already noticed, and he told me about, how classical music brought out his emotions. How he loved to listen to some of that militaristic music of the Austro-Hungarian empire, which was sometimes playing when I visited him in Hinckley. We went to a few classical concerts together in Leicester. I pried, gently at first, about this and he was very open about this background and he told me about his last contacts with his father, who by 1940 was somewhere in France. He told me that his family was Jewish, something which he did not share freely unless he trusted you. I treated him to a grand meal at an Austrian restaurant I knew in a little-known part of Birmingham where I grew up. He told me of the anti-Semitic laws that were promulgated from 1933 onwards in Germany, and how these and the attitudes of his father's non-Jewish accountancy partners led to his father loosing his partnership rights. Eventually, the family decided they had to get out of Germany.

The family procured false documents and travelled to Cologne/ Bonn, probably in 1938. From Bonn they were to go to a border city, Aachen, where they would meet refugee smugglers who would assist them in crossing the border. Eric and his bother spent some time in Bonn and took an excursion to Bad Godesburg where they tried unsuccessfully to go into a cafe but it banned them because they were Jews. I never asked Erich how the proprietors knew he and his brother were Jews.

In Aachen, the family had to wait in a cafe opposite the railway station for the arrival of the smugglers. They waited several hours until late afternoon and thought they had been double-crossed. All had been paid for in advance. Eventually, the smugglers arrived with a car and the family climbed in and were taken to the outskirts of Aachen along a fairly well concealed route in the forest to just out of sight of the border guards. The border was on a level stretch of this road where the old German border post can still be seen. They walked the last last 200 metres or so, They were searched and robbed by the border guards. The guards knew they were fleeing Jewish refugees and took what they wanted.

What Eric explained happened next didn't at first make sense. He said that the family walked over the border for some way and had been told to turn off the road down a track where they would come to a farm which would put them up. By now it was dark, but they found the track and the farm and were put up for the night. There were others similarly staying the night. In the morning, they were loaded up into the false back of a farm truck and told to keep quiet. They were taken over the Belgium border in the truck. What was this, I thought? Walking over the German border, staying in a farm, being driven over the Belgium border, clandestine farm in the woods intertwined with the smuggling.

Next time I was in Aachen, I would find out. I went to the Aachen Town Hall library and asked to see the border maps from the 1930's. The librarian grudgingly obliged and was none to pleased with my request. It then became clear. Following World War I, there had been a no-man's land between Germany and Belgium, It was about 1 km wide and, sure enough, there was a very large, impressive farm about 500m from the German side to the right off the road between the respective border patrols. I took a walk to this farm to have a look. Eric's account now made sense, the family had overnighted in non-man's land. The family made their way to Antwerp. Later Eric and his brother went to London.

Eric did receive letters and vaguely told me that his parents had been discovered and ended up in a camp somewhere near Marseilles in France. He thought the name of the camp was "Gers". He was insistent that it was near Marseilles. Intrigued again, I started studying maps but found nothing of the sort near Marseilles. At that time, in the early 1990's, I had a French girlfriend, and we regularly went to the family home in the Pyrenees, near Pau. I told Eric and as soon as I mentioned "Pau" he said, "That's it", his parents had been somewhere near Pau. I mentioned another place, "Oloron Ste Marie". Same response, in fact his mother had lived in Oloron, he thought! Well, Marseilles and Oloron are about 400kms apart. Talk about wild goose chases! I studied the maps again and there was a small village called "Gurs" about 12kms to the west of Oloron, which, in turn, was about 40kms from Pau.

Next time I was in the Pyrenees, I asked my girlfriend's mother whether there had been any camp at Gurs during the second world war. She said yes, it had been built for refugees from the Spanish Civil War in about 1936. Living conditions were bad for the persons who ended up there. Local people didn't like the food inflation caused by the camp's huge purchases. I decided to get on my bike, literally, and take a look at Gurs.

Gurs had consisted of wooden barracks – it was an internment camp and did hold Jews. I bought a book about the history of the camp from the small museum. Although the barracks have pretty much gone, overgrown by woods, there is a well tended cemetery, an inspection of which revealed that there were a good number of Jewish graves, mainly of Jews who had been displaced from Alsace-Lorraine in 1939 and died in the period 1938-42. I don't recall any Jewish graves where the incumbent had died later than 1942. A relation of my girlfriend worked for the prefecture in Pau and on chatting to him, he informed me that Camp de Gurs was run by the French authorities and the records were kept at the prefecture in Pau. I asked him if he could find out if there was any file on Fritz Lewinsohn, Eric's father. The answer was, "Yes. Did I want a copy?" When I had read the file I asked Eric if he wanted it and he said, enthusiastically, "Yes". It was in French so I translated it for him. Some official documents had been duplicated and I retained any duplicates. There were a few copy letters from his parents on the file, and these were given to Eric.

The documents show (dates are approximate) that Fritz Lewinsohn ("FL") and Blanca crossed the border from Germany into Belgium by May 1940 and been arrested for having false papers with a false certificate, but were not taken before a court. This doesn't quite tally with a police statement account, which may be a mistake, that they crossed the border in 1938 but it may be that the family were 'playing down' the true length of time they had been in Belgium. Their address is given as 26, Avenue de la Brabanconne, Brussels. This contradicts the account given by Eric, but it may well be that Eric's account is correct and that the information given to the French police (in Perpignan) by FL was not true and they may have crossed the border earlier. There is nothing to suggest that Blanca too was detained, although there may be another file on her. They were interned on 10 May 1940 and taken to the Military Forest Prison, Brussels. On 15 May 1940, they were then taken to Cepoy, near Orleans, and this may be where a letter was posted to Eric as it is not far from Chalons (-sur-Soane), the post mark on the letter. Blanca was taken to Gurs on 25 July 1940, and FL was sent to St Cyprien on the Mediterranean coast near Pergignan. Blanca was released, probably because it was normal practice to release an unconvicted wife if the husband was detained. Due to a paperwork error, FL had been recorded as a convicted prisoner on a list produced in Belgium and, as a result it can be inferred, thought not entitled to be at St Cyprien camp. He was taken to the prison at Ceret in the eastern Pyrenees. About 21 August 1940, FL was transferred from Ceret prison back to the camp at St Cyprien, presumably because the error had been corrected. I went to Ceret but the prison no longer exists and is the site of the present tourist information office! I also visited St

Cyprien and spoke to the daughter of a Spanish refugee who had been in the St Cyprien camp. She explained that the camp was tented and on the beach near where there is a tourist information office now. It blew down in a storm and some detainees were relocated to Gurs.

On 11 December 1940, Ernst Lewinsohn, FL's brother, wrote to the commandant of the Camp de Gurs asking if FL could be transferred to the same foreign workers company as himself at Agen. In a letter to the commandant, FL describes himself as a qualified accountant at the Berlin Chamber of Commerce from which he managed a number of industrial enterprises. He went to Belgium where he directed a grease packaging concern. On 2 January 1941, the director of the Camp de Gurs recommended the transfer to the Prefect of the Basses-Pyrenees. FL made a further request for his release explaining that he was in poor health which was not conducive to living in the camp. This was not backed up by a doctor's certificate confirming this. The director was not in favour of release as FL did not have a resident's permit and "given his age of 48". On 7 January 1941, FL wrote to the director of the Camp de Gurs asking for permission for Blanca, his wife, to visit him at the camp. He states she was living in Perpignan which is close to St Cyprien (he says he arrived at St Cyprien on 5 June 1940). Permission was granted. He also asked, in December 1940, for permission to go to Perpignan for two weeks to visit the Prefect there to see if he could be allowed to organise a supply factory (meat and animal products). He also renewed his request to be released on medical grounds and this time providing a certificate from the military stating that he had been unsuitable for military service due to his "bad attitude". The Prefect at Pau was against the request to transfer. Later, in January 1941, FL asked to be allowed to go to Perpignan again, this time to see if he could arrange emigration to Siam. Blanca's address at this time is given as 4 bis Rue Valette, Perpignan. Google Earth does not show a Rue Valette at Perpignan but there is one in nearby Montpelier ("bis" means "behind"), and this is almost certainly where she was staying, a small studio flatlet probably. These discrepancies may suggest that Eric's parents were not being completely truthful, perhaps because they did not trust the French authorities, There is nothing in the file to suggest that she ever lived at Marseilles although it is quite possible she went there to try and arrange immigration to Siam as it was an embarkation port for that country. The police recommended that they be allowed to emigrate to Siam. In March 1941, her address is given as nearby 10 Rue Valette, suggesting something of an itinerant existence? Unfortunately, these are all the documents I retained – there were others, which almost certainly show why they were unable to go to Siam.

With this extra information about what had happened to his family, Eric became more of a celebrity giving talks in schools and colleges about his experience of the Holocaust. The Berlin City Council invited him back to that city, but, as he explained to me on his return, "He blotted his copy book" by telling some of his old school colleagues what he thought of them, particularly those who had joined the SS. It was a mixed visit as far as I could determine. Prior to the visit, Eric had sworn to have nothing to do with Germany or Germans ever again, but on his return he was enthusiastic about Germans and all that had been achieved in recent years. He truly had become pro-German. He reveled about the all-expenses paid visit. German technical and social achievements were well above what had been gained here in the UK, he thought.

I left Hinckley in 1997 for the beautiful Derbyshire Dales, but often returned to Hinckley and would visit Eric, go to the social club and I would overnight at his house. Unfortunately, I was unable to attend his funeral, something I certainly would have done as he was a great friend and someone from whom I learned a great deal about how life for any of us can turn out to be very different from how we might have imagined".

Written by Reginald Cooper (2021).

Having read Reg's testimonial the reader will realise how valuable Reg's efforts were in enabling Dad to expand his knowledge of and verify facts about his parents internment.

He became aware that his parents were arrested on a tram in Brussels as illegal immigrants. Whilst his father and mother were imprisoned in Brussels for about two weeks they were, obviously, not allowed to go home. Grossi, who was living with them in Brussels at this time, must have been extremely worried and fearful about what had happened to them. I can only hope that they were able to write to her and let her know that they were still alive. The Nazis did "visit" their apartment, ransacking it and removing anything of value, therefore leaving Grossi destitute. About two weeks later Dad's parents were moved to France. After the fall of France, which occurred on June 14th 1940 both were sent to a concentration camp in the south of unoccupied France, Camp de Gurs. His mother was freed about four weeks after their arrival there. She was able to visit her husband and he was allowed out of the camp to meet her. This is when she began to work in Marseilles as a language teacher. During this time she applied for her husband to be moved to a camp closer to Marseilles. It was at about this time that Dad heard from his parents telling him of their arrest and asking for blankets, clothing etc. Dad and his parents were able to communicate reasonably well by letter during this time.

It was also discovered that Dad's cousin Heinz was arrested on the same day as his parents. Heinz, his Uncle Ernst and Dad's father all ended up in the same camp. With help Heinz, who was a doctor, managed to escape from the camp. He joined the French Marquis. By this time Heinz, whose first wife was presumed killed when the Germans invaded Belgium, had remarried. As he looked very Aryan he was able to be infiltrated into German held areas with the intent of undermining the German morale.

Dad knew that his cousin Max (Heinz's brother) was in America working as a musical conductor. He had been sponsored to enter America prior to the breakout of war. Did Max wonder how many of his relatives had escaped Hitler's wrath?

In the early 1970s during a trip to Austria (possibly a summer holiday), Dad asked the telephone operator for the phone number of any Dr Heinz Pollak that they had listed. It must be remembered that, at this time, phone calls were made by the caller being connected with the recipient by a telephone operator, not by direct dialling as it is today. Dad was given a few numbers and he called each number until he found the right one. Yes, his cousin Heinz was alive and practicing as a doctor in Vienna. Imagine the joy for both of them! It was the first time that either of them knew that the other was still alive. It was the first time that that they had seen each other or even spoken in over thirty years. How elated they must have both been to see each other and to be together again. They did correspond with each other after this meeting but sadly, as often happens, the correspondence gradually faded out. Dad did visit Heinz for a second time in about 1990. This was the last time they saw each other. When he knew that he had to spend time in Europe whilst completing his Masters Degree Dad wrote to Heinz but he did not receive a reply.

Dad did meet Heinz's eldest child, Susanne Pollak, and I have also been fortunate enough to meet Susanne and spend time with her when she was living in France. Susanne has written a testimonial which can be read in the chapter "Family Memories".

When he arrived in England in 1939, at the young age of nineteen, Dad couldn't speak a word of English. He spent his free time reading the newspapers, working hard to master the English language, which he did. This may have been his first success in England but it was not his last.

Although he was very proud to be a British citizen and stated that England was the best country in the world, Dad also said that being German and a Jew would always come out in him. He maintained that the Germans were very thorough and if they intended to do something then they did it thoroughly. Dad had high expectations of himself at all times and in all situations. He was always very thorough in all that he did and I ask myself whether this was to some extent, due to his German heritage. Another sign of this heritage is that, when he was dying, Dad reverted to his native language speaking in German.

Sûreté publique	**PRISON** à FOREST
N°	

1. Nom et prénoms . . . . LEWINSOHN Fritz

2. Lieu et date de naissance . VIENNE le 17 - 10 - 1892

3. Nationalité . . . . *Allemand*

4. Prénoms. lieu et date de naissance du père. . . . . *alpin ,*

5. Nom. prénoms. lieu et date de naissance de la mère . . . *B*

6. Est-il marié ou célibataire? S'il est marié. indiquer les nom, prénoms, lieu et date de naissance ainsi que la résidence de l'épouse . . . ep. de HAHN Blanca

7. Lieu et date du mariage . . .

8. Nom. prénoms. lieu et date de naissance et résidence des enfants .

9. S'il s'agit d'une femme mariée. indiquer les nom, prénoms, lieu et date de naissance ainsi que la résidence de son époux . . .

10. Occupations et moyens d'existence

11. Conduite (1) . . .

12. N'a-t-il commis. à l'étranger, aucun crime ou delit qui motive sa présence en Belgique ? . . .

13. Résidence hors du royaume .

14. Date de l'arrivée dans le pays .

15. Résidence en Belgique (indiquer l'adresse complète) . .

16. Date de l'arrivée dans la localité mentionnée au n° 15 . .

° 49

(1) Indiquer ici ce que l'on peut avoir appris à cet égard.

Document re first imprisonment in Brussels on 10th May 1940

Fritz's application to support his transfer from Camp de Gurs to Camp de Milles. In it he describes himself as a qualified accountant.

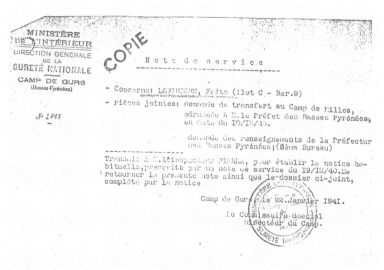

Document from January 1941
re Fritz's transfer from Camp de Gurs to Camp de Milles

MINISTERE DE L'INTERIEUR

DIRECTION GENERALE
de la
SURETE NATIONALE

CAMP DE GURS, le 20 décembre 1940.

ECTION DU CAMP DE GURS.

N°

LE COMMISSAIRE DIVISIONNAIRE,
Directeur du Camp de Gurs,

à M. le Préfet des BASSES-PYRENEES,
(3° Division),

P a u .

Par application des dispositions de la note de service n° I.25.390 du 26 novembre 1940, paragraphe 3, de
M. le Général commandant la I7 ème Division Militaire
(Etat-Major - 2° Bureau), j'ai l'honneur de vous trans-
mettre sous ce pli, avec avis très favorable, les pièces
suivantes :

- requête qui m'a été adressée par l'interné LEWINSOHN
Fritz, ilôt " C " baraque 9

- requête adressée par LEWINSOHN Ernst à M. le Commen-
dant de la 308 Compagnie de T.E. et qui m'a été re-
transmise par celui-ci avec avis favorable.

*Document from December 1940 approving Ernst's request that Fritz
be relocated from Camp de Gurs to Camp de Milles*

PEGGY'S STORY

Both my mother and my father loved me and my siblings very much. We were brought up to be kind and caring people. Mum and Dad both worked hard to give us as much as they could and they were always there for us. As the reader will know from reading Dad's story, both Mum and Dad had children before they met. At no time do I remember either of them treating any one of us differently because a child was or was not biologically theirs. Growing up we children did not know that we were not all full blood siblings. We were definitely brought up as one family. I am very proud of both of my parents for this. We must remember that I am talking about the 1940s and 1950s when life and society's expectations and acceptances about many things, including blended families, were very different from what they are now.

We children were very lucky. We had two wonderful parents. They both took their responsibilities as parents very seriously and they both genuinely loved all of us children. They both always put us children before themselves, caring for both our needs and our wants and we were always shown love. We never had to wonder whether our parents loved us, we just knew they did. Even though we were not a family that hugged and kissed each other often we always knew that we were loved and felt secure. I think that when we children were growing up in the 1940s and 1950s it was far less common for families to demonstrate their love for one another by kissing and hugging than it is today.

My parents were both very clever people, although their skills lay in different areas. Dad was academically very capable whereas Mum was extremely artistic and this showed in her knitting, crocheting, sewing, embroidery and tapestry as well as in her decorating, gardening and cooking.

However, as this story is about my memories of my father, I will be dwelling on my memories of and experiences with him. This does not mean that my mother was any less caring as a parent and as a friend.

How do I remember my father, Eric Lewinsohn? My thoughts and memories of Dad are, obviously, different from those of my siblings. Every human being is an individual and has differing memories and opinions of every other person, including their parents.

Having read Dad's autobiography you will understand that Dad's life, whilst he was growing up, was affected by Hitler's rise to power and the subsequent Nazi regime. Dad and his family suffered many indignities and deprivations. They were robbed of their freedom and the opportunities to work. As Jews they lived in fear of deportation to a concentration camp. By the time Dad arrived in England he had endured more oppression, deprivation and fear than most people these days can imagine. Sadly his parents were gassed in Auschwitz and he also had to cope with the emotion of this loss.

Dad must have often felt very sad and depressed about his life in Nazi Germany, the splitting up of his immediate and extended family and the fate of his parents but he never let this show. I think that he would have suffered from what we now know as PTSD (post traumatic stress disorder), but this result of trauma was not known of then. I wonder how many nights Dad lay awake in bed thinking about his past and his family and wishing that things had been different. I wonder how many years he had "flashbacks" to his life with his family when he was growing up, both before and after Hitler came to power. I never really spoke with him about these very personal issues. I wish I had, but perhaps it is better that I didn't. I would not have wanted to encourage sad, bad memories to resurface.

Dad never let sad memories or regrets affect his parenting. He was a happy Dad. Usually he was cheerful, laughing and smiling. Whatever worries he had and emotional turmoil he went through he did not let it show. He was always my happy, loving Dad. He did not talk about his past. I don't know if, when I was young, I ever wondered why he did not have parents, who would have been my grandparents. I can't remember asking about this, but we didn't have many relatives at all. The only grandparents we had were our great grandmother Grossi and our maternal grandmother who died when I was about six. The only "real" true blood line "first" aunt or uncle we had was Dad's younger brother Uncle Jack and his wife Auntie Ruth. Our few local "aunties and uncles" were my mother's relatives who we called auntie and uncle.

I remember one day when I was walking to town with Dad. There was just the two of us. I can't remember how old I was, but I would think probably between seven and ten. We were skipping along happily and I think we had been singing. I can't remember what we had been singing and talking about, but I do remember Dad making a comment about how bad some people could be and how unbelievable it was that people could be so cruel to other people. As I have said I don't remember Dad's exact words, but I have never forgotten this event. I still remember exactly where we were when the words were said and I now realise that Dad would have been referring to his earlier life, the Nazi regime and the fate of his parents. I also remember that as quickly as Dad's mood had become serious and sombre it changed again and he was my happy, laughing, fun Dad again.

My Early Years.

I have some memories of when we lived in the prefab, but these memories are very few as we moved from there nine days after my fourth birthday. I remember the rooms in the living area, the kitchen was at the front and the living room at the back, but I don't remember the bedrooms etc. I remember waiting excitedly for Dad to come home from work and that he would get down on all fours and I would ride on his back to bed. Once I was in bed he would tell me a story. He was a brilliant story teller. This is my earliest memory of Dad and one that I will always cherish.

My younger brother, Stuart was born when I was about twenty months old. He was born on July 21at 1945, Dad's 26th birthday. Dad was always proud that he and Stuart shared a birthday. In later life they and their wives always went out to dinner together on this day.

As I have said, immediately after my fourth birthday we moved into the house in which my parents both lived until they passed away. My parents got married one week after this house move. They were married in The Registry Office in Hinckley and I remember being taken by the baby sitter to the area where this office was. We hid in a vantage point and I watched as my parents came out of the building after their marriage. Of course my parents knew nothing of this until I told them many years later when I was an adult with a family of my own.

I remember Grossi, Dad's grandmother, my great grandmother. I remember her staying with us, both in the prefab and after we moved. She was very traditional, a real European lady. She loved us all, but Stuart was definitely her favourite. When she arrived in England Grossi did not speak English but she did pick up quite a bit of the language which is both, surprising and commendable considering her age at the time.

Grossi and Mum sometimes clashed, which is to be expected when there are two ladies from very different cultures and born two generations apart together in one kitchen. Mum was very modern in her ways compared to Grossi. I have one very distinct memory of their differing opinions. If the family were all eating together Mum would give us children our meal first and then put the adult's plates on the table. This quite upset Grossi who was used to the traditional European habit of always putting the man of the house first. She would say "feed the papa first, feed the papa first" to Mum repeatedly. Of course Mum took absolutely no notice and ignored Grossi's request to "feed the father first". I think that Mum's refusal to feed Dad first may have caused Grossi quite a bit of anguish. She probably thought that Mum was a very disrespectful wife. How things have changed!

We were not a wealthy family, but we did not miss out on anything. In fact our parents often gave us more than they could really afford. When young we each had a birthday party every year and we were quite spoiled at Christmas. I know that my mother sat up very late at her sewing machine, after we children were in bed, sewing Christmas clothes and presents. Christmas was always very special in our house. We always had a large "real" Christmas tree with glass ornaments and wax candles (obviously a fire hazard when lit) and the living areas would be festooned with decorations, including paper chains made by us children.

Grossi

One Christmas was particularly special to me. I can't remember the year. It was after we had moved house, so it was probably 1948 or thereabouts. Father Christmas gave me the most wonderful doll's house. It was every little girl's dream. The doll's house was double storey. The living areas were downstairs and there was a built-in staircase leading upstairs to the bedrooms, a typical English house. Every room was decorated with wallpaper, as was the English tradition. The outside of the house was covered in a wallpaper with tiny bricks on it, so the house looked like a brick house, just like the one we lived in. Of course there was furniture in the house. So, you might say, what was so special about this house? Well the house had lights. Yes, real electric lighting. Dad had built the doll's house himself and he had put wiring throughout the house and there was a small globe (bulb), the sort that were in torches before LED, in every room. The lighting system was powered by a battery inside the attic of the doll's house. Yes the house even had an attic.

It is important to remember that this was shortly after the war. Materials were not readily available. In spite of working long hours, as the working week then was a minimum of five and a half days, Dad had not only planned such a magical doll's house but he had also sourced the materials and spent the time to build it. He must have built it in the evenings after we children were in bed as I knew nothing about it and do not remember him spending lots of time in the outhouse that was his shed. It must have been freezing cold in the shed as there was no heating in there and the English winter is very cold. Dad must have spent endless hours building my doll's house as this was before the days of power tools.

I loved my doll's house. I remember that it was very special to me when I was a little girl playing with it, and my friends enjoyed it too. I still remember how the lights fascinated me. I don't know what happened to it. Did it get worn out by being played with? Did I just outgrow it? Was it given away? I have no idea. I have never seen a doll's house anywhere nearly as amazing as mine was and it was made for me by my father. I will always treasure the memory of my doll's house.

I was always a Daddy's girl. I spent a lot of time with Dad when I was small. Perhaps I was his "favourite" at that time, as I was the first and, at that time, the only daughter in the family.

When I was a child there was a dolls' hospital in Hinckley and if one of my dolls needed repair it was Dad who would go with me to take my doll to the hospital. It was also Dad who regularly took me to the children's library that existed in Hinckley at the time. These are examples of "special time" I remember remember spending with my Dad.

We knew Dad's brother as Uncle Jack. His name had been changed from Hans Lewinsohn to Harry Lewis when he joined the British Army during the war, but to us he was always Uncle Jack, (Jack being the English translation of Hans). After he was demobbed from the British Army in 1947 and before he and his wife emigrated to Canada in the early 1950s they lived in Sutton, a borough of South London. Dad would travel by train to visit them on some weekends and he would take me with him. I vividly remember these train trips. I enjoyed being with my Dad and I also enjoyed showing off to the other passengers on the train. I was a bright child and advanced for my age. I could tell the time using a traditional (not digital) clock and I could read before I started school. I remember showing off these skills on the train and seeing Dad beam with pride, enjoying the admiration of our fellow travellers. I am sure that Dad enjoyed showing everyone what a clever daughter he had. I know that he was always proud of me and of my achievements.

Dad felt very strongly that academic ability and achievements were something to be proud of and so they are. However, there are many types of achievements other than those tied to academia that are just as noteworthy. I think that everyone is an individual and should be proud of their skills and abilities and that we all continue to learn throughout our lives. What a sad, unproductive world it would be if we were all academics and there were no manually skilled people.

I believe that Dad thought that being successful academically was preferable to having skills and knowledge in other areas. He may have felt this way because he felt cheated as he had left school at an early age as a result of the Nazi regime and he began to work in an engineering shop, whilst his brother was able to continue with his education and in Dad's words his brother "had a good job for all of his life". Dad said he was the first manual worker in his family. Did he feel inferior because of this? I don't know, but I think he probably did. Whilst he had the responsibility of bringing up a family Dad had no option but to continue to work as a manual factory worker in the engineering industry. After he retired he resumed his academic education and he did so very successfully. I am proud of him for doing this. Not because he pursued academic learning but because he persevered and achieved success in what he wanted to do.

Let me get back to my train trips to Sutton. I remember feeling extremely loved and very special sharing these journeys with Dad. We had fun on these trips. We played games such as "I spy" and hand games, we read and we talked. It took quite a time for the journey to Sutton by train, several hours, as the steam trains were very slow compared to the diesel and electric trains of today.

I enjoyed being at Uncle Jack's house. My aunt and uncle thoroughly spoiled me, probably because they did not have children of their own at this time and also probably because we were a very small family as a consequence of Mr Hitler's policies. Even though they moved to Canada when I was seven or eight Uncle Jack always remained a very special person to me. He called me his princess.

Auntie Ruth was also very loving towards me. One thing I remember is that she always had chocolates on her dressing table and I was allowed to help myself to these. At this time chocolate was still rationed but this did not seem to bother her at all. Auntie Ruth probably spoiled me as much as Uncle Jack did, but for some reason unknown to me she never held such a deep place in my heart. Perhaps, as a child, I preferred men to women.

My father had been brought up liberally in the Jewish faith and my mother as a Methodist. However, neither of my parents practised any religion, although they did send us children to Sunday School, as was the tradition at that time. There was a little chapel in the street where we lived and that is where we initially went to Sunday School. I don't know if, in those days, parents sent their children to Sunday School to get a religious education or to enable the parents to have a short time together alone without children!

Sundays were very different in those days. Family life was different in those days. Men and women had specific roles in the family. Men usually did not do chores within the house nor did they participate in the general daily care of the children. These were the woman's responsibility. Men were the "breadwinners". They often worked five and a half days every week and from Monday to Friday they usually did not get home until it was time for their children to go to bed. I remember I was always still up when Dad got home from work and I would be looking out of the "front room" (this is what we called the lounge/sitting room) window eagerly waiting for Dad to arrive home. In the winter the window would be frosted up and I would blow on it so that I could clear the frost and see through it.

On Saturday if the men were not at work, or after they arrived home from work, they were often busy doing household maintenance, gardening, mowing the lawn etc. Sunday was often the only day that the family could spend together and relax and it was a family day. No shops were open. Nobody did their washing on Sunday, or if they did they did not hang it out. Everyone wore their "best" clothes. Children generally were not allowed to play outside.

We always had family breakfast together on Sunday, a full English breakfast at about nine o'clock. Then at lunchtime we had a roast dinner followed by dessert. Dessert, or pudding as it was called, was a daily tradition in our house for the whole of my mother's life. At about five o'clock we would have tea. This usually consisted of sandwiches or salad again followed by a dessert.

After Sunday tea the whole family played games together. We played board games such as Crown and Anchor, Snakes and Ladders, Ludo etc. and card games such as Happy Family, Snap and Lexicon which I really enjoyed. As well as playing well known games we also played a game called "Rapunzel". I think Dad knew this game from his childhood in Europe. It is a listening game that always amazes players. I have never met anyone else who has heard of the game "Rapunzel" and most people are amazed by it until it is explained to them.

In the summer when it was fine weather we would often go for a walk together instead of playing games. We would walk along the canal path to "The Lime Kilns", a pub that is still there. The Lime Kilns is on the banks of the Ashby Canal and has a lovely grassed outdoor area with tables and benches. We children were allowed one soft drink and a packet of potato crisps each and we would sit there watching the canal barges loaded with coal pass by. What a lovely way to spend a family Sunday evening. I was last at The Lime Kilns in about 2014 or 2015 and the only change seemed to be that the barges no longer carried coal. Nowadays some are used as permanent homes, others as holiday lets.

When it was time for me to go to school my parents enrolled me at St. Alberts, the private convent school in Hinckley. This school was probably at least 5km from where we lived, but there were school buses that ran from our nearest bus stop to the school and back again in the afternoon. The local free school was only a short walk from our home and my two older brothers attended this school. As my parents did not practise any religion and neither of them had any leaning towards the Roman Catholic beliefs they did not send me to the convent school for the purpose of the religious education that I would receive there. I think they felt that I would receive a better education at a private school than at a council school as the free schools were called. The convent school was basically a girls school. Boys were only allowed to be enrolled there if they had a sister at the school and then they were only allowed to stay for two or three years. This rule allowed my younger brother to attend the convent school but had prevented my parents from enrolling my older brothers there.

There was one class at each year level. Each class had about thirty pupils, as school students were called in those days. We were taught by nuns. As is usual in primary schools, the nun who was what we now call the home group teacher taught us for all of our academic subjects. There was a strong emphasis on numeracy and literacy. The school was, I think, quite forward in its thinking, as, for mental arithmetic and spelling, each class was divided into ability groups and each group would work in a separate room, tutored and supervised by "spare" nuns and novices. This allowed every child to learn at their own pace, a practice that is always best for each individual. I still appreciate those spelling and mental arithmetic groups. I never have a problem when shopping! I was quick to finish writing tasks etc. Was I competitive? Yes I'm sure I was. I enjoyed being successful.

My parents were both proud of my achievements. The school had an "Open Day" each year. On this day students' work and workbooks were available for parents to examine and parents had a chat with their child's teacher about the child's progress and behaviour. My parents always attended on these days. They enjoyed listening to my teacher telling them what a "good" student I was. I remember that Dad's face would beam with pride.

I think the only negative comment ever made about me as a primary school student was about my handwriting. One year, in my later years at primary school, my teacher told my parents that my handwriting "looked like a chicken had walked across the page". Perhaps I remember this clearly because I was not used to any sort of negative comment being made about my scholastic abilities.

We had a piano in our house. I am not sure but I think it belonged to my maternal grandmother who died in about 1949. I must mention here that our piano was quite unique! It was an old piano and in all the years that this piano was in our house, and it was still there when I left home, I can never remember it being tuned. When I was young I don't think my parents could have afforded to get it tuned. I have never come across a piano so out of tune. It also had notes that did not sound at all. As any pianist can realise, it is very difficult to practise on and play a piano that does not give off a sound when certain keys are depressed.

At the Convent school it was possible for parents to pay for their child to receive piano lessons and Theory of Music tuition. It was decided that I should learn to play the piano and also attend the Theory lessons. The individual piano lessons took place during the school day. The group theory lessons occurred after school, twice a week. I remember they were on Monday and Thursday from three thirty till five o'clock. This meant that theory students could not travel home on the school bus. I had to walk more than two kilometres from school to catch a bus home after these lessons. In the winter it was very dark at this time. Would it be safe today to let a child walk this far alone at a young age? I don't think so. I remember enjoying these walks, particularly in the winter, when it was dark and cold. I felt so grown up.

When I was eight years old I began to sit for nationally accredited piano playing examinations and written theory of music examinations. I also participated in Music Festivals and was successful in these, often achieving "First Place". I think Dad was particularly proud of my achievements in music because he was such a great lover of music.

I was far closer in age to my brothers than I was to my sister. My brothers and I were each born about two years apart and I think I was rather a "tomboy" in some ways. We had trees at the bottom of our very long garden and I used to climb these trees with my brothers even though I was not allowed to "because I was a girl". My brothers and I went to cub scouts and brownies and, on the way home, we would "spirit knock" (knock on peoples' doors and run away). I remember one night we were running away and I ran straight into a street lamp post. I don't think I got much sympathy from my brothers who were far more worried about getting caught than they were about their sister's possible injury! I enjoyed playing "marbles" and "conkers", both popular games in those days.

My brothers and I got on well generally. Obviously we had squabbles as all siblings do. Sometimes I would shout "ouch" during mealtimes and accuse one of my brothers of kicking me under the table. My parents would believe me and the brother would be chastised and told to leave me alone. I probably made other false accusations to get my brothers "into trouble" with our parents too. My brothers got their revenge on me for getting them into trouble. Their nickname for me was the revenge. Their name for me was "scruff", meaning scruffy or dirty and untidy. This may have been an accurate description of me at times as I was somewhat of a tomboy, but I hated being called "scruff". When they called me this I would often have a tantrum and stamp my feet and scream. My brothers obviously enjoyed this reaction and teased me even more which made me scream even louder. Ah! The joys of sibling love!

I think we were a pretty normal family in most ways. I did not have a lot of close friends. As I did not attend the local council school I did not get to know many of the the girls who lived close to us intimately. My best friend was Carole who I met at primary school. She lived near to us and we remained very close until I moved away from Hinckley in 1961. Carole was an only child so our home lives complimented each other in many ways. I think I envied the attention she got as an only child and I enjoyed the quiet of her house. Carole has told me that she enjoyed the "busyness" and fun of our house. Carole and I would often stay overnight at each others homes. We were like sisters. We shared our thoughts, our hopes and our dreams. Sometimes when I slept over at Carole's house neither of her parents would be there during the evening. On these occasions Dad would walk to Carole's house during the evening and call through the letter box in the front door to ask if we were all right. We always were, but this was yet another example of my parents love and caring towards their children that I was allowed to stay there even though it meant that Dad would have to venture out, often in cold wet weather, to check on us. It seems ridiculous to me now that we did not open the door to Dad as we knew it was him because we heard his voice. It's surprising that he believed we were safe just because we told him we were. In retrospect, there could have been an axe murderer inside with us telling us what to say. In those days there was far less crime against people and against children in particular.

I was seven when my sister, Deryn, was born. I don't remember much about Deryn as a baby. I do, however, remember feeling disappointed because she was a girl rather than a boy. No longer was I the only girl. No longer was I Dad's only daughter. I would now have to share my Dad with another girl, my baby sister. I don't think that it was that I didn't love and want my sister. It was just that I believed Dad and I had this wonderful special bond that I must have felt was there because I was his only daughter (and it probably was) and I didn't want anything nor any person breaking this bond and coming between Dad and me. That bond never did get broken. It may have become chipped a few times but it was always there. It was far too strong to ever become broken.

1951 was the year of the Festival Of Britain Exhibition. In the summer of that year, when Deryn was about six months old, our whole family went to London and stayed at Uncle Jack's house in Sutton. We visited the Festival of Britain Exhibition. I have several vague memories of this exhibition but one clear memory that I have is that we children all received miniature tins of condensed milk, a welcome sweet treat. Following our stay in London we went on to Worthing for our annual summer holiday.

In the early 1950s Dad's brother, Uncle Jack and his wife Auntie Ruth left England. They emigrated to Canada where they stayed for the rest of their lives. By this time they had a child of their own, their first daughter was born in 1950, their second daughter being born in Canada. I remember being sad when Uncle Jack came to visit us to say goodbye before they left. He had been like a second Dad to me on the occasions when I saw him and I did not want to lose him. I have met his first daughter a few times but I have never met his younger daughter although we are now in contact via social media.

My childhood was a very happy one. We were not a wealthy family. My parents both worked hard to give us the most that they could. We didn't have a car, but in those days not many people did own a car. My parents never owned a car and never learned to drive.

Most of the things that are special memories from my childhood are the things that didn't cost money. As they say; "the best things in life are free". It is difficult to put my special memories into a chronological order, in fact some of them were ongoing and overlap, so I will write about them in no particular order. Again, I will focus on Dad but do please remember that Mum was always there as well, loving us, caring for us and supporting us, just as Dad was.

One thing that will always stick in my mind was Dad's willingness and ability to laugh at himself. Most people do not like to be laughed at and can get annoyed by this, but if Dad did something silly he would laugh about it and tell other people so that they could laugh with him. If we children poked fun at Dad he would laugh with us rather than get angry as many parents would.

More than once we children put an open container or bag containing flour on top of the kitchen door when we knew that Dad would be the next person to enter the kitchen. The container was balanced in such a way that when Dad opened the door the container would fall and he would be covered in flour. Most fathers would be annoyed by this and possibly become quite angry. I don't know whether it bothered Dad or not but this "trick" never made him show anger. He always laughed. I can still see him standing there, just inside the kitchen, covered in flour, laughing with us at himself. I don't know if he ever knew what he was walking into. If he did he always let it happen and acted surprised and laughed with us. It is important to remember that this was in the early 1950s. Children did not generally have such a close, relaxed relationship with their parents, particularly their father, as they have now. Also people did not have easy to wash clothes in those days and they did not have many changes of clothes.

A young Dad standing behind the door where he sometimes got covered with flour.

Mum deserves a mention here as she allowed us to do this knowing that she was the one who would have to clean up the mess on the floor and wash Dad's clothes. It sounds like we were a bunch of undisciplined, unruly children, but we weren't. We were just a happy family. Being able to "trick" our Dad in this way shows how confident we were in his love for us and his patience and sense of fun. I still remember the excited feeling of anticipation I had whilst waiting for Dad to come through the door and my brothers and I still laugh about this now on the rare occasions that we are together.

When he no longer had to work on Saturday morning Dad went into town, armed with a shopping list written by Mum. One Saturday, when Deryn was a baby, Dad walked to town taking Deryn with him in her pram. When he arrived home, Mum asked Dad where Deryn was. Yes!! Dad had gone into a shop, leaving Deryn outside the shop in her pram, as was the usual habit in those days. When Dad left the shop he had forgotten that he had Deryn with him. Obviously a panic occurred. Dad rushed back to town and there was Deryn, in her pram, outside the shop, exactly where Dad had left her. What a relief! Dad did not laugh on this occasion. None of us laughed at the time. However, we sometimes reminded Dad of this in later life and we all laughed together about it then.

Dad was a keen and I think good chess player. He was a member of a chess club for many years. I don't know how old I was when he taught me to play but we spent many hours playing chess together. It is another of my special memories of him and I doing things together. I might have been reasonably good at chess when I was a child. I know that Dad showed pride in my skills, but now, although I remember the way the pieces move, I don't remember the strategies.

I have no idea when he started to smoke but Dad always smoked a pipe and I can't remember him not being a smoker. Sometimes he would buy a tobacco that was in flat leaves. These leaves needed to be rubbed between the palms of one's hands so that they broke up into flakes before they were able to be put into the bowl of the pipe to be smoked. I used to do this job. It wasn't that I was a particularly helpful child and I did not really like the feel of the tobacco between the palms of my hands. I just enjoyed doing something that was just for my Dad and for no-one else. Today when I think about rubbing those tobacco leaves I get a strong feeling of nostalgia and of happy memories mixed with sadness because those days are long gone. If I see some-one smoking a pipe or smell pipe tobacco, a very rare occurrence today, pictures of Dad immediately come to mind. I still have Dad's pipe rack. It is one of my most treasured possessions.

Dad's pipe smoking did, however, cause him a recurring problem at times throughout his life. After smoking he would sometimes put his pipe into his pocket before the fire in the pipe bowl was fully extinguished. He would only realise this when his leg began to get hot or when he, or some-one else noticed the smoke or the smell of burning cloth. Mum often chastised Dad for this carelessness, and who could blame her, as she was the one who would have the job of mending the burnt clothing. We children thought it was hilarious every time we witnessed this happening. Every time it happened we laughed and, of course, Dad laughed with us. Another example of his sense of humour and his ability and willingness to laugh at himself. He seemed to think it was as amusing as we did. This is something that happened for as long as I can remember, from when we were young children until the end of Dad's life, and however old we were, my siblings and I laughed every time we saw or heard about it. Whenever he burnt a hole in his clothes Dad would successfully make a claim on his Contents Insurance. This meant that he got paid money to enable him to replace the burnt item even though Mum, who was a very good seamstress, was often able to mend the damaged item.

We children received "pocket money" each week. The amount was dependent on our age. As we got older the amount increased. It was not a large amount of money, but I think it was fair. We were expected to save at least a minimum amount of this money but there was enough left to buy a ticket for "Saturday Morning" pictures which were special movie sessions for children and some sweets or other treats, so I think it must have been a reasonable amount. Some children who had no brothers or sisters got more pocket money than we did, but there was only one of them to pay. My parents had four, and later five children to pay this allowance to and I think we were very lucky to get the amount we did. I am pleased that my parents expected and encouraged us to save money as I am sure that this helped us to learn the value of money and the value of appreciating and enjoying what we have saved for. We were not expected to do very much to "earn" our pocket money but one consequence of unsatisfactory behaviour was to lose the right to receive a week's allowance. When this happened I'm sure we deserved it.

On Dad's pay day I would sometimes be waiting at the bus stop for him when he got off the bus on his way home from work. I didn't wait for him walk to the house. I was too eager to spend some of my pocket money. If he had got off the bus at an earlier bus stop which meant that he had gone for a haircut, then I would walk the short distance to the barber's shop and get my pocket money from Dad there. I think a lot of parents would have been annoyed by being pounced upon by their child like this but Dad accepted it and he would put his hand into his pocket and give me my money with a pleasant word and a smile on his face.

During the 1950s in England the usual annual holiday for workers was two weeks. Some people stayed home during this time, probably because they did not want to go away on a holiday or because they could not afford to. Those who did go away often went away for one week and spent the other week at home. We always went away and not for one week. No, we went away for the whole two weeks. When we went on these holidays our clothes etc were packed into a trunk and two suitcases. Dad would carry the suitcases whilst the trunk would be carried by my older brothers Ralph and John each holding the handle that was fitted on to each side of the trunk. The trunk looked huge and heavy. I have sometimes wondered how my brothers managed to carry this burden but, in retrospect, perhaps the trunk was not as big as I remember it to be, as when I was seeing it I was a child.

We went on holiday to the same boarding house in Worthing for, I think, three consecutive years. It was only a few yards from the esplanade. If we were on the beach we could hear the gong sounding to indicate that it was lunchtime or dinnertime. We would leave the beach when we heard the gong, so we probably went onto the dining room with sand on us. Other places that I remember us spending our summer holidays include Scarborough, Bournemouth, Hunstanton and Mablethorpe.

I remember being in the water with Dad when we were on our annual holiday at the seaside and also at the local swimming baths. I don't think Mum liked the water as I can't remember her being in there with us but Dad would always be there. I suppose this was necessary for safety reasons, but I don't remember it for that. To me it was another fun time with Dad. We would all play water games together, and Dad taught us to swim. At least he taught me to swim and I assume that he taught my brothers and Deryn too. I would lie on my stomach across the water and Dad would hold me by having one of his hands under my stomach and the other hand over me on my back. As I gained confidence Dad would gradually loosen his hold on me, but I knew he was there to catch me if I floundered. Eventually I gained enough confidence to swim alone. I have no idea how long it took for me to be able to swim without having him there to hold me. I know that I had a set of "water wings" that I used for a long time. I have never been a strong swimmer but I still enjoy swimming, particularly in pools.

Stuart, John, Peggy, Dad. Early 1950s summer holiday.

When we were on holiday at the seaside, if the weather was fine, we would all go for a walk together as a family in the evening after tea. I remember these walks as happy times. Whilst we were walking we would collect empty soft drink bottles that had been thrown away. These glass bottles were returnable and a refund was paid for each returned bottle. By collecting and returning these bottles we children added to the money available for us to spend whilst we were on holiday.

During these walks we would all talk and laugh together for the most part. However, if I did not like something, perhaps I did not want to walk further or something or someone had upset me, I would stamp my feet, scream and have a real "girlie" tantrum. The family would ignore me, and quite rightly so. This would make me even more upset and I would stamp my feet harder and scream louder. My whole family would then tease me by singing to me. There is a nursery rhyme that begins "Poor Mary is a'weeping". Instead of singing these words my family would sing "Poor Peggy is a'weeping down by the seaside". I hated being teased like this and, eventually I would stop my tantrum. I think Dad was probably the ringleader of the teasing gang, but I deserved it. These tantrums of mine did not only happen when we were on holiday. They also occurred when we were at home at times when I couldn't get my own way and I got the same treatment, being teased until I stopped.

I think that our early holidays were booked by Dad writing to boarding house owners etc. in reply to advertisements that they placed in a newspaper. Most non-business people did not have a telephone at that time and we certainly didn't have one. In fact my parents got their first phone installed in 1972.

There came a time, however, when rather than booking our holiday by responding to an advertisement, a few weeks before the holiday dates Dad would travel by train to the chosen destination and door knock to find suitable accommodation for us. I don't know whether this decision was made because my parents had been dissatisfied with unseen accommodation or because they thought that if they booked shortly before the holiday time they would probably get a discounted rate. It may have been any combination of these factors or nothing at all to do with these factors that prompted the change to the way in which our holidays were booked. I don't know.

What I do know is that this was another exciting time that I spent with Dad as I went with him on these day trips. My best friend Carole came along too. Our destination was usually Hunstanton or Mablethorpe. We would catch the train in the morning. I think the journey took about three to four hours. Whilst on the train we would eat the lunch that mum had packed for us.

Once we arrived at our destination we would walk the streets looking for vacancy signs and knock doors to enquire what accommodation was available for our holiday dates. Towards the end of the day Dad would decide which available accommodation that he could afford would be the most suitable for our family. We would then return to that address and Dad would confirm the booking and pay the required deposit. We had to make sure that we did not miss the train home as our tickets were specially priced "day return" tickets so they were valid for that day only. Also I doubt that Dad had the money to pay for overnight accommodation if we had missed the train home.

I don't know why I remember these days as so enjoyable and so much fun. It was probably because I was with my Dad and, in my memory, he made every outing fun. I'm sure we would have sang and laughed as we walked those streets. I do know that, on the rare occasions that I have seen Carole during my trips back to England she has always commented about how much fun we had on these days and how much she enjoyed them.

As I said earlier, we were expected to save some of our pocket money each week. This saving was not supposed to be optional but it was not strongly enforced upon us. This savings was our "holiday fund" for want of a better word as it was expected that we would spend our savings whilst we were away on holiday at the seaside. Obviously he or she who had saved the most was able to buy more ice-creams, rides etc. than those who had not saved money on a regular basis. This was a good lesson in the value of saving, as those who didn't save every week could not enjoy as many holiday treats as those who organised their money sensibly and planned for the future.

Dad must have been quite community minded as he joined the Civil Defence, an organisation that was trained to help out in times of an emergency. There would be regular practical exercises. This involved the Civil Defence volunteers practising survival and rescue skills and techniques so that they would be sufficiently trained should a catastrophic emergency occur. After the dropping of the two atomic bombs over Japan in 1945 (this ended the Second World War), people were very aware of the damage that could be caused by such weapons and many were quite frightened that England could be attacked by an enemy using this type of weapon.

On practical exercise days there needed to be "victims" to be "rescued". Of course I volunteered! It was great! There I was, spending more time alone with Dad and also often being the centre of attraction as Dad proudly showed me, his daughter Peggy, off to everyone. I think that I was probably the youngest of the volunteers. I can't remember any other young children being there. The Civil Defence members and the volunteer victims would travel by bus to the designated "catastrophe" site.

We volunteer victims were briefed on our role, what had happened to us, injuries incurred etc. There would be sirens, warning alarms and suchlike and the scene would be very realistic, which appealed to my sense of drama (I have always loved the Performing Arts). Eventually I would be rescued and bandaged up as needed. When the exercise was over we would all enjoy tea and cakes together before being driven back to Hinckley. Whenever we were together Dad and I talked and laughed together freely and continuously or, at least, that is how I remember it. I never tired of Dad's company and I hope he felt the same about being with me.

I can't remember when Dad started to bring chocolate bars home on his pay day. It was usually a Crunchie Bar. Obviously I really enjoyed this treat but it was not very fair if Mum and I got chocolate and the boys didn't. Dad was possibly spoiling his "ladies", but, as an adult, I believe the boys should have been included too.

I also don't remember how old I was when Dad began to give me a Valentine's card. He sent me a card every year until 2006, the year he died. As he died in March he was probably not well enough that year to continue the tradition. These Valentine cards were always very special to me. To me they were a sign of Dad's special love for me. I didn't save them all, but I do have the later ones. If I look at them now it makes me rather sad as I wish that, in his later years, I had told Dad what wonderful memories I had of my childhood and how much I loved him.

Dad never smacked me. I do remember Ralph being smacked and John has told me that Dad used corporal punishment on him too. I don't know why I wasn't smacked. It may have been because I was a girl, or did Dad's views on corporal punishment change, as my younger brother does not remember being smacked either. If I did something minor that I shouldn't have done I would get sent to stand in isolation in a corner or in another room. If I did something wrong that was more serious Dad would talk to me in private. He would ask me why I had behaved in such a way and tell me how disappointed he was and that he had expected more from me etc. These "discussions" would make me feel awful. Dad did so much for me and had so much trust in me and I had let him down. I can only remember twice when I did something wrong enough to need such a talk, but I will never forget the feelings of sadness, guilt and remorse that I felt afterwards. I think that corporal punishment may have been preferable to these talks as the physical pain of being smacked would have soon passed whereas, even today, I still remember the emotional pain of knowing that I had let my parents down.

In September 1954 I began my secondary school education. In those days children sat for an examination known as the eleven plus exam during their final year in primary school. Those who passed the examination were eligible for entry into the more academic school, generally known as the grammar school. Those who did not pass went to a secondary school which, in addition to teaching the required academic subjects, had an emphasis on practical subjects, thus preparing students for apprenticeships and manual jobs. Students who passed the eleven plus did not have to go to the grammar school. They had the option to refuse this offer and attend the secondary school. I am sure that, in those days, the decision was made by the parents, but hopefully with the input of the child involved. I think that this method of educating children differently based upon their skills and interests is an excellent idea. Overall it was a win-win situation allowing each child more opportunity to work at their own pace and and within areas where they can achieve success.

As I passed the eleven plus examination I was entitled to enrol at the local grammar school. However, because I attended the private convent school and I had passed the eleven plus I had the opportunity to continue at the convent school for my secondary education free of charge. This meant that my parents did not have to pay school fees for my private school education. I think the convent school probably offered these free scholarships as they did not want their more academically minded students to leave the school as they wanted to boast about the success rate of their students so that more parents would be encouraged to send their girls to the convent school for a supposedly "better education" thus ensuring the financial success of the school.

I can't remember my parents discussing my secondary education options with me but I feel sure that they would have asked what my preference was. It was decided that I would continue at the convent school rather than enrol at the grammar school. This is definitely what I would have wanted to do. Most of my friends were going to continue at the convent school so why would I want to move to another school! I had enjoyed my years at primary school and the convent school had a very good reputation so there was no valid reason for me to go to the grammar school. Staying at the convent school meant that I could continue with my music lessons and this may have been a factor in the decision. I don't know. I do know that I was happy with the decision. I was used to the ways of teaching, the habits, rituals etc at the convent school. In my opinion it was a good school. I enjoyed all of my schooldays and have fond memories of them, even though, in retro-spect, I think that, in some ways, the nuns were sometimes quite emotionally cruel in their treatment of children.

The secondary school was not in Hinckley. Blessed Martin's In The Fields was in Stoke Golding, a small village about eight kilometres from our home. Again I travelled there by bus. I would catch the local bus into the town centre of Hinckley and, from there, a school bus would transport me to school. At the end of the school day the reverse would happen.

Within the school grounds was a magnificent large elegant house. Piano lessons occurred in this beautiful house, in a large room that I'm sure was once a parlour. I felt very small when I entered this magni-ficent house on my own when I went for my piano lesson. The nun who had taught music at primary school was also my music teacher at secondary school. I don't know when she actually moved to Stoke Golding, but Sister Ruth was my piano teacher at both schools and I know that she lived at Stoke Golding whilst I was there. We became quite close, which was not surprising as she was my one-on-one piano teacher for so many years. She told me many stories about her years as a nun in South Africa during the days of apartheid, a time of legalized racial separation and prejudice in South Africa.

During my time at Blessed Martin's I was given the opportunity to learn German. Sister Miriam was giving German lessons to two students during lunch break once a week and I was invited to join the group. This was a great opportunity for me. German was Dad's native language and it was possibly as a result of discussions between Sister Miriam and Dad that I was invited to join these lessons. I remember that Dad was pleased and happy that I was going to participate in these classes. I did attend the German lessons but, sadly, I didn't persevere with them. As the lessons occurred during lunch break I soon began to want to be socialising with my friends rather than forfeit thirty minutes a week of my free time to learn a language. I just stopped attending lessons. I don't know whether there was communic-ation between Sister Miriam and my father about this. I don't remember Dad talking with me about it. Eventually Sister Miriam stopped asking me to attend. I feel sure that Dad would have been disappointed by my decision not to attend these German lessons, but I can only assume that he and Mum understood how important social life is to a child. Of course, since being an adult I have often wished that I had persevered with learning German, both because languages are so useful particularly if one travels and also because German was Dad's native language. I have often wished that Dad had taught us German at home, even if only by using the language at times in our daily life. I am surprised that he didn't as he valued academic education so highly. I think that most likely Dad didn't want to use German because it reminded him of the traumas he had endured and the loss of his parents and other relatives and friends who had perished as a result of Hitler's regime.

Mum and Dad's last child was born in 1954. Mum delivered her babies at home, as was the usual practice at that time in England. I was kept home from school on that day so that there was someone to run to fetch the midwife. I don't know if this decision to keep me home with Mum was made because Mum was in the early stages of labour that morning or whether she had a premonition that she would have the baby that day. Dad had gone to work as usual at about six am. In those days it was not expected that a man would take time off from work because his wife was about to deliver a baby. In fact a man was not welcome in the room whilst his wife was giving birth. Dad had actually been present in the room when I was born. Was this was the beginning of our special bond? In those days there was no such thing as paternity leave, family leave nor sick leave. Even if it had been acceptable Dad could not have afforded to lose a day's pay by not going to work. There was no money to spare in our house, every penny was needed, and often spent before it was earned. I think that there was also possibly the risk that Dad might have lost his job if he had not turned up for work merely because his wife was about to give birth! They were not always really the "good old days"!!

So, on November 29th 1954, two days after my 11th birthday, I was kept home from school to be there for Mum. I knew, perhaps I had already heard it said, that Mum delivered her babies rather quickly after her waters had broken. If I remember correctly, and I seem to have a vivid memory of that day, at about midday Mum called to me. She was standing in the bath and her waters had broken. She instructed me to run quickly and fetch the midwife. The midwife lived about seven hundred metres from our house, not very far. I remember running as fast as I could to the midwife's house. I felt very nervous and wary about what was about to happen. The midwife immediately went to our house. I don't know how, when, nor by whom Dad was informed of the imminent birth of his child but he arrived home before the baby was born. As it would have taken him well over an hour to get home he must have been informed before I fetched the midwife.

I remember sitting on the stairs during the time Mum was giving birth. I must have been quite in the way as Dad went backwards and forwards, downstairs to boil water then upstairs to their bedroom (the birthing suite) with the boiled water. He seemed to do this over and over again. It seemed that this was an endless task. I remember that, to me the whole situation seemed to be very surreal. In those days "the facts of life" were not talked about and children generally did not have any real knowledge or understanding of the birth process. I did know that the baby was in Mum's tummy and was going to be born, but I did not understand nor did I question how this would occur. Dad was not smiling. He seemed to be worried and in quite a panic as he went back and forth with pots of boiled water. I had never experienced anything like this before. I remember feeling quite nervous and afraid.

Eventually, I heard the cry of a baby. My new brother or sister had been born. I was sitting on the stairs when I heard the baby's first cry. I think Dad was in the bedroom for the actual birth, as I have said, an unusual occurrence in those days. Dad told me that I had a new baby sister. It was decided to name her Angela. I later learned that there had been complications during the birth and it was, according to the midwife, a miracle that Angela had survived. I think it is possible that she was named Angela because, when being born, she had almost joined the angels.

I'm not sure what time in the afternoon Angela was born but I think it was about two o'clock or thereabouts. I know it was before my

253

brothers arrived home from school. I don't know where Deryn was at this time possibly being babysat by a a friend or neighbour. I have no recollection of her being in the house. Angela was born a "blue baby", meaning, in simple terms, that her heart was not able to pump enough oxygen round her body. It was decided that because Angela was blue and therefore quite unusual looking, and because she was in a very delicate condition, it would be better if her siblings did not see her on that day as there was a strong possibility that she would not survive. As an adult I can now realise how distraught my parents must have felt.

As I had been involved in the birth by seeing Mum in labour, fetching the midwife and because I had sensed and observed the panic that had occurred during the birthing process, it was agreed that I would be allowed to see my new sister for a few moments on the day of her birth. Both Dad and the midwife spoke with me before I saw Angela. They told me that she was a blue colour and not to be frightened by this. They also told me that she was not well and that the only reason that I could see her on that day was because I had been there and had helped by fetching the midwife. It was probably thought that it was important for me to see Angela on that day as I had been involved in some way during her birth and had heard her first cry. I think they thought that she might not survive until the next day.

I can still see Angela lying in her crib on that day. She was wrapped in a shawl which covered her head and she was also covered with blankets so I could only see her face and really only one side of her face. I couldn't understand what the fuss had been about. She looked lovely to me. I did not notice that she looked different from anyone else in any way. She was a baby, my new baby sister and, to me, she looked quite normal, just like any baby. I was not jealous when Angela was born as I had been when Deryn was born as I was now used to having another girl in the family and also I was getting older and growing up.

Angela did survive the night. She was a Down Syndrome baby (often called mongoloid in those days) and she had a hole in her heart. In those days many families felt that caring for a Down Syndrome child was too difficult for them and these children were often put into residential care homes. Not my parents! Angela was loved as much as we all were, probably more because she was special and I'm sure that my parents knew that she probably wouldn't be with us for very long. I don't think we children were told about Angela's specific health problems. She was our darling little baby and we all adored her. I knew that she needed to be kept warm and my parents were allowed extra coal and coke for our fires. Even in 1954 the amount of fuel available to each household was regulated. This extra allowance was authorised by our family doctor.

Angela was late in achieving the progress goals of a baby. I really enjoyed taking her for a walk in her pram. I felt so grown up taking my baby sister for a walk without an adult there to supervise me. I was only allowed to walk around the block as I was not allowed to take the pram up and down the path curbs in case I tipped it over. Adults would look into the pram and comment on what a beautiful baby Angela was. I felt so proud of my baby sister. In those days it was safe for children to talk with people they met in the streets and most of them knew our family. Did these adults see that Angela was a Down Syndrome baby? Thinking about it now, I'm sure they did. But they were right. Angela was beautiful. I don't know if my siblings thought she looked "different" but I definitely didn't notice any features in her face that were different from those of anyone else. Today when I look at the couple of photos that I have of Angela her Down Syndrome facial features are very obvious to see, but I never noticed them when I was a child. Ah, these innocence of childhood!

In those days, in the mid 1950s, medical knowledge was, obviously, not as advanced as it is today. Sadly we lost Angela. She passed away on March 16th 1956 when she was sixteen months old. The cause of her death was stated as mongolism and broncho-pneumonia.. I still remember how I learned of her death. As I was walking along our street on my way home from school Dad walked down the street to meet me. As we walked together he gently told me that Angela had passed away. I don't remember the exact words he used. Did he meet the boys on their way home from school and tell

255

them in this way? I don't know, but I think that it is highly likely that he did. It really was a very thoughtful, gentle, caring way to break such sad news to a child.

Meeting me and breaking the sad news to me in this way would have, in part, prepared me for the scene at home. We were all heart-broken but Mum was absolutely distraught. Mum was an emotionally strong woman who generally kept her feelings to herself. I had never seen her like she was on that day. She was crying and sobbing loudly. Her crying was punctuated by her saying how much she was going to miss Angela etc. In fact she was quite hysterical. I distinctly remember that on that day and for a while after Angela's death she would cry and list all of the baby products and items that she would no longer have any need for. Never again did I see my mother as upset as she was following Angela's death.

I was not used to seeing my parents so upset. Dad tried to keep a "stiff upper lip" and he would have made all of the necessary arrange-ments. Quite understandably Mum did not seem able to get over the loss of her youngest child. As any mother knows, when one has carried a child in the womb for nine months and given birth to that child, that maternal bond is something extremely special. In my opinion the umbilical cord never really gets cut and a mother will do anything and everything to protect her child.

Mum was the one who had looked after Angela throughout her short life. She was the one who was home with Angela all day every day, as was the usual role for a mother in those days. It was only natural that she would feel the loss more strongly than anyone else because she was Angela's primary carer and because of that undeniable maternal bond.

Mum was such a strong woman and it was very different and quite unnerving for me, as a twelve year old child, to see my super efficient mother not coping as well as she normally did. Looking back now, as an adult and a mother, Mum coped extremely well under such difficult circumstances. She had five other children to care for and she did a marvelous job of trying to carry on as normal and trying to hide from us children the terrible sadness and despair that she must have felt.

I think that although Dad must have stayed home from work on the day that Angela died he would not have been allowed to take any period of time off work to be with Mum after Angela's death, nor could he have financially afforded not to go to work. March 16th 1956, the day of Angela's death was a Friday, so Dad would have been home with Mum for the weekend. Obviously he did take a day off work on the day of Angela's funeral. I am sure that he was as saddened as Mum was by the loss of Angela, but, in those days, men were discouraged from showing their emotions, and he needed to remain strong for the sake of his family. I wonder if losing a child made Dad think about his parents and other family members that he had lost earlier in his life as a result of Hitler's barbaric policies.

At that time, in England, it was usual for a deceased person to remain in their home or in the home of a family member until the day of the funeral and the funeral procession would begin from that address. Every house in the street would have its curtains closed during this period of time, usually three days, as a sign of respect for the deceased person.

I was asked if I wanted to see Angela during the time that she lay in our front room following her death. I did choose to see her. She looked just like she was sleeping.

The day after Angela's death I was due to compete in a music festival. My parents were very aware that I might not want to participate in this competition on the day after Angela's death and they gave me the choice of opting out. I was always grateful that they let me make the decision as to whether I would perform or not. I chose to perform in the competition. It was not that I was not upset about losing Angela, but I think children are very resilient and they suffer and grieve on a different level than adults do. I must have performed well as I achieved "First Place" in the competition. Usually my parents both attended my performances. I can't remember but I doubt that either if them were there on that day.

As already stated Dad's marriage to Mum was his second marriage. He and his first wife had two children, Ralph who lived with us and Peter who had gone with his mother when Dad and his first wife separated. This meant that I had a half brother, one that I did not know about. When we were children we were all treated as equal brothers and sisters and we were not aware that we did not all have the same two parents. We were also not aware that we had another brother named Peter.

I used to often visit one of mum's cousin's, one of my "honourary aunties". One day when I was at her house she was talking to a friend. Sadly she was talking quite openly about my father having been married prior to his marriage to my mother and the fact that he had another son who did not live with us. I don't remember her exact words but I do know that she stated that this unknown brother was going to come and stay with us. I don't know how old I was when this happened but I was old enough to listen to what she said but not to ask any questions. I think I might have been about twelve or thirteen.

I was intrigued! This was the first time that I had any inkling that all of us children were not both Mum and Dad's biological offspring. I think that it was very remiss of my "aunt" to discuss these personal family matters of my parents with another adult and I think that it was even more remiss that she did it quite openly in front of me, a young, impressionable, inquisitive member of the family that she was talking about. As I said, I was intrigued! I was not upset, just intrigued! I did not let on in any way that I had listened to what was said, although my "aunt" should have realised that I could hear her. I would have to have been deaf and stupid not to have heard and understood what she was saying, and I was neither of these.

I did not tell my parents what I had overheard. I don't know why. Perhaps I felt that it would cause some embarrassment for them. Perhaps I felt that I should not have heard what was said. Perhaps I did not want them to think badly about my "aunt". I don't know why I didn't tell them what I had heard but I didn't. I didn't tell anyone.

Shortly afterwards Peter, my unknown half-brother, came to stay with us. Neither my siblings nor I were told about him and his impending arrival. One day he was just there. I can't remember how we were told who he was. I knew who he was of course because of my "aunt's" gossiping. I suppose Dad must have explained to us that Peter was his son and our brother.

Peter had been brought up in London area. From what I learned later he had been brought up more by two elderly ladies, who may have been related to his mother in some way, rather than by his mother herself. I believe he had been brought up according to the Orthodox Jewish faith and as a practising Jew.

Peter was about the same age as John, about two years older than me, and about two years younger than Ralph, who was his full blood brother. Life with us was very different from anything that Peter had ever known. He had been brought up as an only child and his companions had often been adults. We were quite a boisterous bunch and we must have been quite a shock for Peter. I remember him as being quite reserved, but he could have felt uncomfortable as he had really been removed from a quiet lifestyle among people he knew and thrust into the midst of this large family where he did not know anyone. I got on really well with Peter. Perhaps he found it easier to relate to me than to my brothers because I was a girl and there was only one of me for him to cope with as Deryn was still very young at this time. Perhaps sharing a bedroom with three brothers and having them ask him questions etc. was difficult for him to handle.

I do remember that there was friction in the house whilst Peter was with us. I can't imagine Dad and Mum not trying very hard to make Peter feel welcome. I'm sure that they did all that they could to try to help him fit into the family and become one of us. Peter was Dad's son and Mum was a natural mother and would have loved and cared for him in the same way that she did for all of us. Peter gave me a book "1000 Things For Girls To Do". I don't know why he had this book but he gave it to me and I treasured it for a long time. Sadly I don't have it any more and I have no idea where it went to.

Peter found it impossible to settle down in our house. I think our way of life was just too different from anything that he had known, and he returned to London. I was disappointed to see him leave but I am even more disappointed that I did not keep in touch with him after he returned to London. I know that in his later life Dad saw Peter on several occasions and for a while they seemed to get on well together but sadly this relationship did not last.

I think that I had many advantages by being the only girl among three boys for the first seven years of my life. Even after Deryn was born, because of the age gap between us older children and Deryn, my brothers and I seemed to be together as a group and Deryn seemed to be separate as we were growing up. I think that I was rather spoiled in some ways, particularly by Dad. However, my brothers did have some advantages because they were boys. My brothers were able to earn money whereas I wasn't able to do this as the jobs that were available were deemed, by my parents, to be unsuitable for a girl.

In those days it was usual for virtually every household to have a newspaper delivered each day. This delivery service was usually done very early in the morning by young teenagers on bicycles. The "paperboy" needed to complete his paper round and then go home and have breakfast before going to school. My brothers all had a paper round at some time thus earning extra income in addition to the pocket money they received from our parents. I was not allowed to have a paper round because, in my parents' view, this was not a job for a girl. I don't think they were worried about my personal safety. I think that my parents just thought that delivering papers was not a "lady-like" thing to do.

One morning one of my brothers was sick and not able to do his paper round. Rather than my brother's boss be let down it was agreed that I could do the paper round on that day. I was so excited! It still amuses me now when I think about this. I was not allowed to have my own paper round because I was a girl, but I was allowed to step in for my sick brother. There seems to be a double standard there somewhere! I can't remember whether my brother paid me for the day's work I did for him, but I bet he did. I'm sure I would have made a big fuss if he hadn't.

Another way in which my brothers earned money was "potato picking". During potato picking season, in the school holidays, my brothers would pick potatoes at a local farm. They earned what seemed to me to be a good wage for this, giving them extra money to spend. Again I was not allowed to do this because it was deemed to be unsuitable for a girl.

I really envied my brothers because they had these opportunities to earn money whereas I didn't. It was not that my parents were favouring the boys, it was just how things were in those days. There were different expectations of boys and girls. Jobs and other roles in life were very gender based.

My Teenage Years.

One year, just before Christmas, Dad asked me to go Christmas shopping in Leicester with him. I think that it was possibly 1956 when I would have just turned thirteen. He told me that he wanted my help in buying some makeup for Mum as a Christmas present from him. I was proud that he wanted my help. I didn't wonder why he would expect me to know anything about makeup. I also never wondered how he knew exactly what brand and type of makeup he intended to buy, Max Factor Creme Puff. This was the makeup that Mum always used but I didn't even query why he hadn't looked at the colour shade on the compact that she would have had in her dressing table drawer. In the shop he told the shop assistant that he needed advice on what shade to buy and that the one that was best on me would be the best on his wife. The shop assistant was very helpful and tried different shades on my face before a decision was made and Dad made his purchase.

I was genuinely surprised when, on Christmas morning, I found that makeup in my Christmas stocking, or rather, in my Christmas pillow case, as this is what we used to hang on the bottom of our beds on Christmas Eve. I might add that they were always very full the next morning. I was overjoyed with getting makeup for Christmas. My first makeup. I felt so grownup. I realised then why Dad had wanted me there with him when he was selecting the best shade of makeup "for Mum". It was not for Mum at all. It was for me. I felt that Dad had bought me something very special. As I got older I realised that Mum and Dad had planned together to come up with a plan to get the correct shade of makeup for my face. In fact I am quite sure that me being allowed to have and wear makeup would have been Mum's idea rather than Dad's. Dad would probably have wanted to keep his Peggy a little girl rather than have her grow up. Quite a usual way for fathers to think.

Of course, I was only allowed to wear the makeup on special occasions or when going out somewhere quite formal. Nowadays it is quite usual for young girls to wear makeup every day, even for school. That would never have been allowed in any school in those days. I was really quite surprised and even rather shocked when girls began to wear makeup to school in about the 1980s.

At about this time my friend Carole and I were attending ballroom dancing classes on a regular basis, usually twice a week. We were among adults and felt very grownup. I was good at the dancing. I had good balance and a good sense of rhythm, as one would expect given my musical experiences. I don't know when and from where I got my first lipstick. I do know that I thoroughly enjoyed the whole process of getting dressed up in my best clothes, putting on my makeup and participating in these dancing lessons. Carole and I attended these classes for quite a long time. I don't remember why we stopped going, perhaps it was because we discovered Rock 'n Roll, teenage "tanner hops" and boys!

What are "tanner hops" you might ask? The tanner hop was a dance for young people. "Tanner" was the slang term for the predecimal coin the sixpence, which was equivalent to about two new pence. "Hop" was the term used to describe a rock 'n roll dance. Hence the term "tanner hop". The music was loud and fast (for those days) and young teenagers had lots of fun at these dances.

It must be becoming obvious that my parents were very progressive. They were willing to allow me to explore different ventures as long as the venture was deemed by them to be suitable for a young female teenage girl. I wanted to grow up or, at least, feel grown up. I wanted to socialise. I was an emerging adolescent.

This was the mid 1950s, the time of the emergence of Rock 'n Roll". The times of the "Greats" such as Tommy Steele, Cliff Richard, Elvis Presley, Jerry Lee Lewis etc. The list is endless. It was the time of the jukebox and cafes where teenagers would hang out, drinking milkshakes and feeding their money into the jukebox. There were two such cafes in the town centre of Hinckley. My older brothers were allowed to frequent them, but I was not supposed to go into them as my parents thought they were unsuitable, and possibly unsafe places for a young teenage girl to be. I think they thought that I might find the "wrong sort of friends" or meet the "wrong sort" of boys in there.

I was allowed to go to the tanner hops. Hinckley did not have a tanner hop, but two small towns near to Hinckley each had a weekly tanner hop. Barwell held one every Thursday evening and Burbage held one every Saturday evening. They were held in a large hall. There was no alcohol allowed which never seemed to be an issue as we were all there to dance and we were too young to drink alcohol anyway. We danced to vinyl records. Sometimes there was a DJ but usually the records were put on by a person responsible for doing this. If you knew that person and they liked you they would play your choice of record. The music played was rock 'n roll, rhythm 'n blues and, of course romantic ballads. Girls would wait on the edge of the dance floor eagerly hoping that a boy would ask them to dance. If not the girls would dance with each other. It was the time of bobby socks and waspy belts, drainpipe trousers and teddy boys. It was the time when teenagers got a music of their own, a music that most parents did not enjoy and did not approve of.

My father never did understand and accept rock 'n roll as music. His love of classical music blinded him to all other types of music. During the Christmas period at the end of the year 2000, which was the last time I spent time with Dad, he still did not accept that rock 'n roll was music and he still found it difficult to believe that rock 'n roll was, perhaps, my favourite type of music. He thought that, as I was his daughter and had been taught classical piano, I would embrace classical music and see rock 'n roll and other such forms of music for the "rubbish" they were, to quote his words. I do love classical music. It is beautiful to listen to and the composers were brilliant. However, I am more broadminded than Dad in my opinions of music. I appreciate all types of music. There are some types that I do not like, particularly those with loud, headbanging repetitive bass lines. I do not like singers that scream rather than sing and I abhor swearing and inappropriate vulgar lyrics in songs. Is rock 'n' roll my favourite style of music? I don't know. I love classical music and I love musicals. I enjoy these as much as I enjoy rock 'n roll and other music of the 1950s and 1960s. Over the years, and having spent more than twenty five years teaching music in schools, I have come to the conclusion that a person's favourite music is often the one that they enjoyed during their teenage years. However, both classical music and the music of the 1950s/1960s still remain very popular and, in my opinion, they are both timeless.

I was allowed to date boys from when I was about thirteen, which now seems ridiculously young, but my parents did stipulate that they had to meet the boy before I went out with him and they had to know where we were going and at what time I would be taken home.

Obviously I was still at school at this time. I was a student in the academic stream at school and I was still having piano lessons, taking music examinations and participating in Music Festivals. I did not find school difficult and, for a while, I was able to keep up with with my studies with minimal effort on my behalf whilst also socialising on some evenings each week.

However, as I became more interested in having a social life as a teenager my school grades began to drop. I had more important things to do than homework and piano practise. My parents would ask if I had done my homework etc., and I'm sure that I told them what they wanted to hear whether it was the truth or not. I can't remember them showing any anger or disappointment as my grades dropped to average. Perhaps they thought it was a natural decline as the work became more advanced. I think they were probably disappointed, particularly Dad because he held academic achievement in such high regard.

One Saturday night in April 1958, whilst I was at the Burbage Tanner Hop my brother introduced me to the young man who was to become my husband.. His name was (and still is) Bill and when the dance ended he asked if he could walk with me on the way home. Bill was home on leave from the army and I was on school holidays. He invited me to go skating with him the following day. I replied that I couldn't go as I had no money. Bill offered to pay for me, so we had a date for the next day.

On that date at the roller skating rink I discovered that I could not skate. I have tried both roller skating and ice skating on several occasions since then, and I have never been able to even stand unaided on skates.

After our first date Bill and I spent virtually every day together until his leave ended and it was time for him to return to his barracks in Devon. We wrote to each other very regularly and looked forward to being together in three months when his next leave would occur.

During Bill's next leave we spent every day together and by the time that this leave ended we were sure that we were in love and that we wanted to be together forever. I was still only fourteen and Bill was sixteen. Nowadays it seems strange to have a serious boyfriend/ girlfriend at that age, but in those days if a girl was not married, or at least engaged by the time she was eighteen she was thought to be "on the shelf". Some of my girlfriends had boyfriends but I don't think any of them were as serious about each other as Bill and I were.

My parents accepted Bill. In fact my mother and Bill got on partic- ularly well. They were like mother and son. Dad and Bill got on to a certain extent but there was always a barrier there. Fathers often think that a boy is not good enough for their daughter. Bill was not an academic and I think Dad expected me to socialize in circles where I would meet young men who had a professional future.

In April 1959, after we had been going out together for one year, Bill and I got engaged. It seems ridiculously young now, but I think I was always mature for my age, and getting engaged to be married seemed to be a natural progression for us. I can't remember my parents having any objection to me getting engaged at such a young age, but my parents probably thought that our young love would not last.

I was still at school at this time, studying for my GCE O Level exams. By now I was not a good student. I managed to get by and achieve satisfactory grades without putting in any real effort. I did not study as I should have. I was far more interested in spending my time socialising and with Bill than in study. It is not surprising that my grades dropped.

My parents were away on their summer holiday when my disappointing GSC exam results arrived. This was the first year that I had not gone away with them. Whilst my parents were away on this holiday Bill and I decided that I would leave school and get a job. As we intended to get married and my future would be as a housewife and mother we could not see any value in me continuing with my education. Probably a sensible decision if I was not going to put any time nor effort into my studies.

When Mum and Dad returned from their holiday I gave them a disappointing shock when I announced my intentions. They had always expected me to stay at school, succeed in my GCE A Level exams and then to further my education at a higher level. They were probably quite devastated when I told them that I was not returning to school. I do remember having lengthy, sometimes heated, discussions with both of my parents about my intentions. I dug my heels in and would not agree to go back to school, in spite of all of their pleading, cajoling and demanding that I "do as they say". Eventually they gave in. I think they realised that you can take a horse to water but you can't make it drink! How disappointed and upset my parents must have been, particularly Dad who valued academic education so highly. I still think that continuing at school at that time would have been a waste of time as I was not putting in any effort, but I do regret the hurt that I probably caused my parents by my decision, and I regret not apologising to them about this in later life. I got a job! Not a difficult thing to do as jobs were plentiful at this time. My first job was as a receptionist at a hosiery factory at Burbage. The factory was owned by one of my mother's relatives and his business partner but I don't think this had any influence in me getting the job.

In September 1959 Bill was informed that he was to be posted to Germany as part of the British Forces On The Rhine. This was a part of the agreement made following the defeat of Germany in 1945. Various troops were stationed in Germany for a period of time. This was to ensure that the Germans did not make any attempts or show any intentions of taking up arms again. We were devastated! At this time Bill was stationed near Leicester and we were used to seeing each other virtually every day. How would we survive if we could only be together when he came home on leave?

I have sometimes wondered if my parents were pleased that Bill was sent to Germany. They never said anything within my earshot, and they seemed genuinely concerned about how much I missed him, but it must have been pleasant for them being able to enjoy relaxing in their front room without Bill and I smooching on the settee. Also, as we were so young they probably thought that our romance would not survive the separation.

Bill came home for two weeks at Christmas. An exciting time, but, all too soon, it was time for him to return to Germany.

My brother John and his fiancee planned to get married in March 1960 when they would both be eighteen. In our letters Bill and I decided that, if they were getting married then we would get married too. I did not mention this decision to anyone, not even my parents. I was only sixteen at the time and I think I must have realised that they would not support us getting married whilst I was so young.

Bill arrived home on the day of my brother's wedding. I can still remember the excitement I felt on that day, not because of John's wedding but because Bill was coming home. I kept looking out for him, just as I had looked out for Dad coming home when I was a little girl.

When Bill and I announced to my parents that we were getting married we were told quite bluntly and firmly that we were not getting married. As I was only sixteen I needed my parents' permission to marry. There were many discussions, arguments and tears during the next week or two. My parents voiced many reasons for us not to get married, and who could blame them. We were so young.

We dug our heels in, insisting that we were going to get married and eventually my parents gave in and grudgingly gave their consent to our marriage. Obviously we were both overjoyed and it must have been quite a relief for Bill who, as a member of the military services, had been required to make a formal application to be allowed to marry. This request had been been approved and, as a result of this, Bill had been given six weeks leave, rather than the usual two weeks.

Married Life.

Preparations were made and we married on April 23rd 1960. I wonder how Dad felt on that day? He was his usual loving self towards me. I do remember that he asked me if I was sure that getting married was what I wanted to do. I wonder if he thought back to his own first marriage. He had been young and it hadn't worked out. He was probably worried that I might be entering into a marriage that was doomed to fail.

Bill had to return to his unit in Germany ten days after our wedding. I could not go with him as, at that time, the British Army did not provide any housing or other assistance for married personnel who were under the age of twenty one, and we had no money to pay rent for private accommodation.

Whilst Bill was home on leave during the Christmas period of 1960, he and I decided that we did not want to live apart any longer and that, even though it would be financially difficult, I should go to Germany so that we could be together. I wonder how Dad felt about me going to live in the country where he had spent most of his youth, the country where he had encountered such horrific racial hatred, the country from which he and his family had been forced to flee in order

268

to avoid almost certain death in a concentration camp. Germany was the country that was responsible for the splitting up of his family and for the murderous death of his parents.

The flight to Germany in early 1961 was my first experience of being in an aeroplane. When the plane arrived in Dusseldorf Bill was there waiting for me. We travelled by train to Munster, which was where Bill's unit was stationed.

We were quite poor. Initially we lived in a hotel room paying a special weekly rate. We could not afford to eat out so we bought a single cooking ring and virtually lived on canned food which we only had to warm up. We got chastised on several occasions by the hotel management because they could smell "cooking" coming from our room. Of course we denied this!

Eventually Bill and I moved into a furnished room on the upper level of a private house in the small town of Hiltrup. Most German houses had a basement, ground floor and upper floor. The upper floor was a separate unit that could be rented out. In the house we moved into the owners and their two children lived on the ground floor, the upper floor unit was rented out to a German couple and there was a separate room on this upper floor which we rented. The room had adequate furniture and a double ring for cooking. There was no running water nor toilet. We had to go to the basement to use the toilet and to wash and to fill a large jug with water to carry to our room. We were allowed to have a bath once a week. As Bill could have a bath in the barracks I used his weekly bath as well as my own. These living conditions may sound quite primitive, but to us they were wonderful. We had a place of our own. The rent was affordable and the family who owned the house were lovely. They treated us like family and sixty years later we still have occasional contact with their son. We lived there for over a year, until the regiment's deployment in Germany came to an end in 1962. My parents were both overjoyed when we returned returned to England.

Bill's next posting was to Watchet in Somerset where we rented a caravan behind a country pub. After several months there, Bill was posted to Wigston, only about 25km from Hinckley. As Bill was almost twenty one and there was a house available we were allocated an army married quarter there. Wow! A modern three bedroom semi-detached home of our own. Could life get any better? It was easy for us to visit our families as there was a regular train service between Wigston and Hinckley. We would visit my parents almost every week and sometimes we would stay overnight.

On our third wedding anniversary, whilst we were at Wigston, Stephen, our first child, was born. Mum and Dad both adored Stephen, as they did all of their grandchildren, great grandchildren and great great grandchildren.

In the summer of that year, 1963, Bill was posted back to Watchet and Stephen and I went with him. It was sad to be moving away from our families again but that is a normal part of military life. Bill and I have continued to have wanderlust and have travelled intensively throughout our life.

We lived in a farmhouse just outside the small village of Kilve. Shortly after we moved there Bill was deployed overseas on active service. Whilst Bill was away on active service, I kept the house in Kilve, although Stephen and I went to Hinckley for part of the time, making a prolonged visit to my parents. They made us feel very welcome, even though it probably wasn't easy for them to have a baby in the house full time. Stephen and I spent Christmas1963 and New year 1964 with them in Hinckley.

Bill returned from active service in February 1964. In those days there were not any family reunions at airports or seaports. A couple of days before the soldier was due to arrive home one was given the "expected" date of return, but no more information could be obtained. It was a very long day. I waited and I waited It was about 9pm when the gate opened. He was home. I can't express the happiness we both felt when we were reunited. Bill was amazed when he saw Stephen, who had been four months old when he was deployed. Stephen was now a big ten month old boy.

The regiment remained at Watchet for the remainder of Bill's enlistment and we continued to live in the same house at Kilve until he was demobbed in September 1965. My parents visited us when they were able to as work commitments limited their extended periods of free time. We managed to buy an old car and we would drive to Hinckley some weekends and stay with my parents.

Our second child was due to be born in the middle of December 1964, but Chris decided to wait for a special day, Christmas Day, to make his appearance into this world. I was to have a home delivery. It was still unheard of for a father to be present during the birth of his child, but Bill and I had already stated that we wanted him to be present during the birth. We did not have a telephone so Bill had to use our only neighbour's phone to call for assistance. We had contact numbers for four midwives and our doctor. It sounds easy but it wasn't that simple. It was winter in rural England. Some roads were closed. One midwife had loaned her car to a friend, one was sick, one was at church. I can't remember what reasons prevented the other professional persons from attending immediately, but it seemed that Bill and I were going to deliver our baby by ourselves. Stephen was put into his cot so that he was safe and did not need watching during this time.

Luckily a midwife did arrive before Chris was born and she quite accepted that Bill was going to be present and would be assisting her during the birth. When the doctor arrived he told Bill what an excellent job he was doing and stood aside whilst Bill and the midwife completed the delivery.

In September 1965 Bill's time in military service came to an end. We were fortunate enough to be allocated a rental council house in Earl Shilton, about ten kilometres from Hinckley. This meant that we were able to visit our relatives and friends on a regular basis and also they could visit us. We had no money and no work. We managed to buy some second-hand furniture from people my parents knew. Bill soon got a job. Life was good.

Christmas 1965 was a financial struggle. We bought presents for the children and a turkey for Christmas dinner and we were happy and satisfied with our lot. In fact we felt very fortunate. We were to spend Christmas Day at home with our boys and then, on Boxing Day, my whole family and their families would gather together at my parents' house to celebrate together.

On Christmas Eve there was a knock on our front door. It was Dad. He was standing there with a bag in his hand. The bag contained a bottle of port and a bottle of sherry. They were for us. He knew that we could not afford to buy any Christmas "cheer" for ourselves, so he had braved the very cold weather, and travelled by bus, to bring us this gift, thus ensuring that we had a drink to toast each other and our family on Christmas Day. We really appreciated this gesture and I felt that Dad was there for me again in his special way. I still have no idea whether this was Dad's idea alone or whether Mum had some input into it.

Whilst we lived at Earl Shilton we had two more sons. Jarrod was born in March 1967 and our last child, Damian, was born in November 1969. Our family was complete. Bill worked full time and, at times, I worked some evenings after Bill was home to care for the children. Jobs I had were working as a barmaid and as a cashier at a cinema. Eventually we managed to buy a car. It was a Ford Zephyr, a very classy car. Of course ours was old and we paid very little for it, only twenty pounds I think. Having a car gave us the freedom to take the children out to different parks etc.

In 1968 Uncle Jack came from Canada to visit Dad and the family. He brought his eldest daughter who was a teenager with him This was the last time that I saw my beloved Uncle Jack.

One day in 1969 I saw an advertisement in the local paper. A house could be purchased with a minimal deposit. All one needed initially to secure a house was fifty pounds, the remainder of the deposit to be paid after the house was built. A mortgage was not difficult to obtain as the builder had an agreement with a particular mortgage lender. In those days owning one's home was a pipe-dream for people in England from our socio-economic backgrounds.

One problem. We didn't have fifty pounds. However, someone had offered us fifty pounds for our car. We did not hesitate. The car was sold and we had our home deposit. We chose the cheapest style of house on offer, a three bedroom semi-detached. The total purchase price of the house was thirteen hundred pounds.

As we no longer had a car we were back to relying on the public bus service, not an easy option with three small children and me pregnant. However we did not see this as a problem as we watched our house grow. The house was in Hinckley, on the Jelson Estate, about midway between my parents and Bill's mother's homes, an ideal position. We moved into our own home in January 1970, when Damian was just a few weeks old.

Late that year I again got a part-time job, working at the local Bingo Hall. After this job folded I got a job as a barmaid at a local club. At the time Dad was working full-time in Coventry in the engineering industry but he was also working part-time as a barman at the same club. On Saturday evenings Dad and I would be working together behind the same small bar. We had lots of laughs and chats too and I felt that special bond again. It had always been there, but had been less obvious since I had been an independent adult. I really enjoyed working with Dad, in spite of the fact that he was paid far more than I was, even though we were both adults and both doing the same work. Why, you might ask? The simple answer is that he was a man and I was a woman. No equal pay in those days!

I have sometimes wondered if Dad was disappointed in the jobs that I did. Here I was, his daughter Peggy, who had a "good education", was very capable academically and a talented pianist working in a bingo hall, as a cashier and as a barmaid. He had always had such high expectations of hopes for me.

Did he feel let down because I had married so young and not pursued a professional career? I hope not. Hopefully he respected the fact that I was willing to accept any job that was available and fitted in with my responsibilities as a wife and mother. Dad's excellent work ethic rubbed off on to all of us children. We have all always been good workers and willing to work at whatever jobs have been available even if it was not always what we would have chosen to do.

Over the years Bill and I had discussed emigrating to Australia. However, whenever we became serious about the idea I would find myself pregnant and we would put the idea on the back-burner and say we would consider it again after the baby was born.

During 1971 the idea of emigrating became an issue that we talked about again. We made inquiries and the prospect of living in Australia appealed to us. Many people say they emigrate to give their children better opportunities. I don't think that was the reason with us. We and our extended family were all employed, in fact Bill had the best paying job that he had ever had. I think we just liked the idea of the adventure of emigrating to the other side of the world.

When we told my parents that we intended to emigrate they were, obviously, very sad. In fact they and we thought that we would never see one another again. Stephen, Chris and Jarrod, who were old enough to understand, definitely did not want to leave their grand-parents, family and friends and go to live in Australia.

After completing a series of tests we were accepted for the "Assisted Passage Migration Scheme", making us what has become known as "Ten Pound Poms". Under this scheme it cost Bill and myself ten pounds each to travel to Australia and the children travelled for free.

We sold our house and, in January 1972, we moved in to live with my parents until we left England. This must have been quite difficult for my parents as they were used to living on their own, and suddenly they had two younger adults with four boisterous boys aged eight years and under living with them. They never complained and I am sure the boys enjoyed this time with their grandparents.

It was really a bitter sweet time as my parents and I thought that when we left it would be goodbye forever. None of us thought that we would be able to afford to visit the other. Shortly before we left England Stephen's schoolteacher asked me what I would do if I didn't like it in Australia? My answer to her was that I would have to like it as I would never afford to return to England. How times have changed!

If we had chosen to fly to Australia we could have left virtually immediately. Bill was keen to do this and get work. I, on the other hand, wanted to travel by ship from England to Australia, thus having a six week holiday whilst travelling to our new home. I convinced Bill to do it my way so we had to wait until a suitable vacancy on a ship was available. In March we were offered a cabin on the Ellinis. We were given only ten days notice. During this time we had to do our final packing and Bill had to hire a vehicle and transport our boxes to the docks at Southampton. We couldn't afford to pay someone to do this for us. We also had to say goodbye to family and friends, a very emotional experience.

Dad, Mum and Deryn came with us to Southampton to see us off. It's hard to describe how I felt on that day. Of course I should have been excited about beginning the journey to Australia, the country that we had chosen to be our new home, the country where we had chosen to bring up our children, but, when it was time to board the ship, all I remember feeling was grief and sadness at leaving my family. Even now it makes me sad to think that I chose to leave my parents forever. I will always remember standing on the deck with Bill and the boys waving goodbye to my parents and Deryn. I wonder if Dad was reminded of when he had to say goodbye to his parents when he left Belgium for England in February1939, or when he said goodbye to them after their final time together in August 1939. I think that saying goodbye to us at the docks would have made him think about these sad times in his life. Did he feel that history was repeating itself and he was again losing loved ones?

The six week cruise from England to Australia was wonderful. I think we had a a cabin cancellation. All of the other emigrants that we met on board were in dormitory situations on lower decks. The men being in a cabin with several other men and the women and children being with other women and children. Our cabin was on the Main Deck and it was a suite. There was a bed for Bill and I, a cot for

Damian and two sets of bunk beds. We also had a deluxe bathroom, the most luxurious we had ever seen.

The cruise was fantastic. A luxurious holiday that we could never have imagined being available to us. We docked at The Canary Islands and Cape Town and arrived in Australia in late April. We first docked at Fremantle in Western Australia and then in Melbourne, Victoria where we disembarked. During that day we were given a tour of Melbourne and had meals in a hostel in Melbourne before being put on the Overland train to travel overnight from Melbourne to Adelaide, South Australia, which we had chosen to be our new home.

When we arrived in Adelaide, very tired and weary after a twelve hour overnight train trip with four children, we were taken to Pennington Hostel which would be our home until we moved into our own home.

There has been a lot written about the migrant hostels in Australia, but in our opinion Pennington Hostel was very satisfactory. The living accommodation was nissen huts. They were clean and furnished with basic furniture and bedding etc. There was a communal dining room where one could get cooked meals. Packed lunches were available for people going to work and for schoolchildren. Migrants who did not have jobs were paid social security money. The cost of the hostel living were taken out of this but there was still a small amount left for the family to spend as they wished. Another good thing about the hostel was that there were people there to guide and advise the new migrants re employment, schools, housing etc. English lessons were available for non English speaking migrants. I think that anyone who was dissatisfied with the hostel situation would have been a person who expected far too much to be done for them. We will always be grateful that the hostel was there for us as new migrants in a new country.

So many things were different here in Australia than they had been in England. Some things were the same or very similar. The language was the same for us, English. Settling into a new country with a different culture, different laws and different ways of doing things would have been far more difficult if we had needed to learn a new language.

I think of Dad again. He was only nineteen when he first went to England. He was alone and he couldn't speak a word of English. How lonely, nervous and even frightened he must have felt! He had to find his way around London area on his own, keep appointments, accept lodgings in a stranger's home, find his way to work, complete engineering work proficiently, communicate with work colleagues etc. without having any prior knowledge of English. At that time, some people would have been very wary of Dad as he was assumed to be a German. Germans were, obviously, not the most popular people in England in 1939. Dad succeeded admirably, learning the language quickly and integrating into his new way of life in England with virtually no assistance. It is amazing what one can do if the need and / or desire is great enough.

When I think about this, it makes me try to understand how terrible life was for Jews in Europe at that time. It was so frightening that people gave up their homes, abandoned their assets and took great risks to try to escape the horror, terror and fear of Hitler's Nazi regime. It makes me realise how frightening, sad and desperate the situation was for Dad's family. First there was their move from Vienna to Berlin. Then their risky, daring escape from Berlin to Belgium and even then they knew that they were not safe. The family was split up when Dad departed for England, with his brother, Uncle Jack, following him soon afterwards. Dad's parents, my grandparents, must have felt devastated when their sons left them to live in England, even though they would have known that it was safer for them there. They must have been so very worried about their children and they would have missed them so very much as well as being concerned about their own safety in Belgium. I think that it is impossible for anyone who has not experienced it to imagine what life was like for the Jews and other so-called "undesirable, sub-human" groups in Europe during the time of the Nazi regime.

Within three months of arriving in Australia we had purchased and moved into our new home. Bill worked full-time and I got a part-time job as a barmaid. I was amazed when I got my first week's pay. I was paid the same as a man. I had never earned so much money.

Life was good. The three older boys went to school. Bill and I had our jobs. We had a car so family outings were a regular weekend activity and the boys enjoyed the beach. I got my driver's licence during 1973.

Was I homesick? No. We had made a decision to live in Australia and we had our own family, our children with us. Did I miss my family in England? Yes, particularly my parents. It is normal to miss family members when one is separated from them. My parents and I kept in regular contact by mail and telephone. Dad had a phone installed when we emigrated so, on very special occasions, we would telephone one another. Overseas phone calls were very expensive in those days.

I worked on Friday afternoons and every Friday a group of teachers would come into the bar for drinks. One Friday I suddenly decided that I wanted to be a teacher. Was it possible for me, at the age of thirty, with four children to care for, to train as a teacher? Yes it was. As an adult I had two options. I could take an entrance exam or I could study two subjects at Matriculation level. Satisfactory results in either of these would allow me to enter Teacher's College, which was affiliated with the University.

I decided to study two subjects at matriculation level as this would let me know how I felt about studying before I embarked on a Teacher Training course, so, at the beginning of 1974, I undertook the study of Australian History and Economics. I was still able to work in the hotel during this time as the classes did not clash with my working hours. I achieved good results in both subjects and I was accepted as a student at the teacher's college.

During 1974, when we had been in Australia for two years my parents really surprised us. They were coming to visit us for their annual holiday. I don't know how they afforded the trip at that time and I was surprised that they were able to get the extended time off work, as their usual holiday was for two weeks only and they were coming to Australia for six weeks.. We were all excited about their impending visit.

I was so excited when we met my parents at the airport. It was a busy holiday. We showed them many of the beautiful sites in South Australia, including the Barossa Valley as well as just about the whole of the metropolitan area. Our boys, of course, couldn't get enough of their grandparents. Dad really liked Australia and stated that he would like to live here but Mum would never have left England and, quite honestly, I don't think Dad would ever have wanted to live anywhere other than in his beloved England.

I feel sure that both of my parents were happy about my decision to train as a teacher, but Dad, with his high regard for academia, more openly showed his pride and joy in what I had decided to do. I think that he felt that I was finally following a path that was suitable for me and one that I should have taken when I was a younger woman. However, we all need to do things when the time is right for us.

All good things must come to an end and all too soon it was time to take my parents to the airport for their journey back to England. It was a sad day. We all tried to put on a brave face, which was extremely difficult for me and I am sure was just as difficult for my parents as, again, we thought that we would probably never be together again. Yet another reminder of the anguish Dad must have felt when he left his parents.

On the way home from the airport I sobbed relentlessly. Perhaps my parents visit had made me realise just how much I did miss them. Our boys were crying too and saying they wanted their grandma and grandad.

On the way home from the airport Bill promised me that I would see my parents again. We decided that we would save as much money as we could and that we would all go to England for a holiday in two or three years. It seemed an impossible dream, but it was something to strive towards.

As I have got older I have come to think that it was probably quite a cruel thing that Bill and I did to both our parents and our children when we emigrated to Australia. Obviously our family members would miss us and our children had friends as well as their relatives in England who they would never see again. Our boys knew, loved and were spoiled by their grandparents, as most grandchildren are. They had aunties, uncles and cousins as well as their friends. We took them away from that safe, secure situation and brought them to Australia, on the other side of the world. They did not have any relatives or friends in Australia. We did not know anyone when we arrived here.

Don't misunderstand me. I do not regret coming to Australia. We became Australian citizens after we had been here for one year which was as soon as we could. Our sons quickly settled in to the Australian way of life and they have made their own lives and families here. When we arrived here we were the only people with the name "Toon" in the South Australian telephone directory. At the present time, in mid 2021, in addition to our four sons and their wives/partners we have seventeen grandchildren and twenty five biological great grand-children plus five children who are non-blood-line great grand-children, with more additions expected, so our family has definitely helped to populate Australia.

I began studying for my future profession as a teacher in February 1975. I really enjoyed being a college student. I chose Music and Science as my two major area of study. Going back to playing the piano was something that I had thought I might never do. Finding time to practice was sometimes difficult as Bill was working full time and there were four boys and a home to be cared for. By working together Bill and I kept the wheels turning smoothly. I even began to work part time again, as a waitress. I did not work many hours a week, but the money I earned helped to boost our savings for our trip to England.

Our savings grew and during 1976 we knew that we would have enough money to travel to England at the end of that year and spend Christmas with our families, which we did. The six of us lived with my parents for the six weeks that we were in England. It was wonderful spending Christmas in my old home. The boys obviously enjoyed being with their grandparents again and we all enjoyed being with relatives and friends that we had not seen since 1972 when we left England. The boys also enjoyed the snow and ice, things that they could not really remember.

It was on this trip of ours to England that Dad began talking to me in more detail about his life before he arrived in England. I found it difficult to believe that he and his family had suffered and endured so much trauma. It amazed me that anyone who had suffered as Dad had could be such a happy, jovial person. How could he have kept his hurt to himself for so many years?

We returned to Australia and life went on. After three years of study I applied for and obtained a position as a Music Teacher in a government secondary school in a small township about twenty minutes drive from home. I can just imagine Dad's face beaming with pride when he heard this news.

After our visit to England in 1976 it was ten years before I saw my parents again.

The boys grew up. First Stephen and then Chris got married. Like their parents our sons got married at a young age. When Jarrod was planning to get married in 1986 we decided to pay for my parents to come to Australia to attend the wedding. They were both retired by this time and we had two grandchildren for them to meet, as Stephen had a son and Chris had a daughter. This visit was the last time my children saw their grandmother.

By this time, Dad had been back to Berlin at the invitation of the German Government and he had written the part of his autobiography that I have and that was the original purpose for this book being published. He had sent me a copy of "The Journey Back" in November 1984, along with the letter that I used to introduce the chapter "The Rest Of The Story". I know that going back to Berlin was a very traumatic, bitter-sweet experience for Dad. Berlin, that amazing city that he had loved so much, the city of music and opera. Berlin, the city where he spent his adolescent years with his loving family. Berlin, the city where, after Hitler came to power, living there

281

as a Jew he had experienced first hand the fear of every day life under the Nazi regime. Berlin, the city that he and his family were forced to leave because of the ever-present danger of being rounded up and transported to a concentration camp.

During my parents visit to Australia in 1986 Dad spent many hours talking with Bill and myself about his family history. These talks often took place in the late evening. Having read "The Journey Back" made it easier for me to visualise and "know" various family members and I wanted to know as much as I could about my lost family. Dad spoke in depth about his life before he arrived in England and of his return visit to Berlin and the effects this visit had on him emotionally. These discussions made me want to see the places Dad spoke about. I wanted to see Dad's Berlin.

By now Dad had achieved success by getting very good results in GCSE examinations in five subjects at O Level and two subjects at A Level. He was also teaching German, both privately and at local colleges and he was very proud of his achievements. He had worked in a factory for all of his working life and he had worked hard to earn the money to raise his family. In retirement, rather than slowing down, he pursued formal education and worked to achieve his dream of academic success. This gave him great pleasure and pride in himself, and quite rightly so in my opinion. I am proud of him for following his dreams.

After their visit to Australia in 1986 I did not see my parents again until 1995 when Bill and I visited them in England at Christmas time. Again a lovely holiday spent with family and friends. Neither Bill nor I had seen our siblings since our visit to England in 1976, nineteen years earlier. We were all thrilled to be together again. Spending Christmas in the house where I had grown up and with my parents was very special and made me think about when I was a little girl and I got that very special doll's house for Christmas.

During this visit to England in 1995/1996 I went to dinner with a group of friends from my days at the Convent School. We had a great time reminiscing about our schooldays. Since that visit Bill and I have been to England on several other occasions, six times I think, and on every visit a "convent girls night out" is an essential. The group has grown to include other girl friends as well as "convent girls".

I had not forgotten my desire to visit Berlin and see the places that Dad had known in his youth. I had been to Berlin before but I wanted to see the city through Dad's eyes. I wanted he and I to experience "his" Berlin together so we had arranged for the four of us, Dad, Mum, Bill and myself to spend several days there in January 1996. During this time Dad showed us the house where he had grown up and the workshop where he had first worked. We saw streets where he had played and we visited the school that he had attended. I must add here that the students at the school were extremely polite and welcoming to us. Dad also showed us the sites of synagogues that had been destroyed, not during the war, but by the Nazi's on Kristallnacht. Dad had informed the German Government of our impending visit and they supplied us with a vehicle and a driver on one day thus enabling us to have a guided tour of the whole of Berlin, both the West and what had been the East before the Berlin Wall came down on November 9th 1989, exactly sixty years after Kristallnacht.

We spent time at Wannsee Lake, the lake that was a favourite of Dad's. A large, beautiful lake used for boating and swimming in summer and for skating in winter. There is a beach there, made from sand imported to the area and the lake is surrounded by woodlands. This place is very popular for leisure activities throughout the year. As our visit was in January the lake was frozen and we sat watching the skaters. As I have never been able to even stand upright on skates I was quite in awe of their skills. With Bill's help I did venture out and stood on the frozen lake much to my parents fear and dismay. They were worried that the ice might crack and that I could be drowned. I think this would have been highly unlikely as so many skaters were safely enjoying the frozen lake.

Close to Wannsee Lake, is a beautiful villa. This villa was taken over by the SS in 1940 and has become known as "The House Of The Wannsee Conference". The decision to rid Europe of all of its Jews had already been made and it was in this house, on January 20th 1942 that Heydrich chaired the meeting that was responsible for organising the implementation of "The Final Solution", (how to carry out the extermination of Europe's Jews). On January 20th 1992, exactly fifty years after the Wannsee Conference, a memorial and study centre was opened in the villa. We were fortunate enough to be able to visit this house, learning about its history and spending time examining the exhibits on display there. How could such a terrible crime, the intended extermination of all of the Jews of Europe have been planned in such a beautiful setting, or, for that matter, in any setting at all?

Wannsee House

During these days in Berlin we also visited Sachsenhausen Memorial Centre, the site of Sachsenhausen Concentration Camp, which was in use as a concentration camp from as early as 1936 until its liberation in 1945. Although designed as a detention and work camp, an extermination complex was built there in 1939 and it is estimated that approximately 100,000 people were systematically put to death in the camp. The inmates at Sachsenhausen were mostly "antisocial" criminals, their only crimes being that they were Communists, Social Democrats, Jews, Christians, Liberals, Homosexuals, Gypsies, Jehovah's Witnesses etc. All subhumans according to Adolf Hitler! By 1944 the camp held 204,000 inmates representing forty seven nationalities.

We arrived at Sachsenhausen on a cold January morning, it was minus eight degrees Celsius, as I said cold! As I walked around the camp area I thought about the inmates there. It was hard to imagine how they managed to survive the weather let alone the cruel treatment they endured at the hands of the Nazi guards. Try to imagine how they must have felt during those inevitable roll calls, when they would have to stand outside for hours in all weather conditions, undernourished, in fact virtually starving, with hardly any clothing. They had to stand to attention for as long a time as they were ordered to. I tried to visualise their working and living conditions. How did they find the strength to live in these worse than barbaric conditions? They knew that the threat of death was constantly present. The gallows were always there and, later on, the extermination complex. I think that death might have been the easy option and I applaud and am in awe of all of the brave people who survived or tried their hardest to survive in any of Hitler's Nazi concentration camps. Visiting Sachsenhausen was a very sobering experience for me. It made the horror of the concentration camps more real. Since then I have visited Dachau and also Auschwitz, the camp in which my grandparents were murdered.

I felt very close to Dad throughout this visit to Berlin. Being with him and seeing the places he had known and enjoyed in his youth and also seeing places where he had experienced the cruelty and abominations of Hitler's Nazi regime made me more fully realise and appreciate what he and his family had endured. I felt closer to the grandparents and other relatives that I had never had the opportunity to meet. I will always be grateful that we made this trip to Berlin with Dad and I will always remember how he seemed to enjoy showing me the places that he had spoken about, places that were close to his heart and also those that held negative memories for him. I know that Dad was very pleased that I had wanted to experience his life in Berlin with him. As he had never spoken about his life before England when we were growing up, and even after we were adults he only spoke about it when asked particular questions, he probably felt that his family were ambivalent about his past. I can only speak for myself, but I was and still am very interested in learning about Dad's family, my paternal family, a brave, loving family that was destroyed by the Nazi monsters. The memories of this special time spent in Berlin with Dad will always hold a special place in my heart.

This visit to Saschenhausen was Dad's first visit to a concentration camp, but it was not his last. The reader might remember that later that same year, 1996, Dad visited Auschwitz the place where his parents had been murdered. Can we even imagine how he felt? I don't know that we can.

At this time Dad was a part time student at Leicester University where he was completing an Arts degree studying History, Politics and German. He began this course of study in 1989, at the age of seventy and graduated eight years later in 1997. He was also teaching German both privately and in local colleges and giving talks to groups about the Holocaust and about his personal experiences during this time.

Dad's graduation was an occasion that I did not want to miss, so, in mid 1997 we again went to England. At his graduation ceremony I think I felt as proud of Dad as he had felt of me when I achieved my academic and music successes all those years ago. I was so proud of him for continuing to pursue his dream of achieving academic success and also for his high achievements in his chosen subjects. He was also very proud of himself, and quite rightly so. During his working years I don't think that he had ever thought that he would be able to do what he had done since he retired. I have always felt that "age is just a number" and I think Dad must have felt that way too, as he never let age deter him from following his dreams.

Dad would usually go out on Saturday evening. Not to the theatre as one might expect, but to a local club to play bingo. Bill and I enjoy bingo so, on each of our visits to England, we would often go with Dad on Saturday evening. We were not very lucky at bingo, but I felt very lucky being out with Dad. It still seemed special, being out with him. We were not alone as Bill was there with us, but perhaps in a way, in my subconscious mind, it reminded me of when I was a young child and the special times when Dad and I would spend time together.

In a way there was a similarity between Dad and I regarding our academic achievements. We had both left school earlier than our parents had wanted us to, but, as adults we had both returned to school and achieved success at a higher education level in our chosen fields. I was proud of Dad's perseverance and achievements and I know that he was proud of me, both for my achievements and for my eventual choice of career as an educator. He liked the fact that I was teaching Music, an area so close to his heart.

Once Dad started to study there was no stopping him. He was not content to rest and relax once he had obtained his Degree. He wanted to do more. He wanted to complete a Masters Degree but financially he could not afford to do this. Fortunately he received a phone call from a past student of his who had appreciated Dad's teaching methods. This gentleman, Clive Walley, kindly gave Dad a cheque for enough money to pay for the university fees required for him to be able to enrol for a Masters Degree. So, in 1998 Dad began studying part time for a Masters Degree in Philosophy specialising in Holocaust Studies.

Sadly, in 1999, Mum was diagnosed with cancer. Obviously, both Bill and I wanted to spend some time with her so, in December of that year, we again travelled to England to spend Christmas and New Year there. In spite of Mum being very sick it was a good holiday. Christmas at my parents house was always special. Mum loved Christmas. She enjoyed decorating the tree, always a fresh real tree, and she enjoyed the cooking, the exchanging of gifts and the family being together. Seeing in the New Millennium, the year 2000, with my parents and siblings was very special. Mum was very stoic and did not openly acknowledge that she was seriously ill, although it was obvious that she was. I don't think anyone knew whether or not she was in a lot of pain as she did not share her feelings. Her appetite was very poor and she did not have the same energy for life that she had always had.

Saying goodbye at the end of that holiday was heart-breaking. Bill and I both knew that it was the last time that we would see mum. I think Bill was as upset as I was, as he and Mum were extremely close. At the airport mum and I clung to each other, both knowing that it really was our final goodbye. I was as brave as I could be in front of her, forcing myself to hold back my tears, but once we were out of sight my tears fell. It hurt so much, accepting that I would never spend time with my mother again. Even now, as I write this, twenty years later, the pain of that goodbye is still there and tears well up in my eyes.

Do I regret not feeling as close to my mother as I was to my father? Yes I do. I will never regret the close bond that I had with Dad but maybe, and possibly because of this, I took Mum for granted and I did not nurture the same type of relationship with her that I had with Dad. I don't know. What I do know is, my mother was a wonderful mother, the best. I think that nothing was more important to her than her children and their well-being, and later on her grandchildren, great grandchildren and great great grandchildren. I am so very lucky. I had two amazing parents who both always put their children first.

Mum passed away on June 25th 2000, exactly six months after that last Christmas Day. We did not go to England for Mum's funeral. We had always said that there was no point in going back for a funeral as the deceased person could not appreciate one being there. Family in England said that they did not expect us to attend the funeral. We had spent time with Mum just five months before she died and we both had work commitments. Bill did suggest that I go to the funeral but I said no, because we had always said that this would be a futile exercise. Do I regret this decision? Yes I do. Since the day of Mum's funeral I have always regretted not being there to say my final goodbye to her. It is something that I will always regret.

Dad was still studying for his Masters at this time. As the year 2000 progressed I was concerned for him. Even though my siblings were in England I was worried about the prospect of him being alone at Christmas in the house that he had shared with Mum for so long. Bill and I decided to buy Dad an airline ticket and invite him out to

Australia to spend Christmas and New Year with us, an offer which he accepted.

During the time he was with us on this, his last visit to Australia, Dad told us that he had never been fishing and had always wanted to do this, so we took him fishing. We went to the River Murray at Goolwa and Dad experienced yet another success when he caught the first fish he had ever caught in his life. He caught not one fish but two when he reeled in a double header. He was very proud of this achievement even though, as soon as the fish were landed on the bank, pelicans stole them. A theft that we all laughed about together!

We went on a road trip to Melbourne, where our youngest son, Damian, lives so that Dad could spend time with Damian and his family. We travelled to Melbourne via the Great Ocean Road, enjoying the beautiful scenery on this route. As our other sons live in South Australia he was able to see them more easily.

At that time our eldest son Stephen, his wife and seven sons were living in the mid-north of South Australia at Clare, about 200km north of Adelaide. Dad never did get to meet their daughter, Esther, who was born in 2004, and whose decision to complete a school assignment on the *Effects of the Holocaust on Future Generations*, finally prompted me to fulfil Dad's wish of having his story "The Journey Back" published. When we visited them we detoured via The Riverland, a fruit growing area so that Dad could visit Banrock Station, a vineyard and wine producer whose wines Dad enjoyed in England. On the way there we stopped at several wineries and Dad sampled their produce. In fact, by the time we arrived at Paringa, where we were to stay for the night, Dad had sampled quite a few wines!

Dad also spent time with Chris and Jarrod and their families during this, his last visit to Australia.

When Dad's holiday with us came to an end we said our goodbyes. Dad was very active for his age and still studying for his Masters of Philosophy, but he did have some health issues and he was eighty one years of age so I wondered if we would see each other again, or was this to be our final goodbye, which, sadly it was.

Dad completed his Masters Degree and graduated in 2001, after two and a half years of part-time study. What an achievement! I did not travel to England for this graduation Ceremony as I had spent time with him just a few months earlier. How I wish now that I had made the journey to England to be there with Dad on this very special occasion. I know he was extremely proud of himself and he really enjoyed the publicity he received because of his efforts and achievements.

In late 2001 Dad remarried, which was quite a surprise, but it was, obviously what he wanted to do. Dad's new wife owned her own house, which she sold when they married. As Dad had lived in his rented council house since 1947 he was able to purchase this house at a very reasonable price, well below market price, so between them, he and his new wife bought this house. This was another dream of Dad's that finally came to fruition. After paying rent since he had arrived in England in 1939, sixty three years later he finally became a home owner, or I should say co-home owner as his wife owned the home too. Dad expressed to me that he was very proud to own his home, another dream that he thought that he could never achieve.

During the final years of his life Dad became very active within the local community. In addition to teaching German he visited schools and colleges giving talks about The Holocaust in general and also about his personal experiences during this horrific time. He became a regular visitor at one particular college, setting up the "Eric Lewinsohn Holocaust Award" scheme there, and he pledged money in his Will to allow this scheme to continue after his death. Dad was also actively involved in the discussions and implementation of a local annual Remembrance Day Service to mark the Holocaust and he spoke of his experiences and loss at these annual ceremonies. Dad was a great speaker. People never tired of listening to him speak about his personal life and also about the horrors of the Nazi regime in general.

Left: Dad snoozing.

Below: Dad with his pipe.

Both of these photos were taken during Dad's last visit to Australia, late 2000.

Dad was a great teacher. He must have believed that people learn by doing, as students in his classes were expected to participate actively during each lesson. He encouraged student success by his positivity towards each student and their abilities. On more than one occasion during our visits to England both Bill and I have been "invited" by Dad to sit in during a German class. This meant that we had to participate by speaking German during the lesson. Not an easy thing for us to do, but we were always told how well we had done.

I retired at the end of 2002, at the age of 59. Bill had already retired. We sold our property at Willunga, had a caravan built to suit our requirements, and became "grey nomads" for the next ten years. We usually spent about six months of each year in South Australia close to our family and during the colder months we would explore a different, warmer State each year. During this time there was not much of Australia that we did not see. Wherever we were I always kept in regular contact with Dad, generally by telephone.

On March 17th 2006 we were at Esperance, in the south of Western Australia, when I received the phone call telling me that Dad had passed away. I was heart broken. I would never see nor talk to my Dad again. My Dad, who had always been so special to me throughout my life was gone. I cried so many tears.

The question I asked myself was: "should I go to England for his funeral?" Bill urged me to go, but I felt that I shouldn't go. I had always regretted not travelling to England for Mum's funeral but, as I had not attended Mum's funeral I felt that I should not attend Dad's funeral as it would seem like I was favouring him over her and this was not what I wanted.

When I was speaking with our eldest son, Stephen, about this, he said some very wise words. He said, "Mum, if you regret not going to Grandma's funeral don't let yourself regret again by not going to Grandad's". I will always remember these words. They made sense and were responsible for enabling me to make the decision to attend Dad's funeral. A decision that I am sure I wanted to make and one that I do not regret.

Dad had left specific instructions regarding his funeral. He wanted a particular minister, Canon Brian Davis, who he knew and respected, to perform the ceremony and he was to be buried in the three person grave that he and Mum had purchased when Angela had died. Because the grave had already been used permission had to be obtained to open the grave to allow another body to be placed there. This took time, which meant that the funeral was not to be until March 29th. This was good for us as it gave us time to get there as, after I made the decision to attend Dad's funeral, Bill and I had decided that we would both go to England to attend the funeral and to have an extended holiday.

It was a busy time for us. We had to travel home to South Australia as our passports were there, as were our suitcases and clothes that we would need in England. We packed up the caravan and left Esperance on Sunday March 19th at lunchtime. It was a long drive to Clare in South Australia where our belongings were stored, more than two thousand and sixty kilometres. We completed the journey in two days, found our passports, packed our suitcases and were ready to board the plane to England a couple of days later.

It was a bitter-sweet meeting with my siblings. The last time that we had been together was in 1999/2000 when we had been in England during the last Christmas that Mum was alive. It was good to see my brothers and sister and their families, but we were there because Dad was no longer with us, and this was a sad occasion. I had to say goodbye to my very special Dad.

I would never hear his voice again. His voice that had a Berlin accent. An accent that I had never noticed as I was growing up, an accent that I had never really noticed until it was pointed out to me. The only thing that I had ever noticed about Dad's speech was that he did not pronounce "no" as it is usually pronounced. He pronunciation of "no" sounded like "now". We used to have a laugh about this and mimic dad's way of saying "no", and Dad, of course, in his usual way of being able to laugh at himself would laugh along with us. In all of my life I have never met anyone else who was as willing and able to laugh with others at themselves like he did.

I was fortunate enough to arrive in Hinckley in time to be able to spend a short time with Dad for one last time before his coffin was closed. He looked so small in that coffin. My wonderful Dad who had loved me so much and had always been there for me. My Dad who had always raced around energetically now lay so still. My Dad who I had always loved so much and would always continue to love was gone from this Earth, but would never be gone from my heart.

Dad's funeral service honoured him for the person he was and for the contribution that he had given to the local communities particularly during the latter part of his life. Those who knew Dad will understand when I say that I think he would have been very satisfied with his funeral service. His obituary and the tributes made to him were an indication of the respect he had earned for himself.

I have talked about my life with Dad and the influence he had on me until his death. I am now at the end of the story of my years with and my memories of my father, to me a very special man and the best father I could have had. My father, Eric Lewinsohn, had his faults, as we all do. He was not perfect, none of us are, but to me, he was the perfect dad. I don't think he could have been a better father to me in any way. When I began to write my story I thought that it would be finished in a few pages, but I was wrong. Even now, after all that I have already said, I know that before I finish typing I must summarise why I love my Dad so much and why I am so proud of him.

As a boy and a young man Dad endured the horrors of living under Hitler's Nazi regime, the trauma of escape and separation from his family, arriving in England at nineteen years of age, alone with no knowledge of English. He later had to cope with the knowledge that his parents had been murdered in Auschwitz. None of this terrible suffering made Dad openly bitter, even though the horrors he had experienced would have stayed with him throughout his whole life. Dad was always there for me. From as far back as I can remember he always made me feel very special. He was a fun Dad. He would always laugh with us children, even at himself. He never let his past experiences have any negative effect on his behaviour as a father. In fact he kept his horrible experiences to himself, which must have been difficult at times.

He was a very responsible father, working long hours in jobs that he did not really want to do in order to keep his family. It was only after his retirement that he was able to pursue his dreams of achieving academic success.

Dad was not a big man physically. He was short in stature but he had a huge heart and huge dreams. I am proud that he pursued these dreams in his retirement. By succeeding in his own educational pursuits he gave himself self satisfaction and honoured his parents as he wanted to. He also educated many others, both in German language skills and in knowledge of The Holocaust. The successes he experienced in both learning and teaching gave him great satisfaction as he held academic success in great esteem.

Dad, I still use your words today:

"IF I CUT MYSELF MY BLOOD IS RED.

IF A BLACK MAN CUTS HIMSELF HIS BLOOD IS RED

THERE IS ONLY ONE RACE

THE HUMAN RACE".

DAD I LOVE YOU

DAD I AM PROUD OF YOU

THANK YOU FOR BEING YOU, DAD

AND

THANK YOU FOR BEING MY DAD

FAMILY MEMORIES

As we emigrated to Australia in 1972 my sons did not have their grandparents around them throughout their formative years. After we left England the only time that they were able to spend time with their grandparents was when my parents visited us for six weeks in 1974, when we all went to England for a six week holiday at Christmas 1976 and when my parents visited us in Australia again in 1986. They did spend time with their grandfather again when he spent a few weeks with us in Australia during December 2000/January 2001, after my mother had died.

Even though my children did not have the wonderful experience of grandparents as a constant in their lives I have asked them each to write a brief account of their memories of their grandfather.

Stephen, my eldest son was born on my third wedding anniversary in 1963. He has written the following as a tribute to his grandfather:

"Two Jewish boys, leaving Berlin for a safer part of the world. Never to see their people again. This story has etched itself into the collective consciousness of my extended family.

The older of the two was my Grandad. Eric.

The stale smell of pipe tobacco. A group of men playing chess whilst sharing a pint of beer. Collecting football pools on a cold, damp evening. Many a chess game at 11,000 miles, started but never finished. A letter here. A letter there. Shared concerns. Shared hopes for a kinder world to live in. My memories are sketchy, but fond".

Stephen Toon (2020).

My second Chris was born on Christmas Day 1964 and was seven when we emigrated to Australia. He has said the following:

"I remember that we lived with my grandparents for a while before we left England but I don't have any specific memories of my Grandad from before we emigrated. My memories of him are from when my grandparents came to visit us in 1974 and 1986 and when we returned to England for a holiday in 1976.

Grandad taught me to play chess and when we returned to England for our holiday he took me to the chess club where he played. I enjoyed spending this time with him and I particularly enjoyed being allowed to play the game machines of the day.

I enjoyed playing chess with Grandad and when he was in Australia in 1986 he bought me a chess table.

The last time I saw Grandad was in December 2000/January 2001 when he spent about six weeks over Christmas/New Year with my parents. This was after his wife, my Grandma, had died. During this visit he and I spent time talking whenever possible.

What do I remember when I think of Grandad ?

— His smile, often more of a grin.

— His sense of humour.

— Him chewing his fingers, which he did often.

The best thing that I remember about my Grandad is how he made me feel. He always made me feel very special and this is something that I will always remember.

Chris Toon (2021).

Jarrod, my third son, was born in March 1967. He has shared the following memories of his grandfather:

"I left England at a young age in 1972, several days after my fifth birthday, and although I am so glad to have had such a wonderful life in Australia my only regret is that I truly wish that I had spent more time with my grandfather and other relatives.

My earliest memory of my Grandad was when my grandparents came to Australia on holiday in 1974 and came to pick me up from school. He was a man I didn't recognise, but instantly knew I loved. I remember him teaching me to play chess and sitting on the porch smoking his pipe and chatting.

Two years later, in December 1976, I went back to the UK with my family and "met" all my extended family. We did so many things that I don't remember much individual time spent with Grandad. I do remember my grandfather sitting in his chair, pipe in hand and eyes gleaming with the happiness of having his family gathered all together. (Not sure if I never knew, but at that time I certainly never understood the journey he had taken to be where he was).

I recall being told about Granddad going to university after working in a car factory for all of his working life. I took pride in hearing about his studies and how he was able to achieve so much at an age I always considered old and I was also proud when I saw his graduation pictures in his local newspapers. I guess it was around this time that I really started to get an appreciation of the life he had lived and the person he was.

I saw my Grandad again in about November 1986. I was getting married and busy with life but I do fondly remember spending some quality time with him and marvelling at how, at his age, he was still enjoying life and making the most of what he had. My most fun memory of that visit was taking my grandfather to Maslin's Beach (a nudist beach). I then learnt once again that Grandad was sure that age wouldn't stop him doing anything.

The last time that I saw my grandfather was in late 2000 when I got to see him a few times and had the opportunity to have several conversations with him and I remember the pleasure he took in meeting my children and the looks on my childrens' faces when he was smoking his pipe and telling stories.

Although I never knew my Grandad as well as I would have liked, I always knew he was a special person I admired and loved dearly.

My grandfather taught me that you are never too old to learn, you are never too old to enjoy life, to look forward not back and most importantly "we all bleed red".

Jarrod Toon (2020).

Damian, my fourth and youngest child, was born in November 1969. When we emigrated to Australia he was only two years old. Damian has written:

"I have very few memories of my grandfather Eric Lewinsohn as my parents emigrated to Australia in 1972. However we returned to England for a holiday around 1976 and these are the first memories I have of him. Although still very young, I remember walking down to the local shop with my grandfather..... every child likes lollies (sweets).

I feel extremely fortunate that Eric, my grandad, was able to visit Australia in late 2000. He stayed at my house for about a week just after Christmas so I got to spend some quality time with my grandfather, on many evenings speaking at length with him over a scotch or two. I do not generally celebrate New Year's Eve, however, that year I was so happy to spend it with my grandfather and parents and I will always remember singing Auld Lang Syne with them as we moved into the New Year.

It goes without saying that no person should have to live through what Eric experienced during the Holocaust, losing his parents and having to flee to a foreign country. Despite this, when speaking with my grandfather in the last week of 2000, I was amazed and humbled that he held no animosity towards anyone. I remember clearly that he did not judge anyone and he accepted everyone for who they are.

To this day I am amazed by this man's humanity, empathy, and his ability to see the good in everyone. He used to say: "everyone bleeds red" and I still use this saying to this day.

I try to live my life every day by my grandfather's example of forgiveness, empathy and kindness".

Damian Toon (2020).

Two of my grandchildren have shared memories of their Great Grandad Eric:

Jeremiah, Stephen's fourth son, has written:

"The truth about the life of a man is not what he does, but the legend which he creates around himself" *Oscar Wilde.*

My memories of my great grandfather Eric are faint, and I find it hard to distinguish between what is true and what is legend. So perhaps what I share will be a little of both. For me, the story begins with a boy who escaped Germany. That boy became a man who became a father, grandfather, and great grandfather. My great grand-father. Grandad Eric. A man who was thoughtful and fond of his pipe. A man of great focus who would play chess for hours. A man who will remain a legend for generations to come."

Jeremiah Toon (2021).

Jarrod's eldest daughter, Kelly, remembers that when her Great Grandfather Eric was in Australia in December 2000 he attended her Primary School Graduation. She remembers that he always had his pipe in his hand or his mouth.

Susanne Pollak is the daughter of Dad's cousin Heinz, who escaped from Germany with my father's family and who Dad re-met in Austria in the 1970s. Dad first met Susanne in the 1980s. She has written a book about her family and the extended family. My husband and I were fortunate enough to spend time with Susanne when we visited her in 2014 whilst she was living in France. People who grow up knowing that they have grandparents, aunts, uncles and cousins cannot begin to understand the joy I felt at meeting a "new relative", a "cousin" who I did not know existed. Susanne is one year older than I am. I think that she and I have similarities and we definitely bonded as "family."

Susanne has written the following testimonial. I think that she felt as happy and excited when she met my father as I did when I met her.

ERIC LEWINSOHN

"Vienna, late 80s. He is sitting opposite me at the table of the cafe. He seems an older and friendly man. He looks a little bit like my father. He is approximately 165cm tall, thin hair, clear wide eyes and is smiling. Almost an uncle, because he is a close cousin of my father. The son of my father's favourite uncle. This favourite uncle, Uncle Fritz was the brother of Ella Lewinsohn, the mother of my father–Relatives, Family Connections......

Eric Lewinsohn had travelled from Hinckley in England to Vienna to see the place where he had spent his childhood. My father had once shown me where his favourite uncle had lived, with Blanka his wife, "Muschi" was what she was called, and with their two sons, Eric and Hans, who were both about the same age as my father's two brothers. In my father's family there was my father Heinz and his two younger brothers Max and Kurt.. My father told me that Heinz, Max and Kurt all had short names so that when they were called they would be next to you very quickly.

They all lived in Gersthof, in the 18th Vienna district. A noble area, with many elegant houses from the "Grunderzeit". The Lewinsohn Family lived in a large apartment on the third floor of one of these elegant houses which were built in the 1900s. Similar style houses formed a "U" shape inside which there were trees and lawns. There was an iron gate. Narrow walkways led to the houses. My father's family, the Pollaks, lived a few streets away further outbound.

My father told me that Eric was a close friend of the youngest cousin Kurt. They were both in the same class at school and, most likely, sat next to each other. My father said that Kurt was interested in sport and maths whilst Eric loved music, especially Opera. Unfortunately, in the early 1930s Kurt became ill with tuberculosis and inflammation of the brain and had no chance of survival.

In the 1920s, due to financial difficulties, both families moved to Berlin. In 1933 when Hitler came to power my father returned to Vienna to study medicine. My father had a good relationship with his Uncle Fritz and his cousins, and eventually they planned to escape to Belgium together. My father never spoke of any details regarding the "escape", only that it happened very late, at around Christmas 1938. It was Eric, who I met in the 1980s, who told me about it. He left his notes for a biography with information about it with me so that I could use it for my book: "Family Meeting, Tracking Clues", which was published in 1994.

My father (Heinz) tells his story:

"...Early in December 1938 I got married. I went to Berlin several times and met up with Uncle Fritz to finally put our plan into action and migrate. Migrate is a big word. It was more of a quick and costly escape. Luckily we succeeded. There were eight of us. Susi (my father's first wife*), myself, Uncle Fritz, his wife, his mother-in-law, his two sons and Uncle Ernst. We planned to hide in a lorry and cross the border at Aachen into Belgium.*

The so-called "Green Border" at Aachen was between Cologne and Eupen-Malmedy in Belgium. The "Schlepperorganisation" (smuggling ring) there had been established in 1933 and, since then, it had been very profitable. These farmers helped to smuggle Jewish refugees across the border into Belgium, for a price of course. This "helpservice" cost 1,000 marks per person plus 20% of all of the belongings which the Jews were taking with them. These "people smugglers" would have to be paid days before the actual escape. The women would hide any valuable items in their prams to get them across the border. It wasn't a big risk, not for the babies nor the "helpers". The border officers let them pass with no problems. They may have been paid as well.

The day chosen for us to cross the border was December 24ᵗʰ 1938. This date was chosen because it was thought that the border officers would be less alert whilst celebrating on Christmas Eve. Our meeting with the "escape helpers" was arranged for 5.30 pm in a cafe in Cologne. We were told to stay in small groups and to pretend that we did not know one another. Somebody was to come into the cafe and would ask for a Mr Vogel. This was the sign for the first group to leave. Every five minutes after that another group would then leave, following at a safe distance.

Half an hour passed, then one hour. Nobody came. Uncle Fritz started to get nervous. I had already drank four coffees. We could not sit there forever without raising suspicion. Finally at 6.30pm a tall man entered the cafe and called out loudly for Mr Vogel. Each group paid, left the cafe and got into a large black car. The driver told us that he was late on purpose so that the border guards had more time to get drunk.

We arrived at the German border just after 7pm. We were put into a large room. Our passports, marked with "J" and "Israel" or "Sarah" clearly showed that we were Jews. There were a few bottles on the table but the border officers were clearly not drunk. In an efficient German manner they proceeded to ask us questions. This interview lasted for almost an hour. Then they told us that we were leaving Germany legally but entering Belgium illegally. From that moment on we were stateless, without any protection should Belgium send us back.

We walked through a wooden blockade and found ourselves in "No-man's Land". It was dark and cold, the ground covered with snow. After walking for about 300 metres we heard a whistle. Three men with lanterns gestured for us to follow them. After half a kilometre or so we came to a farm. A large, friendly woman greeted us. She served us a meal, something we hadn't had for a while: warm soup, meat, vegetables, and for dessert a home-made cake.

The next day we were told that the escape was postponed and that we would have to stay on the farm for another night. December 26th was the day. At 11am two lorries specially prepared for smuggling people arrived. Between the loading space and the driver's booth there was an area where four people could fit if they were standing up and close to each other. There was a small hole in the roof to allow air to enter. We got into the lorries and they drove off. It was not comfortable. Every time there was a bump in the road we hit our heads on the roof. The journey seemed long, but after about twenty minutes we had already reached the Belgian border. I remember that I could hear the voices of the Belgian border officers very close to my ear but I didn't know what they said. The only thought I had was: don't sneeze, don't cough. Then it was all over and we drove on.

Belgium also had its borders closed, but unlike the Swiss, if we were 50km inland in the country they didn't send us back. We were taken straight to Antwerp.

Uncle Fritz travelled on to Brussels where he believed he would have better work opportunities. I only met up with him and his wife again in Southern France in an internment camp......"

That is the story of the escape of the two families, Pollak and Lewinsohn. Eric and Hans were able to escape and survive. My parents, Heinz Pollak and his second wife Ilse also survived. I was born in September 1942 whilst my parents were fleeing, hiding and living under a false name in France. In 1945 my parents and I returned to Vienna.

Fritz and Blanka Lewinsohn were murdered in the Shoah.

I am glad to have met Eric and many, many years later, in 2014, to meet his daughter Peggy. She visited me at my house in France. We realised that we are both similar, not only in looks but also in personality.

In the years after the war my family, three children and parents lived rather a lonely life in Vienna. There was only us. No grandmother nor grandfather, no uncles, aunts, cousins. They were either dead or far away. That's why the visit of Eric Lewinsohn was like a happy new beginning, an opening to other people who belong to the family and survived. For that I was, am and forever will be grateful.

Written by Susanne Pollak. (2020).

The final testimonial in this chapter is from a lady who remembers Dad from when she was a child and who later became a member of our family.

From Sheena Lewinsohn-Marston:

"My first memories of Eric are as a child of about ten. He used to collect what my mother called "the pools" money – we never won – he always had a smile and a cheery hello.

Later I married his grandson and he became a friend and a mentor. I say mentor as it was he who encouraged me to return to education and realise my dream of going to university and, ultimately, becoming a registered nurse.

Brian and I had three daughters and Eric always insisted we really needed a son, however that wasn't to be so he had to be content with the girls. I'm sure he didn't really mind.

Our girls remember him fondly and they remember him coming into their schools to talk about his life during the war. He was determined to document the struggle of the Jewish population, a lesson that needs to be told over and over.

Eric used to tell me that we can do anything we want to in life if we try hard enough, broaden our horizons, strive to do the best we can and to live and let live".

Written by Sheena Lewinsohn-Marston (2020).

When I received this testimonial from Sheena I assured her that Dad would have wanted her to have a boy only to ensure that the name Lewinsohn did not die out. Sheena's words show how Dad tried to inspire people to pursue their dreams and achieve their potential.

ESTHER'S RESEARCH

My grandchildren are fourth generation survivors of the Holocaust. During 2020 my youngest grandchild, Esther, chose to question and research the impact of the Holocaust on following generations of Jewish communities as a school assignment.

In order to do this Esther carried out intensive research including reading her great grandfather, Eric Lewinsohn's autobiography "The Journey Back" Part Two, and studying many other printed sources as well as creating a survey for relevant second and third generation survivors to complete.

It was Esther's decision to complete a school assignment based on the Holocaust that was the catalyst that determined me to publish my father's story. I will always be grateful to Esther for this.

With her permission I will now share Esther's completed assignment paper.

School assignment completed by Esther Toon in 2020:

To what extent, did the holocaust impact the following generations of Jewish Communities?

The Holocaust was a detrimental time for all Jewish Communities, and the outcome of the Holocaust continues to impact the lives of the following generations to this day. Survivors were left traumatised as they attempted to piece their lives back together and forget the horrors they had experienced. Broken Jewish families tried to bring themselves back together only to find the people they loved most were now gone. The mistreatment of Jewish communities during the Holocaust continues to pain the second generation who grew up with grieving parents, missing family members as well as the passed down trauma they experienced growing up. Similar to the second generation, even though the third generation did not experience the

307

Holocaust first hand they are still trying to process the past events that shaped their family's historical routes. It continues to remain difficult for Jewish Communities to process the pain that their ancestors endured, however it has created a deep sense of empathy in the hearts of many of the following generations of Jewish Communities.

First Generation Jewish communities who experienced the Holocaust first hand were immensely impacted by its effects. The Holocaust took place during World War Two, it was a period of discrimination for many different people groups, including Jewish communities. Adolf Hitler; leader of the German Nazi party was responsible for mass killings of Jewish people through the use of gas chambers. In 1945, Allied troops entered the brutal concentration camps to discover many human corpses, bones and ashes testifying to this. This day is known as Liberation and marks the end of the Holocaust. After the Liberation in 1945, the remaining Jewish Community began to rebuild their lives. To reunite with family, settle down and try to forget. However, Jewish communities found this very hard to do with missing family members, the effects of anti-Semitism and emotional scars and disorders which came as a result of the Holocaust. Many Jews found it difficult to return home due to the anti semitism which was still persistent throughout parts of Europe. On the return home many were greeted with violent anti Jewish riots, which in numerous cases resulted in the deaths of many Jews. Jewish communities were spread across the world before coming together to build the nation of Israel. Six million European Jews were killed in concentration camps which left many children orphaned. First generation survivor; Eric Lewinsohn states that *"he thinks he died that day. He received the last letter from his parents." (Lewinsohn, n.d.).* On top of the grief many survivors were coming to terms with, Jewish Communities also struggled with a psychological disorder which we now identify as Post Traumatic Stress Disorder, making the trauma of the Holocaust not end at Liberation but last for a life time. Jewish communities felt as though they had their whole lives robbed from them. Regine Donner, Jewish survivor of the Holocaust expressed that "*she had to keep her Jewishness hidden, secret, never to be revealed on penalty of death. She missed out on her childhood and the best of her adolescent years. She was robbed of her name, her religion, her zionist idealism.*" (Psychological Pain of Holocaust Still Haunts Survivors, 2020). Eric Lewinsohn supports this speculation in stating that he felt as though "*the best years of his youth were spent looking over his shoulder.*" (Lewinsohn, n.d.). In many ways, first generation Jewish Communities were tremendously impacted in negative ways with missing family members, the effects of anti-semitism and emotional scars and disorders which came as a result of the Holocaust.

Even though the second generation of Jewish Communities did not experience the Holocaust first hand they can still "*be deeply affected both negatively and positively—by the horrific events their parents experienced.*" (How Did the Holocaust Affect the Next Generation?, 2020) These children can be impacted by the Holocaust in that they may have difficulty in their development whereas others may gain from their parents experiences and learn healthy coping mechanisms. Some survivors of the Holocaust talked about the Holocaust too much with their children causing it be very overwhelming and extreme, many others however did not speak about it at all making it difficult for their children to understand and process their traumatic family history. Either way these children were exposed to traumatised parents, Experts in Traumatic Stress state that, "*children of Holocaust survivors may be at higher risk for psychiatric symptoms including depression, anxiety, and PTSD*" (How Did the Holocaust Affect the Next Generation?, 2020). Sinclair; second generation survivor, states that she "*suffers from memories of trauma from events that she didn't even experience.*"(Sinclair, 2020) The Holocaust also deprived the second generation of growing up with lots of family around them as many lost their Grandparents and other family member during the Holocaust. Deryn Lewinsohn, second generation Holocaust survivor states that, "*she found it extremely distressing growing up and not knowing what happened to her grand-parents.*"*(Lewinsohn, 2020).* Although second generations of Jewish communities after the Holocaust have suffered in many ways they have also been able to become more sympathetic towards other people experiencing discrimination. Margaret (Peggy) Toon, second generation Holocaust survivor supports this in stating that she *"hates inequality. She believes that nobody is better or worse than anyone else. We are all individuals, we are all different and we are all equal."* *(Toon, 2020).* Deryn Lewinsohn also confirms that she *"has developed a deep sense of right and wrong, love and hate. She was brought up to think very deeply about how her actions might affect other people." (Lewinsohn, 2020)* The Second Generation of Jewish Communities after the Holocaust were affected in negative and positive ways. Even though their family history is quite horrific and leaves them with missing family members, passed down trauma and at a higher risk for psychiatric symptoms, second generation Jewish communities have been able to grow from their pasts and help others who are experiencing discrimination similar to their ancestors.

The third generation of Jewish Communities after the Holocaust have also been impacted by their family history. Eva Foleman a therapist who is closely related to the topic states that *"Grandchildren of survivors grew up at a time in society when Holocaust survivors had regained their sense of dignity...We have a transformation from shame to pride in the third generation." (Nathan-Kazis and The Forward Association, 2020)* Their family history is "a part of their identity" (Toon, 2020), and even though their families have begun to heal and cope with their horrific past it is still a significant event which continues to shape their lives. The world is constantly changing and is in a completely different place to what is was during the Holocaust. The third generation of Jewish Communities still struggle to come to terms with the legacy of their ancestors, however it has helped them grow into the people that they are today. Stephen Toon, Third Gener-ation Holocaust Survivor states that *"Despite the fact that there are now memorials and many other things put in place to recognise this part of our history, it still doesn't even begin to make up for the things that Jewish Communities went through during the Holocaust"* (Toon, 2020). The Third Generation of Jewish Communities after the Holocaust have been impacted by their family's history as it is an important part of their identity which should continue to be recognised.

The Holocaust impacted the following Generations of Jewish Communities in many different ways. Survivors themselves lost many family members and suffered the ongoing effects of anti-semitism as well as psychological disorders. The second generation were also highly affected in that they also grew up without certain family members as well as passed down trauma. The third generation is also still affected by the Holocaust as it plays a main role in their family history. Despite the pain that the following generations of Jewish Holocaust survivors did endure they have grown a large-scale empathy for other experiencing discrimination.

Bibliography:
Primary Sources:

Lewinsohn, E., n.d. The Following 40 years.

Toon, S., 2020. Third Generation Jewish Holocaust Survivor.

Lewinsohn, D., 2020. Second Generation Jewish Holocaust Survivor.

Toon, M., 2020. Second Generation Jewish Holocaust Survivor.

Secondary Sources:

TheHolocaustExplained.org. 2020. How Did Survivors Rebuild Their Lives? – The Holocaust Explained: Designed For Schools. [online] Available at: <https://www.theholocaustexplained.org/survival-and-legacy/rebuilding-lives-case-studies/> [Accessed 24 May 2020].

ThoughtCo. 2020. How Did The Holocaust Affect The Next Generation?. [online] Available at: <https://www.thoughtco.com/

holocaust-effects-on-children-of-survivors-2076561>   [Accessed 24 May 2020].

Ushmm.org. 2020. *Life In Shadows: Hidden Children And The Holocaust.* [online] Available at: <https://www.ushmm.org/exhibition/hidden-children/insideX/> [Accessed 24 May 2020].

Nathan-Kazis, J. and The Forward Association, I., 2020. *Can Holocaust Trauma Affect 'Third Generation'?.* [online] The Forward. Available at: <https://forward.com/news/162030/can-holocaust-trauma-affect-third-generation/> [Accessed 24 May 2020].

https://www.apa.org. 2020. *Psychological Pain Of Holocaust Still Haunts Survivors.* [online] Available at: <https://www.apa.org/news/press/releases/2010/09/holocaust-survivors> [Accessed 24 May 2020].

Sinclair, M., 2020. *Understanding Second Generation Holocaust Survivors.* [online] The Canadian Jewish News. Available at: <https://www.cjnews.com/news/canada/second-generation-challenges> [Accessed 24 May 2020].

Encyclopedia.ushmm.org. 2020. *The Aftermath Of The Holocaust.* [online] Available at: <https://encyclopedia.ushmm.org/content/en/article/the-aftermath-of-the-holocaust> [Accessed 24 May 2020].

the Guardian. 2020. *The Trauma Of Second-Generation Holocaust Survivors.* [online] Available at: <https://www.theguardian.com/lifeandstyle/2014/mar/15/trauma-second-generation-holocaust-survivors> [Accessed 24 May 2020].

Bbc.co.uk. 2020. *What Was The Holocaust? - CBBC Newsround.* [online] Available at: <https://www.bbc.co.uk/newsround/16690175> [Accessed 24 May 2020].

Also with Esther's permission I am now including Esther's survey questions together with my actual responses to these questions:

HOLOCAUST SURVEY

Q. How have you been personally connected with the Holocaust?

A. My paternal grandparents, Fritz and Blanka Lewinsohn, were killed in Auschwitz in August 1942.

Q. How has the Holocaust affected your family as a whole?

A. In addition to the death of both of my father's parents the Holocaust affected our family by forcing the dispersion of a close extended family. Both Fritz and Blanca had siblings and before the terror enforced on the Jews by the Nazis, the extended families would interact regularly. The fear of the power of Hitler, particularly after Kristallnacht in 1938, forced adult family members to seek safe refuge for their individual family members, which, in general, meant escaping from Germany by whatever means possible, both legal and illegal. This meant that the extended family became scattered across Europe, England and the USA, thereby losing contact with one another. Some were never found after the war.

It also affected the family as a whole by robbing family members born after the family left Germany from the opportunity of knowing other family members and also, obviously, the older family members do not know the people born after the family left Germany.

My father's parents were quite comfortable financially. The Nazi regime destroyed this by making it difficult for them to work in first Vienna and then Berlin. When they escaped illegally they obviously had to leave possessions behind in Berlin, only being able to take what they could carry.

My paternal grandmother's mother, Rosa Hahn, was left to fend for herself after my grandparents were deported to Auschwitz. This must have been extremely frightening for this elderly Jewish lady, being forced to be alone in a foreign country, in constant fear of being sent back to Germany, to the horrors of the Holocaust.

Q. How has it affected you personally?

A. This is a difficult question for me to answer. First and foremost I have to acknowledge that if it were not for Hitler's regime then I would not be here, as it is only because of Hitler's persecution of the Jews that my father's family left Berlin and my father was allowed into England where he met my mother.

The Holocaust deprived me of family. It ensured that I could never know my paternal grandparents. It also deprived me of growing up with aunties, uncles and cousins.

My father didn't speak of the Holocaust when my siblings and I were children, so I did not know anything about it until I was a teenager, therefore, as a child, the Holocaust did not have any effect on me that I realised. As I have grown older I have become very interested in the events of the Holocaust and the events leading up to it. I read books about the Holocaust and watch movies and I would like to get my father's book, which is an autobiography of his life, published.

I have visited Berlin with my father and I have seen where he lived and I have been to the school that he attended. My husband and I visited Sachenhausen Concentration Camp with my parents. My husband and I have also visited Dachau Concentration Camp and Auschwitz where, sadly, my grandparents were murdered. We have also visited the Anne Frank House in Amsterdam.

I would like to see Holocaust Studies compulsory in schools, so that the world never forgets what people can do to other people if they are egged on by someone who has an insane obsession.

Personally, in a word, or perhaps two words, the Holocaust makes me sad and angry.

I hold my father in great esteem. He survived the trauma of Nazi hate and abuse of Jews prior to the war, escaped Nazi Germany illegally in the false wall of a truck, landed in England at nineteen years of age, alone and unable to speak a word of English. He brought up myself and my siblings without showing any signs of the traumas that he had experienced. He always showed love to his children. I don't think that I could have had a better father.

Q. Have you personally experienced any discrimination first hand as a result of your beliefs or heritage?

A. No. I don't think so. Definitely none that I can recall.

Q. How do you think that the Holocaust has effected Judaism? Do you think it has had an effect on people's modern views of the religion?

A. I think that the Holocaust has made people throughout the world realise that hate towards any group of people can be encouraged and grow until unbelievable atrocities can be inflicted on to the hated group. The Holocaust has probably made people more aware of the Jews and Judaism and, in turn, this has made the Jews and their beliefs more noticed and more accepted. I think that, in general, modern views are more accepting of the differing beliefs and opinions of groups of people including Jews and Judaism.

Q. Have the effects of the Holocaust changed the way in which you view the world?

A. Another question that is difficult for me to answer. I don't know how I would have viewed the world if the Holocaust had not occurred or if the Holocaust had not affected my family.

I know I detest the idea of war. I hate inequality. I believe that nobody is better or worse than anyone else. We are all individuals, we are all different and we are all equal.

I have great empathy for migrants and refugees. So many people flee from living in fear in their homeland but they are not readily accepted as refugees needing a safe haven. My father was a refugee twice, first when he left Germany and entered Belgium illegally with his family and again when he entered England legally. Several family members were refugees, moving to the USA and within Europe. How could I not sympathise with refugees?

I also detest racism. We live on a small planet called Earth. If we were to be attacked by aliens from another planet I am sure that all nations on Earth would join together as one and forget about racial and religious differences.

As my father used to say:

If I cut myself, my blood is red.

If a black man cuts himself, his blood is red.

There is no such thing as race.

There is only one race – the human race.

Q. Can you recall any ways in which it affected your father when you were growing up?

A. When I was a child my father did not speak of his past so I did not really see any effect of the Holocaust other than not having relatives. As I have said, my father was a loving, caring parent who worked hard to support his family.

As an adult, my father told me that he found it very difficult not to absolutely hate the German people. The first time that my sister took a German friend home Dad found it very difficult. I do think that, over time, he got over this hatred to a certain extent as he became more involved with German speaking people.

Dad became a British citizen as soon as he could. He told me that he felt British when he started to dream in English, rather than German.

In retirement Dad taught German and he also went back to school. He went on to university and graduated in German and Sociology and he then successfully completed a Masters Degree. He did this in honour of his parents who died in Auschwitz.

Dad also spent time in his retirement educating people about the Holocaust. He gave talks and lectures to adult groups and in schools. At one particular school in England Dad gave his time on a regular basis to teach/talk with senior students about the Holocaust. He set up an award system to recognise excellent work by students on the Holocaust. He left money in his will to enable these awards to continue.

I think that, whilst I was growing up, Dad was a typical father of the 1940s/50s. He worked hard to provide for his family and he ignored his own feelings and emotions re the Holocaust and its effects on his life. After he retired, and his children were independent adults, he had time to dwell on his past and to honour his parents and, in some ways deal with the horrors that he had experienced because of Hitler's Nazi regime and the Holocaust.

Q. Even though you did not experience the Holocaust first hand would you say that it has had an influence/effect over your life? If so, how has it done so?

A. As previously stated, I think we are all equal. Different, individual and equal. Obviously my life has been influenced and affected by the way I was brought up. I had two loving, caring parents. I think I was always closer to my father than I was to my mother. As he must have been affected by the Holocaust the effects on him may have been passed on to me in some ways. However, as Dad didn't talk about the Holocaust or the war when I was a child, the fact that I know that my family suffered so much during the Holocaust is, I am sure, the main reason that I want to learn as much as I can about the horrors of the Holocaust, and I want the world to remember and never forget. An atrocity such as the Holocaust must never be allowed to happen again.

Q. If so, why do you think that the Holocaust still affects Jewish families today?

A. There are still survivors of the Holocaust alive among us. Obviously they could never forget the horrors that they endured, and this is bound to affect how they feel about many aspects of life, e.g. their belief in God, their feelings towards the German people as a whole. They must realise how precious life and family are. They probably have flashbacks and nightmares. The atrocities that survivors endured themselves and the horrific actions and behaviours they witnessed would have, in my opinion, affected them for life. We must remember that, after World War 2 there was no such thing as grief counselling. PTSD was not even heard of. Every survivor has had to cope and deal with their own issues.

The effects on descendants of survivors would vary I imagine. It may, to some extent, depend on how much the Holocaust has been spoken about within the family and the manner in which their family survivor dealt with their personal life story.

So many Jews lost some or all of their family and this must still affect their feelings and behaviour today.

So many Jewish families today must have links to persons who were directly affected by the Holocaust that I think it would be impossible for them not to be affected to some degree.

It is often questioned whether Jews are members of a Jewish race of people or "merely" people of all races who believe in the beliefs and customs of Judaism. Whichever is correct, the Jews are human beings and I think that it would be impossible for the horrors of the Holocaust to happen to any group of people without it affecting that group's emotional feelings and behaviour to varying degrees.

End of survey.

Recently, about one year after she completed the assignment, I asked Esther three questions relating to her choice of topic. Her are the questions and Esther's responses:

– Why did you choose this topic?

"I chose this topic because I had always known that it was part of my family history that I never had the chance to learn about before in detail".

– Did being a fourth generation survivor influence your decision?

"I was definitely influenced by being a fourth generation survivor and think that it is super important to be educated about your own family history".

– Did completing this assignment have any effect on how you think or feel in any way? If so how?

"I was definitely influenced after completion of the assignment about the realness of what Jewish people had to go through as I now had a personal connection to it".

I find it interesting that Esther was affected enough by knowing that she was a descendant of a survivor to want to research and learn more about the ongoing effects of this terrible time in history and also that by learning more she now feels more connected to it.

A MEMENTO OF MY DAD, BY DERYN

Earliest memories

I began this contribution to my sister Peggy's book prior to the discovery by my son, Adam, of the interviews that Dad recorded for the Shoah Foundation in February 1997. With these interviews Dad has added quite considerably to his own life story.

But until then, like the rest of the family, I was left wondering why Dad ended his fascinating written autobiography so abruptly, or whether maybe he continued it but never had the rest of it typed up. With this in mind, as his youngest surviving daughter, and being the child that spent the most amount of time at home during the years that followed on, I was probably best placed to contribute in some way to the continuation of his story.

It is clear from his memoirs the pride he felt as each of his children were born, but they only reach as far as 1947, when he and Mum married, and they moved into their first home together with Ralph, John, Peggy and Stuart.

I came along in 1951, so the first of their legitimate children (an amusing family anecdote repeated many times over the years). The first, and one of the most significant, 'memories' I shared with Dad was created the very moment I was born on a very harsh January evening, as it was Dad himself who brought me into the world, owing to the absence of the midwife, who was unable to get to us on time due to the thick snow covering the ground that night. Dad was always extremely proud of the fact that he delivered me, was the first person ever to see me, and I think we both believed that the strong bond between us was forged right then – I suppose you could say it was love at first sight? It wasn't until I read his aforementioned autobiography that there appears to have been a very similar experience with Peggy's birth!

There was a six-year gap between Stuart and myself, and though I can't speak for Mum, I know that Dad was delighted to have another daughter to fuss over. I always think of him as a very loving father and stepfather but I know the boys would argue, and there is no denying, that he was generally warmer and less strict towards the girls in the family. Looking back, I think Mum made up for this by often seeming to favour the boys, though generally she treated us all equally. She never referred to Ralph as her stepson, nor did I ever consider either Ralph or John as half brothers. For most of my life I thought of us as just one big, happy family, and home was my haven.

The first and no doubt most significant time this was tested came with the loss of our younger sister Angela when I was five. Angela was born in November 1954 but sadly suffered from Down's Syndrome, and was quite poorly throughout her short life which tragically ended when she was just sixteen months old. My memories of her are rather hazy, as I was so young, but I can still recall the worry and sadness in the home that surrounded her illness and then the overwhelming grief that descended on my parents when she died. Of course, at such a young age, I wouldn't really have a full under-standing of just how tragic and life-changing her death must have been for them. It is only since becoming a parent myself that I can even attempt to relate in any way at all to what such a loss must have meant.

Mum went out to work not long after Angela's death, having previously been a hosiery 'outworker', and I always had the impression that this was a deliberate change to escape from the sadness of being at home alone every day. Growing up I don't remember us talking about Angela very much as a family, and it came as quite a shock when one of the friends Mum had worked with told me many years later, at Mum's funeral, that "she never got over Angela's death". I know that several times over the years I wanted to ask both parents more about her and how their grief had impacted on our lives, but somehow I was always afraid of opening up old wounds. For many years I carried the feeling deep inside that I should have been able to console and make things better for them, even at such a young age.

Despite this tragic event, I recall those early years as very happy ones, especially when I was in the secure bosom of the family. School life wasn't always great, and there were times when bullying and other things, such as embarrassment at not being from as wealthy a family as some of my school mates, reared their ugly heads, but I know that I always felt very closely protected and extremely loved by both parents, which even then I recognised was worth more than anything money could provide.

High days and holidays

Some of my happiest memories are of family summer holidays during my childhood. Our annual trip away to the seaside – always the same fixed fortnight in July, when the firm Dad worked for closed for the summer break – was a huge highlight for all the family. Dad would sow the seeds of excitement each spring, once he and Mum had agreed where we would go that particular year, by taking a trip to the chosen seaside town to find and reserve what he felt was the best available bed, breakfast and evening meal accommodation on what must have been a fairly tight budget.

Because we lived in the Midlands, and since neither parent ever drove or owned a car, we would travel to some point east, west, north or south by train, always beginning by carrying a multitude of luggage, on foot, to Hinckley station. The journey to resort and back was also a significant part of the ritual and often quite eventful, as you can imagine, but it was generally good fun, despite the chaos. Providing this holiday for his family every year was very important to Dad, and I believe he took great pride in finding the best accommod-ation for us that he could. He was very mindful of the fact that this was the one short break in every year when Mum didn't have to get up, sort us all out for school and work (including herself), as well as undertaking a myriad of household chores and providing three cooked meals for her family on a daily basis.

I have no really negative memories of these times - come rain or shine we would find interesting things to occupy ourselves. Most of the time was spent on the beach or in the sea of course, whenever possible, but there would also be penny arcades and trips to the cinema laid on if the weather deteriorated sufficiently. And when I was older, visits to the theatre, shows on the pier and so on would round the days off perfectly.

Two outstanding and contrasting memories of these holidays that I have are the time I accidentally poured a bottle full of sea water down the back of a totally innocent stranger, relaxing in his deckchair (of course I thought I was playing a prank on Dad), and the other was when I got carried quite a way out to sea on a lilo, because I had ignored Dad's advice to stay near the shore, and had to be rescued by a stronger, more muscular swimmer than Dad, as the tide was carrying me out quite rapidly. If I say that it was the latter rather than the former incident that caused Dad to smack me on the one and only occasion in my whole life that I recall him doing so, it may seem odd but to me not surprising. I remember him almost in tears berating me because he was so worried that I was going to drown! When I read in Dad's autobiography about the boat accident he had as a young child it reminded me of this incident and I wonder if at the time my 'near miss' brought memories of his own brush with death flooding back.

Swimming is one of the important features of my life that I always associate with Dad, because he taught me (and probably all of us?) how to swim, often taking us to pools and lidos at weekends. He wasn't a particularly strong swimmer, but he enjoyed it and thought it was a vital skill for all kids to learn. He was right of course! It soon became a favourite pastime of mine and even now as a regular, almost daily, swimmer I often think of my original teacher with great fondness when I'm splashing up and down in the sea or local pool.

No doubt there must at times have been other problems and stresses associated with these holidays, but if so they were always well hidden from me, and my overall feeling is that these were some of happiest times in life for every member of the family. That annual break was of huge importance to both parents, who worked endlessly and extremely hard all year round to make sure we could always afford it, and no matter how financially stretched they must sometimes have been, as far as I'm aware the idea of missing our regular holiday was just not entertained.

Other strong memories of childhood are associated with Christmas. Again both parents loved this time of year, and the preparation that went into making it so special for all of us was second to none. I can't speak for my siblings but I always felt our parents' determination to buy wonderful gifts for us every year, hide them so cleverly and keep the magic of Father Christmas alive for so long was very admirable considering there were so many of us, such a restriction on space and so little spare cash.

One of my fondest recollections around Christmas is how each year, for a period when I was quite young, the company Dad worked for would provide free of charge for employees and their families a party and a trip to the pantomime. I can remember looking forward to this with great excitement each year, as did both parents. Our day would start with an early bus ride into Coventry, a visit to Santa's grotto followed by lunch in Owen and Owen department store, before going on to the panto matinee and then the party. I will always look back on that as a truly wonderful and magical start to Christmas.

There was also the annual ordering and collecting of the turkey – or sometimes goose – by Dad from a local farm. Plucking it of its feathers was also his responsibility, which I think I reluctantly helped with once or twice. I may be mistaken but I think this was probably unusual compared to many families, as would have been the parcels of unfamiliar European food sent by Dad's brother or perhaps other relatives in London. Added to this was the excitement of buying, bringing home and decorating the Christmas tree each year, always a real one. There were no fairy lights in those days, only real candles burning in their clip-on metal holders - a very dangerous ritual when I look back on it now! There was then the traditional playing (by Peggy on the piano) and singing of carols (some of them in German) beside the tree. Christmas was truly magical in our house, and whilst I recognise that in many ways we were no exception, I can't help feeling somehow it had a more exotic and 'foreign' flavour for us due to the influence of Dad's background.

Family ties

While reminiscing about relatives of Dad's whom I barely ever knew, I feel I must mention my half brother Peter. I have only the faintest memory of meeting him when he once came to stay with us. Unimaginable now to realise that Dad and his second son hardly ever saw each other, and that Peter's older brother Ralph, who lived with us, had the same virtually non-existent relationship with his birth mother. When Dad and his first wife separated, they each had custody of one child but I believe that Peter didn't live with his mother for long and that eventually he was raised by two aunts. My vague memory is that there was a falling out between his aunts and my parents after this stay, and as a consequence the visit was not repeated. I certainly don't recall ever seeing him again. I know Peter upheld a strong Jewish faith and that after a separation of many years, Dad was reunited with him in later life and was invited to attend the Bar Mitzvah of one of Peter's sons or grandsons. Although I never fully understood the reasons why, this was a short-lived reunion. I contacted Peter by email when Dad died and he sent condolences but didn't come to the funeral and sadly has not responded to a couple of attempts on my behalf since to reconnect.

Peter's older brother Ralph played a much larger part in our lives. There was an eleven-year age gap between us, so although we didn't share a lot of common interests, he was an ever-present figure in my childhood and we were always fond of each other. Unlike my other siblings, he lived with us on and off through much of his adult life, so in some ways he occupies a more prominent place in my recollections. Sadly, from his teenage years, Ralph suffered with quite severe mental health issues, in a time when much less was understood about this area of illness, and treatments were often harsh. Over a number of years I remember clearly visiting him during several hospital admissions. He would undergo a regime of unpleasant treatments, return home, and then after what seemed like quite a short period of recovery, the cycle would be repeated again. I know that Dad particularly struggled to comprehend the complexities of Ralph's illness – this was after all still a period when mental illness was seen as a weakness by many and carried a lot of stigma. Because of his strong work ethic, Dad felt that if only Ralph could get a job and stick to it, all his troubles would be over! This led to some difficult times at home which I don't want to dwell on here, but suffice it to say that there was enough love in the family to support him through most of these episodes, and that Mum's nurturing instincts never failed.

Finally I would like to mention briefly here Dad's brother, Uncle Jack, his wife Ruth and their daughters Bianca and Michelle, our only first cousins. I don't have any memories of them before they moved to live in Canada, but they came to visit us once every couple of years. They would rent a flat in a very prestigious block in Pimlico, London and I recall these visits as times of great excitement and extravagance, as Uncle Jack was comparatively wealthy and would spoil us. Bianca came to live and work in London for a couple of years when I was in my early twenties and we became quite close for a while.

Dad and his brother Jack in later life

I suppose it wasn't until reading Dad's memoirs that I could appreciate all that they had been through together as children and young men, nor just how close a bond there was between them, but I do vividly recall standing on a railway platform, seeing them off at the end of one of these visits, with Jack and Dad hugging each other tightly and renewing their promise to honour their parents' final wish that they should remain close and strong, and ensure that they lived happy and fulfilling lives.

Learning about Dad's story and early parental influences on me

As Dad explained in his autobiography and later interviews, he did not speak a great deal about his Jewish origins or what was actually the very recent history of losing his parents. My first awareness of a Jewish connection was when I was taunted one day as I walked home from school. I must have been about six or seven years old. A few of the kids that lived in the same street, who until then I'd considered to be my friends, were out playing, and as I walked by one of them called out, "There's the Jew girl", followed by a tirade of insults. I had no idea what they meant so went home and asked. This was the first time that Dad explained his background to me, but I was so young that I don't recall exactly how either their taunts or his story affected me at the time, except that from then on I perceived myself as somehow different from my peers.

Dad speaks of tolerance and fairness in his memoirs, and offers advice to others on anti-racism. I certainly acquired my strong belief in equality from both parents and there was never any question of racism being an issue for us as a family. I remember Dad's mantra in those days was "Always feel free to do what makes you happy as long as it brings no harm to others", and there was a deep sense of 'live and let live' instilled in me, which I've upheld until this day.

I feel extremely proud that he managed to engender these beliefs in us considering all the harm that had been done to him and his family, and not forgetting that his hatred of Germans for many years following the war didn't quite sit with his other views on racism. Was it because this basic principle of 'live and let live' had been so profoundly shattered by the Nazis that he never lost his conviction that justice should be done and the arbitrators brought to trial? Fortunately his attitude to the German race as a whole softened over the years as the realisation dawned on him that the younger generation were not responsible for the sins of their fathers.

Looking back, I think this mitigation started when I began to study German at school. This was certainly the first time I remember being aware of his reticence to speak German and his dislike of all things Germanic, though after a short while he couldn't resist the temptation to help me with homework. I think at this point, despite all the years of trying hard to improve his English and feeling like he truly belonged in his adoptive country, he was reminded of the fact that German was his native language and that it would be strange if his daughter started to learn it and he didn't share his knowledge with her. As I later went on to specialise in French and Classics rather than German, I think it's a pity that I missed out on the chance to become bilingual.

Dad making friends and enjoying life

At this point in my life, my early teens, as I began to study languages in depth, and we started to travel abroad, Dad told me more about his story and his escape from Germany, but he always ended any conversation by saying he didn't want to dwell on it. Perfecting his knowledge of the English language, becoming a British citizen and looking forward rather than back was very important to him. Unlike many refugees and immigrants, from the moment he arrived in England, he was committed to being integrated and embracing everything about his adoptive country. He speaks passionately and eloquently about this in his own recollections so no need for me to say more.

Although he maintained some contact with other members of the German/Jewish community, mostly in London, he no longer observed the few Jewish customs that he had previously adhered to. Being surrounded by English speaking friends, family and work mates no doubt obliged him, but also helped him, to learn the language faster than he might otherwise have done. He often told me that he knew he was really British when he started to dream 'in English', but he always maintained a very unique and wonderful accent, which was a blend of Germanic, London and East Midlands vernaculars, and along with his incessant pipe smoking, became a 'trademark' characteristic.

Along with a desire to be accepted and seen as British, Dad was extremely sociable and very keen to make friends. When I was around six years old, he and Mum started to have what was at first a fairly modest social life, both together and separately. Dad would enjoy spending time at his beloved Labour Club, whereas Mum not only discovered the pleasure of a night out with the girls, but also what became her very significant talents as a darts player! Friday nights out at the pub together soon became the norm, often followed by nightcaps and card games with groups of friends back at our house. I believe these activities played an important part in the lives of our extremely hard-working parents, allowing them a well-deserved escape from the daily grind as well as the opportunity to let their hair down and increase their circle of friends.

When I was older, their geniality and generosity were also widely extended to my friends. It must have been a novelty for my parents having me live at home for so much longer than my siblings who had all married and/or moved out at quite an early age. For me, enjoying a social life as a relatively impecunious teenage schoolgirl, before I was old enough to take on a Saturday job, was never going to be easy, but it could have been so much worse if I hadn't had such outgoing and tolerant parents. They never seemed to tire of company or object to me filling the house with friends, and our home was undoubtedly one of the few where the parents were almost always out themselves on a Saturday night and where there were no younger children to take into consideration or babysit!

Even if Mum and Dad were unusually home, a weekend evening would frequently find a gathering of several friends in my bedroom, where I had been allowed to paint the walls dark green 'to create the right atmosphere', and where we would play music, dance, and have many deep and meaningful conversations into the early hours! Due to poor availability of public transport this might occasionally lead to one or two friends staying over, but far from complaining, the next morning Mum would happily cook them breakfast while Dad enjoyed chatting to them about current affairs.

I genuinely believe that both parents loved getting to know my friends, and this was very much reciprocated. Many of them look back fondly on these years and love to reminisce about the hospitality they received. I think our family was something of a novelty compared with their own and most others that they were acquainted with, certainly as far as tolerance and broad mindedness was concerned. I imagine that some of this is due to the fact that I was the youngest child in our home, whereas many of my friends had younger siblings, and at this stage in life my parents had more time to get to know them. Sixty years on these friends still speak fondly of Dad's unwavering friendliness, his 'cool' accent, interest in education and politics, as well as Mum's famous obsession with sport, culinary skills and 'trademark' Woodbine dangling from her lips as she busied herself in the kitchen!

All these years later I feel immensely proud of their joint generosity, gregariousness and enjoyment of life. I probably didn't appreciate these things as much or realise how unusual they were at the time but their legacy speaks for itself. I realise how very fortunate I was to live with this specially gifted couple and now know that my own sociable, outgoing nature is a direct result of what they bestowed on me.

Sharing Dad's passions

I would say this period in my life, during those famously metamorphic, swinging sixties, as I moved into adulthood and became ever more increasingly aware of political and current affairs - especially issues around poverty, racism, nuclear disarmament, freedom of speech, etc - was the time when Dad had the most influence on my life and when we grew the closest. Because of the age gap between my siblings and me, I was the only one still living at home with my parents by the late 1960s. Mum didn't really share his political allegiance and so I think he was delighted to have another adult to discuss and share his interests and beliefs with. These weren't always calm or peaceful conversations, indeed at times there were heated arguments, but we shared the same basic principles about fairness, equality, and tolerance towards others.

Dad was a dedicated member of the Labour Party and from an early age he would take us on regular visits to the local Labour Club, although for many years we were obliged to sit outside with a bottle of pop and a packet of crisps. When I was old enough I started to accompany him there voluntarily and gradually found that more and more I was sharing his political beliefs.

It's worth mentioning here, because it was such an important part of his life for many years, that throughout the sixties Dad was a huge supporter of Harold Wilson's government and it wasn't difficult to understand why. He felt strongly affiliated to so many of the social reforms that Wilson achieved, in education, health, housing, gender equality, price controls, pensions, provisions for disabled people and child poverty. This time of political change had a huge influence on his working life too, encouraging him to become a shop steward and an assertive campaigner for workers' rights. I remember vividly his shock and dismay when Wilson got defeated in 1970; he was in tears as we walked home from the club that night.

Around this time, again thanks to Dad, I started to develop an interest in classical music. Until now I had always thought of myself as a sixties 'rock chick' and fully embraced the rapid development in pop music. This was a genre of music that Dad could never see the point of, let alone enjoy, but given the fact that my friends and I were completely engrossed in it makes it even more surprising and complimentary to him that he was able to persuade me to take an interest in classical music, which was one of the great loves of his life. Even now I can picture his broad smile and excitement when I asked him to recommend a few classical pieces that might appeal to a beginner like me. He took great pride in and gave considerable thought to this, and still now I remember the three recommendations that were the result of this contemplation: Dvorak's New World Symphony, Tchaikovsky's 1812 Overture and Beethoven's Symphony No.6. In fact somewhere I still have the vinyl LPs that I bought then and played dozens of times. Although I never became as deeply interested in classical music as Dad was, or would have liked me to be, I've continued to appreciate and enjoy it, and am grateful to him for broadening my cultural horizons.

No doubt these shared interests, together with the associated education and discussions we engaged in, both together and separately, were a huge influence on my life going forward. Along with the newly acquired political interests this was a particularly formative time for me as far as social consciousness was concerned. As I began to learn and understand more about Dad's life history, his beliefs and ideals, the more aware I became of the many injustices and inequalities in the world, and developed the desire to become involved in any kind of campaign that might help to improve things.

There is one particular incident in my adolescence that illustrates this perfectly and had such a profound effect on us both that I have never forgotten it. On our first holiday abroad together, to Italy in the mid sixties, I encountered my first ever experience of destitution. We came across several beggars by the roadside; I became tearful and pleaded with Dad to give them some money. He was very moved by my reaction, and many times throughout his life referred to this as the time he first realised that I had inherited his principle of showing empathy for the plight of others less fortunate than myself.

This was also a very significant era of revolution in the world, particularly for young people who began to loudly voice their objections and protest against the suppression, discrimination, racism and warfare that they were witnessing the world over. I joined the Campaign for Nuclear Disarmament, which was extremely active at that time, and started to take part in local protests and marches, before moving to London in the late sixties and becoming involved in larger national campaigns.

While admiring my principles, I'm not sure that Dad ever really condoned the idea of marching and openly protesting. No doubt the need to internalise his feelings and object more silently about the many injustices of his earlier life had left its mark on him, and understandably he hated the idea of mob gatherings or violence of any kind being used to achieve the positive changes he knew were needed. Apart from this, I believe he worried deeply about my safety, so this became a more argumentative time between us and mostly we had to agree to disagree about our methods!

Returning to the strong bond we formed during my teens, one of the most striking aspects of this of course was our shared love of literature, languages and education in general. As he refers to many times in his memoirs, although giving up his own education at the age of fourteen to acquire the manual skills that doubtlessly saved his life a few years later, Dad never lost his desire to further that education that he so longed for and was so deserving of. He was a strong advocate of further education so was thrilled that I stayed on at school to take 'A' levels, and when I became the first member of the family to go to university, he was exceptionally proud. Throughout my three undergraduate years, and equally any periods of postgrad study, he was genuinely and profoundly interested in my progress, and it's not meant unkindly when I say that to some extent I think he lived that period of his 'lost youth' through my achievements at that time. I'll be forever delighted that twenty years later he was able to experience that much longed for education himself, and in his early eighties achieved higher grades in his degree than I did!

A sense of adventure, love of travel and broadening horizons

As my parents didn't drive, apart from the holidays already mentioned, many of our outings were limited to local walks and occasional coach or train trips to the towns and countryside nearby, but the biggest treat of all came once or twice a year when we would venture to London. Dad had developed a real affection for the capital in the short time he lived there, and this grew as the years went by.

I know that the whole family came to London for the Festival of Britain in 1951, when I was around six months old and a babe in arms. In those days this was surely very adventurous for a couple with five young children, from a small provincial Midlands town, and I have great admiration for them even attempting it. Some years later, when Dad was treated for stomach ulcers at Manor House Hospital in Golders Green (courtesy of a company sponsored health scheme), he would often take me with him on day trips to attend his follow-up appointments. The two of us would explore London together, occasionally lunching with his uncle and aunt in Swiss Cottage or wandering over Hampstead Heath eating smoked salmon and cream cheese bagels (how exotic!), then rounding off an exhausting day with a trip to the theatre before catching the last train home. There is no doubt that these exciting expeditions instilled in me a love of London that resulted in me making it my home from 1969.

Being able to spend time in his beloved 'first city' never lost its charm for him, and as I then settled and have lived just outside the capital ever since, I know both parents enjoyed their many visits south during the following years. I have fond recollections of numerous adventures on the Thames and visits to famous landmarks - often repeated with their grandchildren once they came along - as well as to the theatre, ballet, musicals, and even to the opera with Dad. One of the most memorable of these has to be seeing in the New Year with them, dancing beside the fountains in Trafalgar Square (I think in 1973/74), thus fulfilling a long-held ambition of theirs.

Having moved home several times and lived in three major European cities during the first twenty years of his life, Dad developed a lust for travel and a general sense of adventure at an early age, that remained with him throughout his life. He only ever saw excitement and never any obstacles in arranging holidays, and his enthusiasm quickly rubbed off on Mum and me. In fact this love of travel developed considerably in both parents over the years, and I would say was probably their most common interest and the one that brought them the most shared pleasure. They never missed an opportunity to travel together and I know they had some wonderful holidays in the UK and abroad. I was lucky enough to share some of these with them, even after I had left home, married and had children. They were great company, very energetic and curious about everywhere they visited, and this is a trait they have definitely handed down to both of their daughters, and I to my own children.

Regaining the love of his mother tongue and returning to Germany

I mentioned briefly that Dad's hatred of all things Germanic started to soften as he helped me learn the language, and this improved gradually over the years as he began to discover the joys of imparting his knowledge to others and ultimately having so much of his expertise and experience appreciated when he became a teacher. He talks about this in detail himself but I just want to touch on the life event which we both agreed was a major factor in kick-starting his acceptance of the German race again. In his memoirs Dad mistakenly associates this with my time at university, but in fact it took place a few years later, in the mid 1970s.

I was working in London and needed to find somewhere to live to escape the horrible little bedsit that I'd been renting for about a year. I ended up sharing a flat in south west London with three other young women, one of whom, Andrea, was a German national whose home city was Hamburg. She had spent a year as an au pair to a local family but by then was working for the Deutsche Bank in central London.

I don't know why but for some reason we hit it off as soon as we met and very quickly became firm friends, which we have remained for almost fifty years.

There were never any feelings of hostility on my part towards Andrea or any of the German people that I started to meet, but I do recall being anxious about taking her to Hinckley and introducing her to Dad. It was a long time before I plucked up courage to 'ask his permission' for this, and indeed his first reaction was very guarded. However, he did agree eventually and we visited not long afterwards. This was the beginning of a long and happy association with Andrea and her family, and Mum and Dad joined me on one of many visits to Hamburg, in 1983, and stayed with Andrea's parents.

In fact Andrea's mother was from a family with Polish connections, some of whom had been very badly treated by the Germans during the War, so this gave them some common ground, and it soon became apparent that Dad was thoroughly enjoying conversing in his native language again as well as sharing many of the familiar customs, food, etc that he had known as a child and young man.

More than forty years had passed since his escape from the Nazis; times of hatred, deep-seated racism and prejudice were beginning to change, particularly among the younger generation and I believe all this helped Dad to start seeing the world through different eyes.

I will touch just briefly here on the point where he started his written memoirs, with his trip to Berlin. This was a few years after he had got to know Andrea, but I have vivid memories of all the heart-searching and anxiety he underwent while trying to decide whether to accept the invitation to return. It certainly wasn't a decision that he took lightly, and I remember discussing it with him and trying to encourage him in what I thought might be the beginning of some form of healing process. I'm sure I wasn't alone in this and I believe his autobiography shows he made the right decision by agreeing to go.

The journey that I know would have been extremely difficult for him was the one to Auschwitz. When interviewed Dad spoke eloquently about that himself, so no need for me elaborate further.

Re-discovering the joys of education

There is little doubt that reconnecting with his German roots helped Dad enormously to come to terms with the past and begin his journey onwards. As we know, a major part of this involved studying Languages, Literature and History, most specifically the Holocaust, which in turn enabled him to realise his long-held dream to return to education, and complete a part of his life that was so unfairly taken from him as a young boy.

Crucially it brought him into contact with many like-minded and learned people, and finally opened up to him a world where he had always felt he belonged. All who knew him well were aware how important this was for him and were in awe of the efforts he was able to put into such intense studies when in his eighties, as well as very proud of the success it brought him. Probably Dad's most significant achievement in all this was his natural progression from student to teacher. There are many who look back fondly at the man they first knew as a teacher, with gratitude for his educative style and patience, particularly his students of German. Others will continue to benefit indefinitely from the sharing of his in-depth knowledge of the Holocaust, and his message of hope that the lessons be well learned.

Enjoying grandchildren
and passing on the legacy to the next generation

I believe we were very fortunate to grow up with parents who lived by these strong principles of equality, justice and fairness towards others and did their best to instil these morals in us, and I am proud to say that their legacy has been handed down to my own children.

Rebecca (or Becky-Lou as Dad loved to call her when she was little) was born in 1982, not long after Dad had accepted early retirement and put his long career of manual work behind him. When they learned that I was pregnant both parents were very excited, as this was to be their first grandchild since the late sixties. They both had more spare time on their hands now than ever previously in their lives, and while Mum began furiously knitting baby clothes, Dad embarked on a project to make a cot for their eagerly awaited grand-child. This gave him a much-needed focus at a time when he was feeling rather lost and not sure how he would manage the relatively slow pace of retirement. It also allowed him to employ his manual skills making something of his own choice for a change.

When Becky was born, Dad was particularly over the moon to welcome another girl into the family, the first for over twenty years! But there was no less excitement when Adam came along three years later. Mum and Dad saw quite a lot of my children when they were growing up - not living nearby each other meant we would often pay extended visits to them and vice versa. They were amazingly active and hands-on grandparents, and from this time on I came to understand what an important and wonderful relationship this was, and to regret that I had been denied grandparents of my own. Despite this I have always been immensely grateful that my children were blessed with the precious gift of four exceptional grandparents.

It gave me great pleasure to witness the renewed youthfulness this engendered in Mum and Dad, and to see the loving bond between them grow. It was like revisiting the happiest times of my own childhood through the experiences of my kids. There were numerous sightseeing trips in London, theatre and ballets, holidays by the sea, and equally enjoyable times just spent at their home or ours, playing games, having fun, and making hundreds of wonderful memories together. One of my own particularly fond recollections is, for the first time since I was a little girl, being able to witness Dad reading (or inventing tales) to them, particularly at bedtime, and recalling what a brilliant story-teller he was.

Both parents were always genuinely interested, and took great pride, in every aspect of the lives of all their grandchildren. I believe that Becky and Adam's educational progress was especially interesting for Dad because he was a student at the same time as they were. He loved to share his passion for literature and history with them, as well as his wealth of knowledge and experience. When Adam was in the sixth form at school, Dad helped him to gain a work placement at the Imperial War Museum in London, where he was involved in the setting up of the now permanent Holocaust Exhibition.

I know how immensely proud he would be now of Adam's role as Assistant Professor of History at a university in the United States, where he specialises in anti-discrimination and anti-slavery studies, and equally proud that Becky has just set up her own literary agency which she has named after him, thus fulfilling his wish to have the Lewinsohn name carried on for prosperity.

She feels very close to her Jewish roots. Although she doesn't practice the religion, she has studied it and celebrates some of the festivals with Jewish friends. Whilst he would have disapproved of the 'medium', I know that Dad would be very touched by the fact that she has the last words that his parents wrote to their sons tattooed on her arm: 'Stark bleiben' ('Stay strong').

As a family we maintain a strong awareness of the tragic circumstances in Dad's past that shaped his life so irrevocably. When he was 16, Adam went to Auschwitz as part of a government funded scheme that enabled two students from each secondary school in the country to make an educational trip there each year. Becky and I went to the camp together in 2017 - all of us feeling a compulsion to pay our respects to the grandparents and great grandparents we never knew.

In his interviews for the Shoah foundation, Dad is asked to give two bits of advice for the young people of today. His first is: If you really want to achieve something and have enough determination, you will succeed. Both of my children have faced their own particular struggles achieving success in life, but have always persevered just as Dad would have recommended.

His second piece of advice is: Never believe that you are inferior or superior to another human being because of the colour of their skin, their religion, or the race they belong to. He concludes with: There is only one race, the human race. I can only speak for my own small family, but can truthfully say the three of us steadfastly adhere to this dictum. Adam and Becky practice Dad's advice in their daily lives, both having extremely strong social consciences and never hesitating to speak up for others who they feel are unfairly treated or less fortunate than themselves.

I believe there is no greater tribute to Dad than that his legacy lives on through his children and grandchildren.

NOTES FROM NANETTE

Nanette Edwards (now Nanette Aldred) and Deryn became very close friends when they were young children and this friendship has continued to this day. Nanette has written the following words for inclusion in this book:

Notes From Nanette.

"These notes possibly do not reflect any chronology but are rather fleeting moments of knowing the parents of my best friend mainly between the late 1950s and early 1970s when I was almost part of the family.

I can't vouch for the accuracy of any of them.

I must have first met Eric and Elsie when I was at junior school – I have a feeling that it was when Deryn was still sleeping in their bedroom because the boys Ralph, John and Stuart were all in the back bedroom and Peggy with her handsome boyfriend, glamorous net underskirts and exciting rock and roll music (the first time I heard Elvis!) was in the little front bedroom that Deryn would have later (before she moved to the back bedroom when everyone else left!). I loved the energy in the house but I can't really remember Eric and Elsie so much at that point, it was more that I thought the family was very exciting – Peggy was shortly to go off and get married to Bill and John to Annis. I remember Candy the dog and a budgie in the front room, which alongside Eric's accent was very exotic to me.

It must have been later when I remember in the school holidays, Elsie rushing home at dinner (lunch) time to walk the dog – not sure why Deryn and I couldn't do it – I expect she came to feed us too! Eric must have been off early to work and back late, as I don't remember him being around except on Thursday evenings, which were, I think, Pools nights, when he dropped off, picked up, or both the forms that he sent off to Littlewoods. The kitchen table would be given over to his paperwork that evening, though Elsie still managed to make us

340

endless cups of Nescafe on the gas stove in the corner. Their weekend evenings would include a few drinks at The Sweet Pea Club – we loved being left on our own whilst they were out and would always hear them coming in the front door after closing time. I think the chocolate cakes were probably just a late night treat at the weekends but it seemed they were always being offered and were usually made with the healthy addition of the ash from Elsie's endlessly burning cigarette. Eric smoked a pipe and the strong smell of tobacco followed him, as did the sound of his frantic patting of his right pocket to stop it smouldering when he put his pipe away. They were both very welcoming and generous to Deryn's friends, even when we started taking boys round and there were loads of us there.

I should not really have thought Eric's accent was that exotic because some of the nuns at the convent Deryn and I went to spoke with similar accents – especially one nun called Sister Herlinda who told us scary Gothic stories. Maybe because each nun had a different accent I thought it went with the universality of Catholicism – whereas Eric was the only "civilian" I knew with that way of speaking. Later I gradually found out, firstly through watching (rather patriotic) British war films and later studying history, a bit about what had happened in Austria and Germany in the build-up to and during the Second World War – and gradually discovered some aspects of Eric's own story from Deryn. Then, rather than merely being a Coventry car worker with a part-time job delivering the Pools to support a large family and a bit distant compared to his friendly wife, Eric became someone who taught me to consider the back-story of individual people and specifically of someone who had lost family and lived through the horrors of the Holocaust but who was now leading an apparently ordinary life in the Midlands in the 1960s. I realised the significance of his tragic early personal experiences.

I didn't see much of Eric after I left Hinckley. He retired and went to university. His time there must have coincided with mine (in a different university) because I knew that it was ok to be a "mature age" student at 31 as he must have been about 40 years older than that when he went to university.

His talks in schools were well known in Leicestershire and must have had a great influence on people's understanding of the Holocaust. I understand that schoolchildren and others appreciated it when, during his later life, he shared his memories with them in an attempt to warn people of the dangers of populism and in particular fascism and hatred of others. A lesson we all need to pay heed to now.

I went to Eric's funeral – Jewish in an Anglican church, seen off to Wagner being played at a volume to wobble the church spire".

Written by Nannette Edwards (Aldred) 2020.

THE END OF THE JOURNEY

My father, Eric Lewinsohn, passed away on March 17th 2006.

Following his death, several articles were printed, both in local newspapers and in other publications, paying respect to my father and showing admiration and appreciation of the work he had done within the local community as a teacher, Holocaust Educator and as an advocate for equality and humanitarianism. Some of these articles are very long. The following phrases are just a few of the many words used in them to describe Dad:

Canon Brian Davis referred to Dad as "a truly remarkable man" and also as "a very special man".

The principal of William Bradford College stated "I think the students have all been very moved by his visits". She also described Dad as "a wonderful man".

When he heard of Dad's death, Simon Lake, who was at that time a curator at the New Walk Museum and Art Gallery in Leicester, wrote the following words which are an indication of Simon's respect for my father.

"I was saddened to hear of Eric Lewinsohn's death. I was privileged to meet him in 2001, when he visited the museum exhibition, A life Divided, on German artist Johannes Koelz.

Mr Lewinsohn was a knowledgeable and compassionate communicator with a lightness of touch and enthusiasm for life which shone out.

For those who never experienced the Second World War, it is hard to imagine the terrible experiences he went through.

He will be very much missed".

Written by Simon Lake. (2006).

As previously stated, Dad had left specific instructions regarding his funeral. These instructions stated that his funeral service was to be carried out by Canon Brian Davis of St Mary's Parish Church in Hinckley. Dad had got to know Canon Davis as they were both involved with planning and participating in Holocaust Remembrance Day services. Prior to his death Dad had discussed his funeral wishes with Canon Davis who has said that he felt very honoured when Dad asked him to take his funeral when the time came.

Dad's instructions also stated that he was to be buried in the same grave plot that his youngest daughter Angela had been buried in. This plot had been dug deep enough to allow for more than one body to be interred in it. Council approval had to be acquired to allow the grave plot to be opened and this obviously took some time. The date of Dad's funeral was set for Wednesday March 29th, thirteen days after his death..

This was beneficial to me as it allowed the time needed for me and my husband to travel from Australia to England to attend the funeral.

The large number of people who attended the funeral service, including the Deputy Mayor of Hinckley, was an indicator of how well liked and respected my father was.

The service included music by some of Dad's favourite composers, Tchaikovsky, Bruch, Mozart, Mahler and, of course, Wagner. I think that Dad probably personally chose these pieces of music. As said by Nanette Edwards (Aldred) in her testimonial: "seen off to Wagner being played at a volume to wobble the church spire"

In some ways Dad's funeral seemed to reflect his ideals of inclusivity. Dad was a Jew. His funeral service, in an Anglican church, included christian prayers and bible readings including Psalm 23 "The Lord Is My Shepherd".

Three tributes were read out during the service. The first one, read by Canon Davis, included input from the family:

TRIBUTE TO ERIC LEWINSOHN

"Where do you begin to tell the story of the life of Eric Lewinsohn? Many of you here today will know some of the details of Eric's highly eventful life, others may know less, and there will be those of us who have so many facts and anecdotes swirling around in our heads but would have trouble putting them into words. But does that really matter? – all we need to know is that this great man led a very full life – and we are here together today to celebrate that.

So let's open this story in Eric's own words: "In the beautiful rose gardens of Beth Shalom Holocaust Centre in Nottinghamshire, there is a white rose bush and a plaque dedicated to the memory of Fritz and Blanka Lewinsohn who died on the same day, 19th August 1942, at Auschwitz. This rose is dedicated to the memory of my beloved parents who never had the chance to know my family, and their grand-children never had the privilege of knowing them.

Despite the sad truth of these words, luckily we all had the privilege of knowing Eric – the survivor of a family decimated by war and prejudice – in fact, if we had to sum him up in one word, perhaps it would be "survivor".

Eric was born on 21st July 1919 in Vienna, Austria, into a loving Jewish family, whose business commitments would soon bring about a move to Berlin – where they would remain until the fateful Kristallnacht destroyed their livelihood. Fritz and Blanka instilled in Eric and his brother Jack, a deep-seated feeling of duty and love for the family that was to stay with them all their life. This love forced them to take action to ensure that Eric and Jack escaped Nazi-occupied Europe to find refuge in England while they themselves remained and eventually perished at Auschwitz, although not before Eric reciprocated this love by risking his life on a journey back to Belgium to see his parents one more time before they died.

It is difficult now to picture Eric, aged 19, arriving in this foreign country, having suddenly lost the security of life with his parents but gained the responsibility of caring for his younger brother, and literally regarded as an alien. He had little knowledge of the language, even less of the customs – and had to endure the prejudice of those who resented or feared the "invasion" of such refugees.

It was due to his qualifications in Engineering (and the shortage of skilled labour here because of the war) that Eric was allowed to enter the UK, and lived for a short time in London before accepting the only job available to him at the time, in a munitions factory, which brought him to Hinckley. Whilst struggling to be accepted in a world where he was largely rejected, he worked extremely hard, sometimes on 12 hour shifts, firmly believing that he should earn the respect of the people whose country had adopted him and whom one day he would proudly call his fellow countrymen. At one time he was even nicknamed "Rommel" but he accepted this with a sense of humour – his ability to laugh at himself remained one of his more endearing characteristics.

There followed many years of happiness as well as hardship. Eric met Elsie who was to become his wife until her death in June 2000, and together they raised Ralph, John, Peggy, Stuart and Deryn. There were financial struggles, with Eric never too proud to take on secondary employment to make ends meet – he worked as a coalman, barman, and for many years as the local football pools collector, but the family never went without the "luxuries" of a holiday each year, regular treats, and above all a loving and secure upbringing. What is perhaps most amazing about Eric's life is how, with Elsie, he built such a large, strong and caring family, despite having had so little of the benefit of his parents' guidance in the way that so may others have. It is a testament to his success that so many of his family members are here today.

There were however times of great personal loss and grief as parents, losing their daughter Angela, aged only 16 months, and in later years Ralph, Eric's eldest son.

346

Eric's main occupation after the war years was in car production where he formed many friendships – the most important one being with Don, who is here today, a friendship which continued throughout Eric's life. He served for many years as a respected Shop Steward and became a keen member of the Labour party. He developed and instilled in his children a strong sense of fairness, and firmly believed that people should be allowed to "live and let live", so long as no one was hurt in the process.

As his family grew and times got easier, Eric's interests broadened. He led quite a full social life, enjoyed a visit to the pub, a game of cards, dominoes or chess and attending football matches. But his great love throughout his adult life was classical music and he would attend concerts whenever he could. Eventually he caught the travel bug and after some trips to Europe ventured to visit his brother Jack and his family who were living in Canada, and daughter Peggy who with her husband Bill and family had emigrated to Australia in the early 70s.

The surviving children all married and Eric proudly boasted of 10 grandchildren, numerous great grandchildren and even great great grandchildren. A loving father-in-law to Annis, Bill, Carol and Graham, he took great pride in his ever-extending family.

Whilst he came to detest racial prejudice, never forgetting how this had robbed him of his parents, nevertheless for the same reasons he found it difficult for many years to accept Germans and all things connected with Germany. Then fate seemed to take a hand in presenting Eric with the opportunity for a major life and career change. At the age of 60 he was offered early retirement from the motor industry and at roughly the same time he received an "olive branch" invitation from the Berlin authorities to return to the city that had been his home for many years before the war. He warily accepted both of these challenges and thus unconsciously opened the door to a whole new area of his life. Free from the daily grind of the car factory job he never would have willingly chosen, he began to study many subjects, and then to teach German. It was through one of his pupils that he was later able to trace documentation that verified exactly the dates and nature of his parents fate in Auschwitz.

Eventually Eric was able to visit Auschwitz, a hugely momentous occasion in his life, and he was able to leave his parents a hand written message of love in this dreadful place. To visit the location where his parents perished took great courage, which Eric repeatedly proved he had an abundance of. However, this was by no means the end of his quest to understand his past.

Goethe once said:

"What you have as heritage, take now as task: for thus you will make it your own".

This is exactly what Eric did. The return to Germany and the trip to Poland enabled him to, in many ways, "lay the ghost" of his terrible past, but he never tired of using his painful experience for good. As well as being interviewed for newspapers, he wrote articles and gave talks describing his own painful experience of the Holocaust, so that through understanding, the next generation might prevent it happening again. Those who listened always did so with great interest and respect, deeply moved by what he had to say. Because of this Eric's passing is not only a loss to us, his family and friends, but to a much wider community as well.

Throughout the next 25 years of his life Eric devoted much of his life to study. As a result he gained qualifications in teaching and lecturing, then went on to achieve a BA in the combined studies of History, Politics and German followed by a Master of Philosophy in Holocaust Studies – most amazing achievements at the ages of 78 and 82 respectively.

It was during this time that much also changed in Eric's personal life. His brother Jack, with whom he had kept in close contact, died, and then in 2000 Elsie, his wife for over fifty years, sadly passed away.

In time Eric took another turn in his life when, aged 81, he married Meriel, whom he had met as a fellow student many years earlier, They offered great comfort and companionship to one another, despite their

348

increasing frailty, and we are sorry that they were not blessed with more years together.

Eric continued to teach and give speeches about his experiences for as long as his health would allow and during this time developed a special relationship with the William Bradford College where he recently set up an annual prize fund for the best essay about the Holocaust.

Eric was justifiably proud of his academic accomplishments, as were all his friends and family. His son Stuart remembers fondly a fitting story from his second graduation ceremony in 2002:

On the balcony at De Montfort Hall, a man came up to Stuart and said:

"It's a proud moment when your children graduate". Then looking at Stuart's grey top the man said, "In your case, I expect it's your grandchild".

"No" replied Stuart, "Actually it's my father".

"You're pulling my leg", said the man.

"No" replied Stuart again,- "and what's more, he got married last week"!

"Now I know you're pulling my leg", said the man.

"No I'm not, there they are, out on the lawn, with all the press people around them. Eric and his wife Meriel, and yes, we are proud".

Sadly, as we all know, Eric's health had been gradually failing of late and in the early hours of Friday 17th March, he passed away.

This story has been our tribute to Eric, and it seems only fitting that it should end with the words of advice that his father, Fritz, gave in the last ever letter Eric received from him:

"Stick together, whatever they may do to us. Bring up your children with the same love as we have tried with you. If a father's blessing can give you happy hours, please take it with many kisses. Stay strong".

Eric certainly heeded this advice and if his own children can do the same and be comforted by these words, they will be an appropriate epitaph to a great man".

Elegy read by Canon Brian Davis at Dad's funeral.

The Principal of William Bradford Community College wrote and read a moving tribute at the funeral. In it she thanked Dad for the time he had given to William Bradford College in both Language and Humanities departments and she said that "the "Eric Lewinsohn Award" was prestigious, very special and something to be proud of".

She went on to say that my father was "a man who looked for the good in people, a man who loved and cared, a man with a big heart who conveyed important messages about humanity, a man who had touched the hearts and lives of so many".

In closing she thanked Dad for sharing his personal story, his wisdom and his friendship. She also stated that the students would never forget him or his message.

From the massive response that I received in reply to my request for people who knew and respected Dad to contact me it seems that she was right. It seems that the students never did forget Dad. In addition to the testimonials/tributes that have been printed in this book I received many more replies from people who preferred not to be included in the book. Every comment was positive and meaningful. I did not receive any negative comments which is an indication of Dad's overall demeanour and manner towards everyone he met.

The third elegy read at Dad's funeral was written by two students from William Bradford Community College on behalf of all of the students with whom Dad had interacted.

In it the students described Dad as "a valued member of our community". They said he was "an emotionally strong man with great integrity and a great and unshakable belief in human kindness", "a fantastic man that helped the human race as a whole". They concluded by saying that Dad's death was "an immense loss" and that " his benevolence and powerful message shall continue to shine".

If Dad had been able to hear the tributes read at his funeral I am sure that the tribute written by the students would have been the one that he would have been most proud of. He knew that it was the young people who had the responsibility to work towards a peaceful, humane world for the future. I know that he would be proud to know of the lasting effect his story and message had on people and that it has not been forgotten.

If published death reports and notices, obituaries, floral tributes and numbers of people attending a funeral are anything to go by then Dad was definitely a very known, respected and loved member of the Leicestershire and Warwickshire communities. I believe that he would have been proud to have known of the large number of people who paid their respects to him when he passed away.

He must have known that his parents would have been proud of him and of his achievements. He must have been very proud of himself, as it is no mean feat for a man of his age to embark on such an academic venture. To persevere and to succeed in the way he did is something that he had every right to be proud of. I am very proud of him for following his dreams, the successes he achieved and for the time he gave and the manner in which he educated people about the horrors of the Holocaust and the dangers of racism and the mass hysteria that can be evoked by propaganda and hate encouraged by people with fanatical views and beliefs.

I will end this book about my father's journey with two statements made by him.

"We must not forget such horrendous crimes against humanity – whether it is the Final Solution or ethnic cleansing in Rwanda or Kosovo or elsewhere in the world. We must not be complacent about racism today and the way minorities are treated in our society. We are all an equal part of humanity"

And, finally, the statement that he used the most and, I think, will always be remembered for.

"If I cut myself, my blood is red,

If a black man cuts himself, his blood is red,

There is no such thing as race,

There is but one race – the human race".

ACKNOWLEDGEMENTS

Many people have helped me to complete this book.

I am grateful to each and every one of them.

First and foremost my thanks go to my husband Bill for his ongoing support and help. From day one, when I began to retype Dad's manuscript, he has been there for me. He has been my sounding board, listening to the wording of my text and voicing his opinion as well as being my co-editor. He has been there for me at all times, cooking meals, supplying drinks, sharing the joy of hearing from so many people and, perhaps most importantly, giving me continuous, never-failing moral support. Thank you Bill. I really have appreciated you being there for me.

A big thank you to my brother Stuart for the papers and information that he sent to me and for the support that he has given to me and also to my sister Deryn for sharing her memories.

Special thanks also to:

*Ava Farrington for sending me letters, a tape and other items relating to my father and his brother Jack.

*Reg Cooper for sending me paperwork relating to my grandparents internment and transport to Auschwitz.

*John O'Donovan for sending me the powerpoint presentation and other items that he had made to assist Dad when presenting his talks.

*Clive Walley for sending me relevant photographs.

Thank you also to the Hinckley Times and the Leicester Mercury for allowing me to utilize articles and pictures owned by them.

When I decided that I wanted to honour my father by fulfilling his dream of having his autobiography "The Journey Back" published, I knew that I wanted to do more. Yes, I wanted people to know of the fear and deprivation that the Jews experienced on a daily basis in Nazi

Germany and of the horrific treatment, traumas and murders perpetrated by Hitler's Nazi regime, but I also wanted to celebrate the fact
that, in spite of what he had endured and survived during his youth
and in spite of the murder of his parents my father was a real survivor.
He rose above the lifelong memories of his family's suffering. After
retiring from full-time work he not only pursued an academic
education for himself, he also became an educator. His success in all
aspects of his life can, to some degree, be measured by the words you
have read in the testimonials in this book.

I would like to thank all of the people who have written testimonials for inclusion in this publication. A big thank you to each of them
for taking the time to contact me and for the kind words that they have
written. These people are:

Andrea Shires	Andrew Brown
Ava Farrington	Charlotte Towe
Chris Hopkins	Clare Taylor
Clive Walley	Cori MacGregor
David Duke	Deborah Abbott
Diane Frost	Frank Mitchell
Hannah Webb	Hazel Herbert
Holly Barnes (nee Beasley)	Istvan Kemeny
Janine Yarwood	Jayne Mayne and Karen Parkyn
John O'Donovan	Kath Morton
Kay Otter	Laura Shipley
Lis Walton	Lorraine McClintock
Malcolm Davison	Margaret Wilson (nee Fletcher)
Martin Dunn	Michael Gibby
Nanette Edwards	Pat Harris

Acknowledgements

Phil and Carole Herbert	Professor Aubrey Newman
Reginald Cooper	Robert William Irving
Ruth Duke	Sarah Fell
Serena Baker and Dean Russell	Sheena Lewinsohn-Marston
Shirley Elsby	Simon Carnall
Simon Lake	Stephanie Brentnall (nee Taylor)
Susanne Pollak	Suz Morton
Tina Swift (nee Alcock)	Tom Waugh
Wendy Prince	Zoe Shires

Thank you also to the people who contacted me with kind words and memories but chose not to have their words published and to those who took the time to find and contact people on my behalf.

I would also like to thank my immediate family members who live in Australia and therefore were unable to spend regular time with their grandfather and great grandfather for sharing their memories.

Damian Toon	Chris Toon	Kelly Wade (nee Toon)
Jarrod Toon	Stephen Toon	Jeremiah Toon

Thank you also to my youngest grandchild, Esther Toon whose decision to complete an assignment on the effects of the Holocaust on future generations sparked me into finally completing this book.

Without the help of so many this book would not be what it is.

A TRIBUTE TO ERIC LEWINSOHN
A SUCCESSFUL SURVIVOR

Lightning Source UK Ltd.
Milton Keynes UK
UKHW021422030122
396550UK00004B/111